# BORN TO REFEREE

# BORN TO REFEREE

## MY LIFE ON THE GRIDIRON

# JERRY MARKBREIT
## AND
# ALAN STEINBERG

WILLIAM MORROW AND COMPANY, INC.   NEW YORK

This book is dedicated to my wife, Roberta;
my daughters, Kathy and Betsy; and my
parents, Henry and Rena Markbreit.
    A special dedication to my good friend
Charlie Stacey.

—Jerry Markbreit

Library of Congress Cataloging-in-Publication Data

Markbreit, Jerry.
    Born to referee : my life on the gridiron / Jerry Markbreit and
Alan Steinberg.
        p.  cm.
    ISBN 0-688-07938-5
    1. Markbreit, Jerry.  2. Football—United States—Referees—
Biography.  3. National Football League.  I. Steinberg, Alan,
1945–  .  II. Title.
GV939.M293A3 1988
796.332′092′4—dc19
(B)                                                                          88-12824
                                                                                  CIP

Printed in the United States of America

First Edition

1 2 3 4 5 6 7 8 9 10

BOOK DESIGN BY JAYE ZIMET

# PREFACE

**I** was born to referee.

I was meant to be out on the football field. It's where I feel most natural, most at ease, most in control of myself. I know the boundaries of this special world and, once I'm inside them, real life vanishes. Everyday problems can't reach me, nothing can interfere. No bills to pay, no secretary running in, no family conflicts, no intrusions. There's nothing but the ultimate personal test: How good can I be?

I love standing at my position just before the ball is snapped. The crowd buzzes with anxiety, the officials are primed, the center leans over the football and waits. The quarterback starts barking signals, and in that instant before the ball is snapped, everything is in slow motion. I glance around the horn at my crew—head linesman, side judge, field judge, back judge, line judge, umpire—and my heart skips because I'm so damn happy.

Here are the best friends I have in the whole world, every one cocked and poised, waiting for the snap. Another instant from now, all hell will break loose. But for this moment, we're all frozen in perfect peace. I feel a surge of camaraderie and pride. I'm thinking: "I love

this crew, I love this game, I love being here. God, what a wonderful place to be."

How often in life are you tested to find out if you're the best you can be? It's almost impossible to find that kind of situation. But on a football field, a referee is tested on every play. If you have the guts to take the risk and stand in that spotlight, you're in the right place. Because for at least one time in your life, you'll have the chance to display your wares and find out what you can do.

I've often asked myself: "How did a little Jewish guy from Skokie get to be one of only fifteen referees in the National Football League?" I think the answer is that I always have to *know* if I'm the best that I can be. In an NFL football game, I can find out on any play: The quarterback fades back and just as he's set to throw, bang, he gets hit and the ball pops loose and it's recovered and I rule fumble, not forward pass, and it goes the other way. And I'm standing there killing the clock, pointing downfield, and everything stops. And I walk away feeling so competent and proud because everything I have is right there on that play. I just showed my wares in a quarter of a second and then it was over. But for that instant, I met the test. I didn't panic, I didn't lose concentration, I didn't overreact. I watched it, slowed it down in my mind, ruled on it, and signaled—everything I could possibly do.

When my mentor Tom Kelleher was on my crew, and I had the game rolling along like an orchestra conductor, there was Kelleher playing an imaginary fiddle and doing a little jig to let me know: "The tempo's perfect." And none of the eighty thousand people in the stands or the millions watching on TV knew this. But when Tom played that fiddle, I felt like I'd just sculpted the David or painted the Mona Lisa.

Where else can you feel that sense of proud accomplishment every week? And it keeps happening. Every game is just as exhilarating as the previous one. Before a game, I always feel like I used to when my dad and I were going fishing. I'd lay awake in bed all night, thinking: "I can't wait till morning comes when we'll

drive out to the lake and watch the sun come up." That was the most exciting part of my youth. Well, the night before a football game I feel that same excitement. I toss nervously in bed all night because I can't wait to get out on the field.

What an extraordinary feeling to be a fifty-two-year-old man—an adult, a family man, a businessman—who's so excited about something every week that it's more fulfilling than anything else in his life. In the dressing room, I still get those pregame butterflies and that wonderful rush of fear: "Will I make the right call? Will I be good enough?" Yet *that's* what makes my job so special. Even after a lifetime of officiating at every level—from college intramurals to the Super Bowl—I'm *still* discovering how good I can be.

# ACKNOWLEDGMENTS

The authors wish to acknowledge gratefully the help, encouragement, and support of Lisa Drew, Jay Acton, Paul McCarthy, and David Means. Special thanks to Jack and Estelle Steinberg, Debra Constantini, Michael Constantini, Jack and Mary Jane Helder, Don Flagg, Steve Fiffer, Vince Aversano, Ruth Wiener, and Mike and Carole Steinberg.

Thank you, one and all.

# CONTENTS

# PART ONE
# HOW GOOD CAN YOU BE?

# 1. INTRODUCTION

**A**t the end of the 1986 season, I worked a Green Bay Packers-Chicago Bears game—my first regular-season Bears game since I became an NFL referee eleven years ago. It used to be that referees seldom worked the cities in which they lived. The more prominent you were, the less likely you'd work your own city, because if you made a controversial call, some irate fan might throw eggs at your house. Then league policy changed and they figured: "Markbreit lives in Chicago, give him the Chicago-Green Bay game. The season's almost over, Green Bay's only won a couple all year. What could possibly happen?"

How could I know that in this "What could possibly happen?" game I'd face the most significant test of my ability in my thirty-two years of officiating?

The game was murder. They were ready to kill each other right from the gun. One personal foul after another—shoving, kicking, late hitting. The tension was unbelievable. We knew it was going to be one of those tough, miserable games with a lot of fouls. And that's how it went for most of the first half. Until "The Incident" occurred.

My main job as referee is to watch the quarterback.

15

So I was watching Bears' quarterback Jim McMahon as he rolled out to his right and threw the football. I knew it had been caught, but I didn't know if it was a reception or an interception because my eyes were glued to McMahon. As the play ended, he drifted slightly toward the sideline and was looking downfield dejectedly, so I assumed the ball had been intercepted. Normally I would've already hustled downfield to set up the next play, but something kept me standing there. It was just Jim McMahon and, five yards behind him, Jerry Markbreit.

About ten seconds elapsed. McMahon was ready to walk off the field when, for some reason, he stopped and glanced downfield again. Out of the corner of my eye I saw Charles Martin—number ninety-four, Green Bay—coming around his defender, who'd stopped blocking him to look downfield. Suddenly Martin grabbed McMahon right in front of me, picked him up, turned him over, and *stuffed* him into the ground. Instantly I threw my flag where McMahon fell.

It was a simple, routine call. Anybody in the officiating business—even any fan—could've called a fifteen-yard penalty on that. If you talked to any official in the league, he'd say, "Markbreit's call was the easiest call of the year." And it truly was. But here's where the test came, here's what made me feel so tremendous about that call.

The second my flag hit the ground, I said to myself: "This guy's out of the football game." That's rare. I can't remember a time when an official ejected a football player for a foul other than fighting. I'd never seen a personal foul severe enough for a disqualification. In fact, it was the first ejection I had ever issued in the NFL.

Martin was on his knee now, hovering over McMahon. I didn't know whether to dive in and pick McMahon up and try to help him, or what. I was just kind of frozen there. As Martin got up, Jim Covert, the Bears' left tackle—and probably the only Bears player who saw what happened—ran at top speed into Martin's back and knocked him over hard. Two of the of-

ficials on my crew, unaware of what I had called, saw Covert run into Martin's back and threw their flags. Now there were three flags on the ground. I immediately said to myself: "Offset." But then I said: "No. There isn't any way I'm gonna offset. That could create a real disaster out here."

Technically we had offsetting penalties, but I didn't think Covert's hit was a foul. Martin had been hovering over the fallen McMahon, so Covert was protecting him by knocking Martin out of the way. He didn't club him in the head, he didn't punch him, he wasn't trying to hurt him. I also knew that if I called an offset, Martin would still be disqualified, but there wouldn't be any yardage walk-off. It would seem as if there were no enforcement of the penalty. So I told myself: "I'll have my two men pick up their flags and we'll disregard that shove."

You're not supposed to touch a player, but I grabbed Martin by the arm because I felt the place was going to explode. I looked him in the eyes and said, "You're out of the ball game. And don't give me any trouble." Martin's about six-four, 280. He glared down at me and said, "I ain't goin' *nowhere.*" I said, "I want you to look around at the faces of the Bears. If you don't walk off the field with me right now, I can't be responsible for your safety. Now let's go." I pulled his arm and off we ran.

I deposited him in front of Coach Forrest Gregg and said, "Coach, this man's out of the ball game." Gregg said, "What'd he do?" I said, "He stuffed the quarterback into the ground." He said, "The ball was intercepted. The quarterback is fair game." I said, "Coach, I don't have time to talk to you here. He's out of the game and I want him removed from the stadium before we have a riot. If you want to talk to me after I enforce this penalty, I'll be glad to come back and talk to you."

When I ran back onto the field, I was immediately confronted by Mike Ditka. When Ditka's mad, he's very tough; as a player, he'd do anything to gain an extra inch. He said, "Jerry, I know there are three flags on the

play, but there better *not* be an offset." Whenever I tell
this story I always say, "Now, you don't think that easy-
going Mike Ditka would ever try to intimidate an official,
do you?"

Actually, he wasn't trying to intimidate me. He was
fighting for his rights. He knew that Covert had run into
Martin for a reason. So I walked Ditka off and I said,
"Coach, this will be handled properly. There will not be
an offset." I gathered my two men together and I said,
"Gentlemen, I don't think you have a foul. I'm going to
rule that Covert was protecting McMahon. I'd like you
to pick up your flags and let that be the end of it. Does
anybody object?" No one did. They picked up their flags,
I signaled the call, and I announced the ejection. We
walked off a fifteen-yard penalty from the interception
spot and gave the ball to Green Bay, and it was over.
That call settled the whole ball game down. From that
moment on, I had the game under control. The players
knew it, and they started playing serious football. Nobody said a word to me about the call.

When the game was over, I started worrying. I'd seen
the play for only an instant, maybe a tenth of a second.
Did I overreact? When my supervisor, Joe Gardi, came
in I asked him, "How bad was the body slam? Was it
severe enough for ejection?" Joe said, "We won't know
how severe until we review the film, but we feel you
did the right thing."

I sat in the locker room and reflected. I began to
realize that I'd been tested critically and that I'd done
what my instincts and all my accumulated experience
over the years had taught me to do. I thought: "You
*handled* it, Jerry. You did everything right." It was a big
jolt of pride. Because I knew that a lot of what I did
wasn't in the rule book. It was common sense. This re-
flection was interrupted by a phone call from the press
box informing me that the pool reporter (a designated
member of the press) was coming down to talk to me
about the foul. I went right back to worrying. I thought:
"Oh boy, he'll want to know why I didn't offset the penalties."

But when the reporter came in, he never even men-

tioned the offset. He talked about the severity of the foul and he said the officials had done a very fine job controlling the game. I started to feel that I had done the best I'd ever done as a professional football official in handling a very delicate situation. It wasn't the foul and it wasn't the ejection—it was everything put together.

Later, the supervisors reviewed the game films and graded me on all my calls. They grade every call from 1 to 7. A routine call is a 5, a good call a 6, an outstanding call a 7. In 224 games that year, maybe they gave out three 7's. That Monday, when Commissioner Rozelle reviewed the play, I heard that he asked a supervisor in the league office, "What grade did Markbreit get on that call?" The supervisor said, "He got a 7." Rozelle said, "Is that *all*?"

That one call helped get me my second Super Bowl. But the biggest satisfaction was knowing that I handled it exactly the way I would've wanted me to handle it, had I been overseeing the National Football League. The most rewarding part was that I didn't have to *think* about the call when I made it. It had been waiting all these years to come out. Until I made the call, I didn't know how I'd react to a play like that. What if I hadn't ejected him? What if it took me five minutes to decide to eject him? What if I'd offset the penalties, which I had a right to do?

I wouldn't have wanted the league to say to me afterward, "You should've ejected Martin right away. You should not have had a discussion. You looked indecisive." As it turned out, I did all the right things. Was it by accident or design? Was I always ready to handle something like this, or was I just lucky? Will I be ready the next time it happens?

That's the challenge that drives me to officiate. Routine plays are easy for everybody. What brings greatness is displaying your wares in a once-in-a-lifetime crisis, knowing that the rest of your career might be judged on how you handle that one situation. Do you come through like a top-notch pro, or do you fall on your face?

The wirephoto of me escorting Martin off the field

ran in nearly every major newspaper in the United States. It was featured prominently in *Sports Illustrated* with the caption "Ref Jerry Markbreit unhesitatingly made a big point when he banished Martin." I got more publicity and national notoriety from that one call than from anything I've ever done. It was a dream come true. A lineman dreams of intercepting a pass and running for the winning touchdown. An official's dream is to have something happen in a football game where you not only react correctly, but you also contain the animosity, you control the game, you save the day.

And brother, that's exactly what I did.

## 2. "TAKE THE RISK AND DON'T GIVE UP"

**T**he game started for me at Passavant Hospital in Chicago on March 23, 1935—Henry and Rena Markbreit's firstborn. Four years later my sister, Marilyn, joined the team. My Uncle Johnny—a football star in his day—gave me two presents at birth: a football and a contract to play for the Detroit Lions. I got plenty of use out of that ball, but the Lions wouldn't honor the contract. My mother always felt that Johnny's gifts were a sign. "As the twig bends," she used to say, "so the tree is inclined." In a way, she was right.

For most of my childhood, we lived in a South Side apartment on Merrill Avenue near O'Keefe Playground. I remember more about O'Keefe than our apartment because I lived in that playground. It was my shrine, my sanctuary. I played there day and night—softball, football, basketball, hockey. I was so sentimental about it that, in 1955, my mother commissioned a famous Chicago artist to do an original watercolor of O'Keefe, and she gave it to me as a wedding present. It's still hanging on my basement wall. Sometimes I stare at it and think: "See, Shmuckmeyer. Look how far you've come."

It was an uphill climb, believe me. Because I had a very ordinary childhood. I was a nebbish (see Glossary

of Yiddish Markbreitisms); I was nothing special. For one thing, I was such a serious kid. I always had this ferkrimpta punim face. Even today, people say, "Don't you ever smile?" I do, but in between I look like a grouch. For another thing, I was a little fatso. That was from my mother's six tuna fish sandwiches and five glasses of whole milk for lunch every day. My house was like the gingerbread house in *Hansel and Gretel*—it was practically *made* of food. My dad loved to eat, and both my mom and my Grandma Zolly loved to cook. They nudjeled me, "Don't nibble like a bird! You wanna be strong, eat everything on your plate!" I ate everything on my plate—and everything on my sister's plate. I figured: "Good, now I'll be *twice* as strong."

Aside from food, sports was the center of my life. Nearly every day, I had a game of some kind at O'Keefe. The only times I missed were the Saturdays my father dragged us off to visit relatives. I was a respectful kid, but that annoyed me. To me, missing an O'Keefe game was like missing a visit from Moses: "I can't stay, Moses. I have to visit my Aunt Cilly." So I'd bellyache every inch of the way, "I don't want to go! I want to play ball!" It amused my dad. He'd say, "You play ball every day. What's a few hours out of your whole life?"

As a kid, those few hours *were* my whole life. I'd go to school, come home, change clothes, run to the playground, and play ball until dark. There weren't any hardball diamonds in our neighborhood, so every summer we played sixteen-inch softball. I was one of the better players—hit in the .600s, always on base, pretty good defense. Since O'Keefe was so small, we soaked the softballs in water so you couldn't bang 'em over the fence. We had a helluva team. Challengers came from all over Chicago to play us, but we beat the daylights out of them. I still remember those games; I played sixteen-inch at O'Keefe until I was thirty-five.

Football was more addictive. I listened to Notre Dame games on the radio and I rooted for Terry Brennan. But I didn't have heroes like kids do today because there was no TV. Greats like Brennan didn't have the massive

exposure of a Lawrence Taylor or a Jim McMahon. My heroes were always people in my own life, like my dad and my Uncle Johnny.

Johnny was my dad's cousin, though I called him Uncle. He was older than my dad and had been an all-city quarterback at Hyde Park High School at 105 pounds. We went everywhere with him—fishing, baseball games, football games. He knew the intricacies of football, so he'd explain to me about formations, blocking assignments, strategy. He was a very strong football influence on me as a kid.

In fifth grade, I went crazy for tackle football. I wasn't a star, but I did have a knack for organization. There wasn't enough competition, so I formed a grade school team and arranged tackle games with other schools. We bought our own equipment and played in Jackson Park without officials. We used the honor system—we just marked off the field with our coats and we played. My mom always wondered why every winter I'd go through coats like Kleenex. Because, Mother: We had to have a *goal line*.

Every Sunday morning in the fall, we played two-hand touch at O'Keefe. The same group of guys played from the time we were ten until we were thirty-five. On Thanksgiving Day we played the "Turkey Bowl." We started at 8:00 A.M. and played one continuous game until dark. It didn't end until the football either ruptured or started knocking out our teeth. Guys would come over, play until two, go home for dinner, and return for more. The game developed into a tradition. Even as older men, we came back from all around the country to play the "Turkey Bowl." I looked forward to it every year, not so much for the game (the score was always something like 98–86) but for the camaraderie. That's what I missed most when I stopped playing. Luckily, I found it again in officiating.

Sports was obviously a shaping force in my life, but my character was molded by my family. My people were strong, willful, independent. Home was like a college of emotions and ideas, and I learned something

important from everyone who lived there. For example, Grandma Zolly. My fondest memory of her is an afternoon when she was preparing gefilte fish for the holidays. Zolly never wore shoes in the kitchen, just nylon stockings rolled below her knees. Nothing distracted her; she really concentrated on her work. So there I was at age six watching this large, powerful, Hungarian woman prepare gefilte fish like a jeweler sculpting diamonds. She was grinding this one magnificent fish in a meat grinder attached to a chair when, suddenly, a huge water beetle scurried across the floor. Zolly shot her foot out and crushed that bug without losing a count on the grinder. I can still see that to this day. I'm sure I absorbed some of Zolly's concentration because when I reflect on her influence, that incident always comes to mind.

One other memorable Zolly influence: My grandfather died before I was born, and Zolly ended up marrying five more times—which got my father crazy. Their relationship was volatile; she always hounded him, and they constantly argued and yelled. That's why I'm such a yeller, a screamer, today. Because when my dad got frustrated—especially at Zolly—he hollered to drown her out. And as my wife and my fellow officials will confirm, whenever I get frustrated, I holler louder than that. I try to drown *everybody* out.

I had wonderful relationships with both my parents. I can trace every strength I have to them. From Rena Markbreit, I inherited my sense of caring about others and my need for order, proportion, control. She painted and wrote poetry and was always there for emotional support. Because my father worked nights, he was never home when I got back from school, so my mom listened to all my problems and helped me with my schoolwork. When I was in high school, I was too exhausted after football practice to read my English assignments. One time, I had to read *A Tale of Two Cities* in five nights. The first two nights, I fell asleep on the book. For the next three straight nights, my mother read me the entire book, chapter by chapter. She was more than just a

mother, she was also a great friend who really understood me.

One thing I learned from her—by osmosis—was emotional control. I was always impressed at how she handled family turmoil. When my father got angry about something and ranted and raved around the house, Rena stayed cool and calm—the voice of reason. Henry was much more emotional. He cried easily. If I said, "Tell me about Grandpa Markbreit," his eyes would well up with tears. I only saw my mother cry twice: when her mother died and when Henry passed away. She was the family stabilizer, she never lost control. I'm that way, too—and that trait has served me well on the football field.

Though Rena was warm and caring, she could also be—in my father's words—"one tough cookie." She was compulsively neat. Like any normal American boy, I'd dump my shoulder pads, jersey, and cleats on the dining room table and go to my room. When I returned, the table would be polished and clean, and all my stuff piled in the trash. Like me, Rena wasn't subtle, just firm. I'm the same way now as an official: good planning, orderly execution, everything under control.

And she could get things done. When I was seven, we took a cottage at Union Pier and went down to the beach. In the water, I gashed my foot on glass and it bled profusely. Immediately, Rena carried me up a steep hill—and I was no light load—trudged me to the car, drove me to town in her bathing suit, and found a doctor to stitch me up. She didn't *think* about what to do, she just did it. That left a lasting impression on me. Today, I'm exactly like her in that way: I know what has to be done and I do it.

Hank Markbreit—who passed away in 1985—was a boisterous, flamboyant, fun-loving man. In Mom's words, "Henry was typically Hungarian. When they say 'Wine, women, and song,' they mean it—but they will give up the song if absolutely necessary." He loved to shmooz and tell jokes, so people always crowded around him. That intimidated me because I was quiet and shy. He'd

always introduce me proudly—"My son this," "My son that"—and it embarrassed me. If you put him in Soldier Field and sang "Happy Birthday" to him, he'd bow and tell jokes and shmooz the crowd. I'm exactly the opposite; you can't sing "Happy Birthday" to me in my own room.

Henry was a great father. From the time I was eight until I was thirty-four, we went hunting and fishing together. He was a city man, but he was an outdoorsman at heart. He loved the solitude of a lake at dawn and the freedom of the woods, where he could walk for hours. Yet he also relished laughing and kibitzing with friends. Those early trips with him showed me how much fun it was to do sporting things with other people.

We also shared an intense enthusiasm for sports. My dad wasn't really an athlete, he was more of a spectator-athlete. As a kid, he had to work after school instead of playing ball. But he loved competition, so he always found time to watch me play or take me to White Sox, Cubs, and Hyde Park High School games. He knew the Hyde Park football coach, Ellie Hasan, who would later become *my* coach, and the man responsible for my officiating career.

Though my dad wasn't an athlete, he taught me more about sports than all the great athletes I've known. His lessons came off the field. For example, when I was nine I belonged to the South Shore Temple and they decided to form a boxing team for a boxing show. In those days, nobody had boxing teams—especially Jewish temples. When they asked for volunteers, we all coughed and stared at the floor. They asked me to be on the team, but I said, "No, thanks." I was a shy, baby-fattish, pampered little shmendrick. Someone said, "Markbreit's afraid of his own shadow." Maybe so. All I knew was, if my shadow had boxing gloves on, I wasn't getting in the ring with it.

My father changed my mind. He said, "Give it a try." I said, "No, it's scary." He said, "All the unknowns you encounter in life will scare you. You must test yourself against them anyway. If it don't scare ya, it ain't worth-

while." He explained that if I didn't challenge myself against the unknown, I'd never find out how good I could be at anything. I can still hear him saying, "*Take the risk and don't give up.* You'll surprise yourself. You'll find out you're better at things than you think you are."

So I volunteered for the boxing team. They installed a ring in the gym, and twelve of us trained for three months for the show. The entire temple membership showed up, we had six bouts, and it was a huge success. I was so frightened before my bout, I thought I'd pee in my shorts. But once I climbed in the ring and the bell rang, I was all right. Just as my father had said, I wasn't as bad as I thought. In fact, I can remember punching my opponent around pretty good, thinking two things: "It's fun to hit somebody without getting in trouble" and "I'm actually *beating* this guy!" We fought three one-minute rounds and I won. The kid I boxed that day is now my eterinarian in Skokie. He has never mentioned the boxing match, but he always gives my cats the evil eye.

My father's lesson about risks really took. Every summer from 1943 to 1947, he sent me to Camp Menominee, a sports camp in Wisconsin, where I tried everything—volleyball, golf, track, tennis, swimming (I swam after girls and I caught a few), even Ping-Pong. I wasn't the best at anything, I was the classic "jack of all trades, master of none." I won a lot of tournament medals because I always finished in the money, but I never finished first. Somehow, that didn't bother me. I didn't realize it then, but I enjoyed competing against myself more than against somebody else.

That was partly the result of something that happened at camp. Shortly after I lost a three-hour tennis match to Buddy Sherman, the best athlete in camp, I had a talk with my dad and he told me something I never forgot: "Son, you can't do more than your best. You may not have the ability the other guy has. Certain fellas can run faster than most, and if you run a thousand races with them you'll lose a thousand. Don't compete against them, compete against *yourself.* If you do your best and you don't win, you'll still be a winner with

yourself." He was talking to a little kid, but he affirmed something in me that would always influence how I looked at sports and life.

Probably the biggest legacy my father left me was my ability to sell. Because selling is one of the key ingredients in officiating. Not only do you make the call, but you also have to sell it to everybody. A confident attitude and presentation make believers out of people because everybody wants to believe in someone who's strong and confident. And those were my father's best traits.

Hank Markbreit was the consummate salesman. He was the guy who *could've* sold you the Brooklyn Bridge. He understood people. He knew that nobody wanted you to walk in and start selling. They wanted to talk about the weather, they wanted to talk about sports— *then* they'd talk about business. He was a genuinely interested listener. People felt comfortable telling him their problems. And he loved the little guy; he could relate to the waiter, the doorman, the car-hiker. He wasn't just out to make a buck for himself, he really *cared* about people. That's why he was a success in life.

He'd say to me, "Son, if you can sell, you'll always make a living. And selling will carry over to everything else in your life." I was an adult before I understood that. I found out that whenever you present anything to anyone, you're selling. You're selling an idea, a product, *yourself.* He told me once, "I may not leave you much money, but I will leave you salesmanship." He left me very little money when he died, but he kept his promise about the salesmanship. Whenever I step onto the football field, I have that confident, take-charge, sell-yourself personality that people always comment about wherever I go. I'm very proud of that personality. Because that's the Henry Markbreit in me.

# 3. LIVE TO TELL ABOUT IT

**I**n the cloistered world of O'Keefe Playground, I always dreamed about competing in something in high school. But when I entered Hyde Park High at age fourteen, I didn't have enough experience playing baseball; I wasn't strong enough for track; I was too short to play basketball. So I tried out for football. The tryout was in the gym, where they started off by weighing everyone. When they announced my weight, guys laughed. "Boy, that Markbreit's a tank!" . . . "Hey, Markbreit, why don't you try out for *tackling dummy*!" They were right—I was a Fatty Arbuckle. At five-three, I was a *barrel*. But I made the team because they needed every shlub they could get. So what? I was excited to get my first uniform.

The freshman jerseys were these thick, ancient, striped things we called "zebras." They looked like they'd been worn in aught-five. A few top freshman got regular team jerseys, while the rest of us shlemiels got the zebras. Along with grubby, baggy pants and a pair of moldy shoes that Amos Alonzo Stagg might've worn. It was hideous—but I was so *proud*. I marched home with those rags in my duffel bag, thinking: "I made the team." Didn't matter that *everybody* had made the team—*I* had made the team.

The freshman coach was Lloyd Rohrke, a former All-American at the University of Chicago in the old days. He lined up thirty of us and assigned our positions by what we looked like: "This guy's tall, he's an end." "That guy's stocky, he's a back." I didn't care. I knew that, physically, I was destined to be a lineman. When Rohrke reached me, he said, "What've we got here?" Eagerly I blurted, "*Lineman*, Coach." Rohrke looked at me like I was an out-of-order phone. "Markbreit," he said, "you're a rolling guard. Do you know what a rolling guard is?" I didn't know, but it sounded important. I said, "No, Coach." He said, "It's any guard that's so fat, he's gonna roll instead of run." Everybody laughed—except Markbreit. He was too busy trying to roll into a large crack on the floor.

That season I did not play "rolling guard," I played "sitting guard"—I never got into a game. In the off-season, I decided to grow five inches. When I returned as a sophomore, I was a more substantial five-eight. *Too* substantial—I'd also ballooned to 210 pounds. I made the varsity, but Coach Ellie Hasan—my dad's friend who knew me since I was five—didn't play me. Two of my best friends, Jerry Much and Stu Musick, were starting halfbacks, while I was Joe Fatso riding the pine again. I spent the whole year gnawing on my envy.

As a sixteen-year-old junior, I sprouted up to a respectable five-ten and I really wanted to play. I needed to find out if I was any good. So I stopped eating my mother's tuna fish and started running and lifting weights. By the football season, I was in the best shape of my life. At 180, I'd finally shed my baby fat. It paid off because Ellie made me starting center on offense and linebacker on defense. But I still didn't know if I was any good because our team was awful. We won only one game. We were sixteen- and seventeen-year-olds playing against nineteen- and twenty-year-olds—mean, tough, Back-of-the-Yard kids who had either flunked out before or started school late. They kicked our tochis. They were *men*, they had beards. We were babies, none of us had even shaved.

Senior year I played every game, but again we won only once. Despite all the losing, I loved playing football. I loved the contact, the teamwork, the camaraderie. And I felt so good about myself. Nothing else was as exhilarating. Unfortunately, I didn't accumulate enough exhilaration to fill a scrapbook. No heroic interceptions, no winning touchdown blocks, no fumble recoveries to save the game. Just ordinary bumps and bruises. I remember only one moment of triumph in my entire career. It came in the Fenger game my senior year, 1951, the year when Fenger went undefeated.

Late in the game, Fenger was called for pass interference in their end zone, putting the ball on their one. Three straight plays I blocked to save my life, but we gained only two feet. Finally, Jerry Much dived in to score, and my close pal Don Cole kicked the point. We lost, 52–7, but I was ecstatic. That was the only touchdown scored on Fenger the whole season—and they went on to win the city championship. I was so starved for victory that, to me, that touchdown *was* the city championship.

It was in these high school games that I first began to appreciate officials. The guys who worked our games were the best around because Ellie Hasan was a high school and college official himself. Seasoned college officials would work our games as a favor to him. Even professional officials worked some of our games. In those days there were no restrictions. NFL officials could work high school, college, *and* pro games. We had Bill Downs, an all-time great NFL referee; Lou Gordon, a veteran NFL umpire who'd played with the Chicago Bears and who is now in the Jewish Hall of Fame; Mike Delaney, who'd been one of the premier referees in the Big Ten for twenty years; and a gentlemanly field judge, Bill McCue.

I was so impressed that these men cared enough to work our ball games. I had always liked and respected officials. They treated us with such dignity. I don't remember a single game where they took us to the cleaners or let things get out of hand. Other coaches used to

tell their teams, "No matter how bad the officiating is, play over it." Ellie never had to mention the officials to us. The guys he selected for our games were the best in the business. Maybe their excellence imprinted on me. If so, I didn't know it then. I never dreamed in a million years that I would someday be one of them.

Ellie Hasan was to become the most influential person in my life, aside from my dad. Ellie did so many things: He was track and football coach at Hyde Park High, an insurance man on the side, a basketball and football official, public speaker, father, and husband. He was such a respected basketball official that every summer he traveled around the world refereeing for Abe Saperstein's Harlem Globetrotters. And he knew both sides of football—coaching and officiating. He worked every major playoff and championship game in Chicago. One day, I realized that *my* high school football coach was working Notre Dame-Michigan State and Ohio State-Michigan games, and that he was one of the premier field judges in the Big Ten. He became a role model for me. As a person and a professional, he was what every man would want to be, or want his son to be. I thought it would be great if I could come out of college and be as successful as Ellie Hasan.

In 1952 I started my freshman year at the University of Illinois. When I left home, my father told me, "When you're through with college, you'll have to work for the rest of your life. So enjoy it, and find out as much about yourself as you can." I adopted that attitude for college, and I've had it ever since.

I belonged to a wonderful Jewish fraternity—Tau Epsilon Phi—and they were very sports-oriented. We were all-university intramural softball champions two straight years. Senior year, I made the all-university softball team. But my first love was still football. Although I had no scholarship, I decided to go out for the college team and, like my dad had said, find out about myself.

The varsity coach was Ray Eliot, and he didn't know who the hell I was. They gave every freshman a uniform and watched us practice for one week. If they thought

you had potential, they let you stay. I stayed, and they played me six games at right guard and knocked the daylights out of me. I was overmatched, but I stuck it out and earned my freshman numeral. As a sophomore, I attended the team's summer training session and made the varsity. I was now a defensive linebacker. We didn't have face guards in those days, so I got my cheeks gashed, my nose busted, my teeth knocked out. This was in *scrimmages* before the season started. Seasoned varsity linemen would explode across the line and tattoo my face with fists, forearms ... cleft hooves. During practice, the stars I saw were not in the sky.

I had never come up against shtarkers like them before. So I lifted bigger weights and grew stronger. I was just starting to feel like a bulvon when I had a rude awakening in the form of an unexpected nap. In practice, they had me at left linebacker on the "Hamburger Squad"—the shmos whose sole mission was to defense the varsity offense in scrimmage. However, the offensive line had Billy Bishop, whose sole mission was to eat raw Hamburger meat at every scrimmage. Of course, no one bothered to tell *me* that.

One afternoon, Bishop blasted through the line and pulverized me with a sledgehammer disguised as a right forearm. They told me later that I was out for twenty minutes. I told them they were full of it because I distinctly remembered Bishop's cleats crunching into my shoulder pads as he ran over me. *Then* I was out for twenty minutes. I blacked out twice when they carried me back to the TEP house. When I finally came to in my room, I felt like somebody had been storing cement blocks on my head. I looked in the mirror and saw a one-eyed purple basketball where my face used to be. I thought: "Jerry, why are you *on* this team? This isn't for you. This isn't even for *Charles Atlas*. You're kidding yourself. You're not big enough, you're not tough enough, you won't enjoy life in a cast. Get out of it now. Live to tell about it."

That was the end of my football dream. It was a major letdown. It wasn't that I'd ever really hoped to

play pro, I just loved playing the game so much that I wanted it to last. And I was proud of being on the varsity team. It made me feel important. My fraternity brothers admired my chutzpah. Even if I didn't succeed, nobody else in the house had the guts to go out for varsity football. Nevertheless, common sense—and an almost permanently swollen face—won out, and I quit. But when I did, it created a vacuum in my life and in my self-esteem.

I needed something to replace varsity football. Somebody told me they were looking for officials for intramural fraternity games, which I was already playing for TEP. Out of curiosity, I went over to the intramural office and asked questions. It sounded exciting—and they paid $3 a game. My dad had borrowed a thousand dollars to send me to Illinois, and I'd been working at odd jobs to supplement that. I sold programs and sandwiches at the football games and, for a nickel, I'd take a TEP brother's shirt to the laundry. I figured the $3 a game would help, so I signed up.

They gave me an orange T-shirt with a white Roman "I" on it, a red flag, and a plastic whistle. No instructions, no rule book. They said, "Okay, you're an IM official. Show up at three." My officiating career was launched. But I didn't know one touch-football rule from another, so they paired me with a veteran official. He didn't know much more than I did. In fact, as soon as I stepped on the field, I realized that *nobody* knew the rules—or much cared. The only calls you needed to know were: maiming; disembowling; dismembering. Fifteen yards, loss of down.

When I walked onto the field for the first time in my orange shirt, I was very nervous. I didn't know if my calls would be accepted, or even if I'd know what to call. Before the game, the players were fooling around in warm-ups. I knew a few of them from school, and they started smiling and nodding at me, as if to say, "We know you'll help us win this game." But I felt serious. When I put that orange T-shirt on, it was like wearing a policeman's outfit. Suddenly I felt the burden of moral

responsibility—even though the three bucks were hardly commensurate.

I was tested on my very first call. The quarterback shot through the line untouched and ran for a touchdown. The guys who knew me started screaming, "You *missed* it, Markbreit! He was *tagged*!" I said, "No. I was looking right at it. *Touchdown.*" I was surprised at how tough I sounded. They were, too. They scowled and muttered, but they accepted it. I thought, "Hey, this is easy. This is fun. I wish I could get Billy Bishop out *here*." I wasn't feeling competent, just a little cocky.

Later in the game, inexperience started blocking me. I was running around out of position, trying to spot fouls I didn't even know how to call. And the other official was calling fouls I had missed. I started getting those smiles and nods again from my friends—like I'd been looking the other way on purpose. I ignored it. But late in the game, after I nullified a fifty-yard run of theirs for holding, their smiles turned into, "You're *blind*! You don't know your butt from a hole in the ground!" I kicked a hole in the dirt and pointed at it. "*That's* a hole in the ground," I snapped. That shut them right up. They knew I was for real. Of course, even *I* didn't know I was for real. But the orange shirt had summoned the toughness in me—and I never forgot it was there.

After that game I got a rule book, took it home, and studied it for five hours. I was intrigued with officiating. It was a little like playing because I was running around on a field, but it was much *better* than playing because I was making tough decisions. As a player, I just knew that if I knocked the daylights out of somebody, I'd come out on top. As an official, every decision I made affected everybody on the field. I could actually *control* the whole environment. It was a tremendous ego boost. I wanted to be somebody important, and here I'd gone from a nonentity, powderpuff athlete to a touch-football authoritarian merely by donning an orange shirt. There was an irresistible mystique in that. I'd ventured into the unknown—and I had to know how I would handle it.

So I taught myself the rules, talked to the supervisors,

picked up tips from other officials. After maybe a dozen games, I developed a reputation. The players knew that Jerry Markbreit was serious. And since most of my games went flawlessly, other officials requested to work with me. It turned out to be the perfect challenge for me. I was competing against other officials for ratings to get play-offs, but I was mostly competing against myself to see how good I could be. Within weeks, I was one of the top intramural officials at college. I was in demand. Teams asked specifically for me: "We got a big game. We want Markbreit." Along the way, I'd trained two of my fraternity brothers, and we instituted three-man of-ficiating teams. I had my own crew—"The TEP-House Boys"—and we worked all the playoff and champi-onship games in the independent and fraternity leagues.

For three years at college, officiating was a welcome release and a needed ego massage in the fall. But I never thought more of it than that. My major was phys-ical education and, as my senior year loomed, I planned to become a gym teacher. I would've been wonderful teaching phys ed to kids. But then along came the ponytail—and everything changed.

One August afternoon in 1955, I was sitting idly on the TEP house porch when I saw this cute, ponytailed blonde bouncing toward the sorority house across the street. I'd been dating a couple of girls in that house, so I found out that the blonde's name was Bobbie Wei-ner. Turned out that her sorority and my fraternity were in Stunt Show together. After our first rehearsal we all went out to Kam's, a local watering hole, and got drunk on beer. I sat next to Bobbie and gave her a line— something intellectual about the three different ways to drink a beer. By the time I asked her out, she was drunk enough to say yes.

Four months later, on New Year's Eve, I gave Bobbie my fraternity pin. On my birthday the following March, we got engaged. On June 17, 1956, the day after I grad-uated, we were married. That day was momentous in more ways than one. Ellie Hasan was there, and he asked me what my plans were. I told him I was working

for my father as an advertisment salesman at *Where* magazine. He said, "What about officiating?" I said, "What about it?" He said, "The Central Officials' Association has its first meeting in July. I'll call you and give you the address and you come down." I said maybe, and then forgot all about it. Over the next few weeks I adjusted to married life and a regular job by playing a lot of softball at O'Keefe.

# 4. "THE GREENHORN SHOW"

**N**ear the end of July, Ellie called: "The COA meeting is at the Illinois Institute of Technology at seven o'clock. Pick me up at six-thirty sharp." I didn't want to disappoint him, so I went. In the car, he talked about the challenge of officiating Chicago Public League games, and it appealed to me. I had handled touch football, but how good could I be at tackle?

At the meeting I became fast friends with Bob Fallon, a Public League official who joined the COA to get more games. He piqued my interest even more. The meeting focused on rules. Afterward I said to Fallon, "The rules are fine, but how do we get *games*?" He said, "I don't know. But we'll find out." And I thought, "Okay, we *will* find out." Only then did I realize how anxious I was to test myself at this.

Fallon advised me to go to Jarvis & White to buy my uniform, and to ask for Stu Popp. So one afternoon I walked to Jarvis & White, as excited as the day I got my high school "zebra" shirt. I was thinking: "This is your commitment, Jerry. You're going to be a high school official."

The store was in a dingy old building—now long since gone—on Van Buren. I tramped up to the second floor

and entered another world. It was an old-time sporting goods *palace:* warehouse rooms; sawdusty wooden floors; sooty boxes that hadn't been off the shelves in fifteen years; equipment scattered everywhere—basketballs, footballs, helmets, jerseys, cleats, mitts, hardballs, softballs. There must've been three hundred softball bats lying around. "This is great," I thought. "I gotta buy some bats." As I was trying some out, a salesman walked over. I said, "I'd like to see Stu Popp." He said, "I'm Stu Popp." I said, "I'm Jerry Markbreit. I'm going to be a football official, and I need an outfit." He grinned. "You came to the right place." I grinned back. "So what do I need?"

He hauled out everything—pants, shirts, shoes, a dozen boxes of this and that. It was like Christmas. Stu was also a high school basketball and football official, so he knew this stuff inside out. I said, "I want a real good whistle. The plastic ones don't give me the volume I want. And when I bite them, they crack." Stu said, "You need the Acme Thunderer. It's the best whistle made." He unveiled these silver gleaming beauties and I put one in my mouth and it was solid. I said, "How many should I get?" "One," he insisted proudly. "They last forever." I said, "Terrific. I'll take six." (I still have those whistles. They *all* lasted forever.)

Along with the whistles, Stu Popp sold me long- and short-sleeved official's shirts; pants; T-shirts; sweat socks; hat; shoes; jock straps—the whole shmeer. I even bought a bag to carry everything in. The bill was $25. I went home, pulled out the stuff, put everything on, and stood in front of the mirror. At first, it looked strange. Maybe it was the convict stripes. Or the little hat—certainly less imposing than a helmet. But it *did* have the look of authority, and I liked that. I stuck an Acme Thunderer in my mouth for the full effect and gave it a blast. "Oh, my God!" Bobbie yelled from upstairs. "What was *that*?" She came down to see. "That," I proclaimed sarcastically, "was illegal procedure, Roberta. On number nine, Markbreit. For scaring the hell out of his wife. Five yards." She shook her head. "When you're finished walking off the five," she ordered, "keep walking to the store for

eggs. We're out." I've always loved needling Bobbie—and she's always loved reminding me to keep officiating in perspective.

That fall, I packed my uniform in my car and took it to work every day, anxiously anticipating the call for my first game. I attended all the COA meetings, took notes, asked questions, passed all the state exams—and never got a game. My feelings were hurt, but I was too embarrassed to complain about it. I was the only rookie in the COA; everybody else had experience. I figured they were afraid to send me out.

When the '56 season ended, I was so discouraged that I decided officiating wasn't for me. In July of '57, Ellie Hasan called: "Why weren't you at the COA's opening meeting?" I said, "Ellie, I didn't work a single game last year. It's a waste of time." He said, "You were better off *not* working your first year because you didn't know anything, and you would've made a lot of mistakes. You have no right to be discouraged yet. You haven't found out what officiating *is*."

I was ashamed of myself for giving up so quickly. I went to the meeting and they promised me some frosh-soph games. Every day at work, I waited. The first call came in September: "You've got the Tilden Tech-Marion Catholic freshman game at Washington Park." I couldn't believe it. I was finally getting what I wanted —and I felt like throwing up.

The game was at three, so I left work early, drove to the park, and dressed in the field house bathroom. It was exactly where I belonged. I was a basket case; I broke into a cold sweat just trying to figure out what to put on first and how it should look. I was literally scared stiff to go outside. I must've hit the can ten times in twenty minutes. I harassed myself with worry: "It's been two years since I worked a football game, and that wasn't *tackle*. I won't be a big shot out here, like in intramurals. I'm low man on the totem pole. I just hope they paired me with an experienced guy."

At two forty-five, as I waited in my car at the field, up drove Bill McIntee, a veteran official I'd never met.

He greeted me warmly; he could see how nervous I was. He assured me that everything would go fine. When I admitted I'd never worked a tackle game, his face paled. He was thinking: "*Why me?*" To McIntee, this was a game you could work blindfolded. These were fourteen-year-old high school kids—their pads were bigger than their bodies; they didn't even know what football *was* yet. And here he had an *official* who didn't know, either. He thought he would have to work the game by himself—which, basically, he did.

When we started walking toward the field and I saw the teams warming up, I suddenly felt ridiculous in my uniform. I was an imposter. I was pretending to be experienced when, in fact, I knew from nothing. I didn't have any *bad* habits to break, I had *no* habits. I was *lost*. I felt like a guy walking into a masquerade party naked, with everybody staring at him. A total greenhorn. I was embarrassed. I wanted to disappear.

McIntee started advising me about what to do on the kickoff and where to stand. He said, "Just look for the things they taught you at your COA meetings and let's see what happens." But I was thinking: "I won't *see* anything, I won't *know* anything, I won't *hear* anything. I'll just stand there like a bump on a log and not react, and it'll be the shortest career in the history of officiating."

McIntee pointed out we'd have to work opposite sides of the line of scrimmage. "Don't worry," he said unconvincingly. "As soon as you have your first play from scrimmage, you'll know how to react." After the kickoff, I positioned myself on the right sideline for the first play. I remember saying aloud to myself: "I don't know what the hell to do, but at least I know where to do it." Then, bang, the halfback swept right and headed straight for me. As he turned the corner, my first instinct was to move into the action and pulverize him. Then I realized, "You're not a *player* anymore! You're an *official*!" At the last second, I drew back and the kid scooted by. McIntee broke up laughing. He came over and said, "You'd've made a good tackle, but it probably would've been the last game you ever officiated."

Things got worse. The first time I started to run, my socks fell down. And they *kept* falling down the whole ball game. Finally I asked McIntee, "How do you keep the damn *socks* up?" He laughed. "You use either tape or a garter. Didn't they teach you that at your association?" During a time-out, one of the coaches handed me two thick rubber bands. "Use these," he said. I did, but they were so tight they dug two red welts. I was too distracted to deal with it, so I worked the rest of the game distracted—and in throbbing pain.

One other memorable screw-up: On my first penalty, I tugged out my yellow flag and chucked it hard in the air, but it just fluttered and dropped on my shoe. I couldn't understand it. McIntee sauntered over and asked, "What happened?" I said, "Nothing! That's the problem. The damn thing wouldn't *go!*" He restrained himself. "Where's your *weight?*" I looked at him like he was speaking in tongues. Was he asking if I was off-balance when I threw the flag? It didn't register. When he showed me the fishing sinker in his flag, *then* it registered. Stu Popp had explained that I'd have to weight my flag so it would go somewhere when I threw it. In my excitement to buy the uniform, I'd obviously forgotten about the weight.

That Monday, I visited Stu at Jarvis & White. He showed me how to tape my socks and how to blouse my pants properly, and he weighted my flag with BB's. I showed up at the next COA meeting with a list of questions as long as my arm. I peppered several experienced officials until they answered all my questions. When the meeting started, I recounted my first-game fiasco, and everybody had a belly laugh. But they promised that next week an official would bring his outfit and demonstrate how to get dressed. And that's what happened. In this matter I compare myself to legendary Chicago Bears center George Trafton, who, around 1930, invented the one-hand center snap that's still the standard today. Well, because of Jerry Markbreit's sloppy socks and floppy flag in 1957, the COA still gives the dressing demonstration every year. In my own honor, I refer to it as "The Greenhorn Show."

After my initiation game, I expected a horrifying year. But, in many ways, 1957 was the crucible of my officiating career. I ended up with a total of ten frosh-soph games, in each of which I felt glaringly inadequate. I was a fish out of water. I knew the rules and passed all the written tests, but there was no *mechanics* test, nothing on field technique. The things I didn't know were so elementary: where to stand; how far I should be from the football; how to move; how to carry myself. There was so much more complexity to officiating than I'd imagined: signaling style; whistle technique; psychology of player-official and player-coach relationships; manner of address; body language; tone of voice. I assumed that with my athletic prowess and general knowledge of the game, I'd be a "natural" official. I discovered there is no such thing. You have to be *taught*. You can be the greatest natural athlete in the world, and your socks can still fall down.

Midway through the 1957 season, I got discouraged at my lack of progress. I've always been impatient; if I want to improve, I want it *now*. If not for some helpful fellow officials and, later, the B'nai B'rith Touch Football League, I probably would've quit.

I worked several games with a wonderful character by the name of Leroy Clark. He was a six-five insurance man with a walrus mustache and a slightly offbeat soul. He'd show up in a grubby official's shirt that had been ungeladen with shmutzick in his trunk, an oily, flat-top official's cap; and his suit pants rolled above his ankles. The first game I had with Leroy, I was dressed to kill: pressed white pants, starched shirt, "peaked" cap, shiny shoes. He studied me and said, "You look terrific, son. How many flags do you have?" I said, "I only have one flag." He nodded. "What do you do if you get two fouls on a play?" I said, "I throw my hat for the second foul." "Good," he said. "Throw the hat. But what if you get three fouls?" I was stumped. "First one," he said, "throw the flag. Second one, throw the hat. Third one comes, rip your pants down and crap on the spot—just be sure you mark it, son." I didn't know if he was serious or not. Lucky for me, the situation never arose.

Leroy didn't know the rules very well, but the players respected him. He taught me something I've used all through my career: how to treat the players with dignity. He used to say that even at the lowest level of football, where the kids don't know their left feet from their right, you should treat them like professionals. He would talk to thirteen-year-old kids like they were men: "Are you *gentlemen* ready to go?" He told me, "Don't talk down to 'em. Make 'em feel like men." Interesting that Leroy Clark had that insight because, years later, I would get the same advice from Howard Wirtz, the premier referee in the Big Ten. Howard preached, "Never say, 'All right, *boys*' or 'Hurry up, *boys*.' Refer to players as *men*." And I've always done that. Even when I break up a fight, I'll say, "Back off, *gentlemen*." Or in a pileup, "Okay, *men*, let's unload." It's unconscious now, but I heard the concept first from Leroy Clark.

Eddie Dygert provided my impetus to be a referee. Usually, in frosh-soph games, both officials worked the line of scrimmage. Occasionally, one guy would line up behind the quarterback and be referee. In my fourth game, Dygert said, "Markbreit, lemme put some pressure on you. You be the referee today." I was terrified; I'd always been the linesman. He said, "You can be head linesman for the next twenty years, but you'll never learn anything. Take the whistle, walk off the penalties, learn how to control a game. Once you build a reputation, you'll start getting varsity games." Good advice. I started refereeing most of my games with Dygert and all my games with Leroy, and it boosted my confidence.

But I was still too harsh on myself. Because now I was making mistakes and embarrassing myself at *two* positions. I had players on my case, coaches on my case, my wife on my case, *me* on my case. I was twenty-two years old, struggling through marriage, working at the magazine at $80 a week—I certainly wasn't the most mature guy in the world. I wanted more satisfaction than I was getting. I'd work a freshman game and then I'd watch another crew work a varsity game, and I'd want to be working *that* level. I wasn't succeeding fast enough. And

I knew I'd need more than just ten games if I was going to improve. So I was tremendously discouraged.

Then, at a COA meeting, one of the fellas asked me if I'd like to work three games every Sunday in the B'nai B'rith Touch Football League—all Jewish high school kids. I said yes. It turned out to be a godsend. The atmosphere was more relaxed: "Hiya, Jerry, good to see you." The players made me feel important. In city league games, I was a nonentity. The coaches didn't pay attention to me unless I screwed up. And they *knew* I was inadequate. At the B'nai B'rith, there *were* no coaches—just the players and me and a second official. *I* was the authority, and they looked up to me. It was like moving into a new neighborhood. Nobody knew my history. Nobody knew that I was a rookie or that I felt inadequate. They welcomed me, they looked forward to seeing me. Boy, if Markbreit worked their game, they were so happy.

I got only $3 for each touch game, as opposed to $7.50 for tackle, but I would've worked B'nai B'rith for free. Most people slept on Sunday morning, but I was up at 6:00 A.M. and down at Grant Park by eight. The first game wasn't until nine, so I'd kibitz with the players for an hour. They loved that league; nobody ever missed. Some of them would play a high school tackle game on Saturday and get the daylights kicked out of 'em, then come back on Sunday and hobble through touch. They *wanted* to be there, just as I'd wanted to be at O'Keefe every day. They came for the camaraderie. So did I.

I took every game seriously, and the extra work speeded my improvement. I was becoming a decent referee. And for the first time, I understood what Ellie Hasan had meant when he scolded me, "You haven't found out what officiating *is*." He was referring to a sense of accomplishment and self-esteem that's hard to find off the field. I felt some of that in B'nai B'rith games because they appreciated me. That's the greatest feeling there is. And, though I didn't know it then, this new football self-esteem was just a prologue to my future.

# 5. "OFFICIALISM"

**I**n 1957 I earned $179 as a football official. The next two years, my career took off. In 1958 I worked fifty-five Public League and B'nai B'rith games for a grand total of $466.37. It was a year of exciting firsts for me: I had my first varsity high school game; my first Public League playoff game, at Soldier Field; and my first contact with one of the finest football players ever to come out of Chicago.

I remember the Morgan Park-Chicago Vocational game on October 29, 1958, at Palmer Park. Tony Antonides, the Vocational coach, told me before the game, "Jerry, we have an amazing kid this year. He plays fullback and linebacker. You're gonna be impressed with him. His name is Butkus."

I *was* impressed; Dick Butkus was a big, rawboned, fifteen-year-old freshman who, even then, was blessed with football savvy. He was as tough as a ten-cent steak. He made all the big yardage as a fullback and was in on virtually every tackle on defense. He was so strong and determined, he literally carried the team. For four consecutive years he was the big Chicago high school star—name in the papers all the time; a reputation for ruggedness and guts.

The best example was a game I refereed in his senior year. I noticed he was wearing a bulky ring, so I remarked, "I suggest taking that ring off. You'll wind up hurting yourself." Butkus was a man of few words—in fact, *no* words. He just grunted and turned away. In the second quarter, he ran the ball into a gang of defenders who had to wrestle him down. I unloaded the pileup and found blood on the ball. Then I noticed Butkus' finger was gashed around the ring. He'd probably caught it on someone's pads. He trotted to the sideline, where they cut the ring off with a pair of pliers.

When he came back onto the field, his ring finger was heavily taped. "What happened?" I said. "Nothing," he said with a growl. I needled him: "What's all that blood on the bandage? Isn't that the finger you had the ring on? The one I told you to take off or you'd get hurt?" He gave me the poker face. "Yeah," he bragged. "They're fixin' it so I can wear it on the *other* hand the second half." I thought, "This kid's ready for the NFL right *now!*"

That year, also, Bob Fallon, his friend Frank Strocchia, newcomer Don Hakes, and I discovered we all shared the same dream: to make it someday to the "big time"—the Big Ten. So we formed a crew: Markbreit, referee; Strocchia, umpire; Fallon, head linesman; Hakes, field judge—"The Four Musketeers." We started getting all our Public League games together. Quickly, we developed the sort of closeness I'd had with my "TEP-House Boys" at Illinois. We were the third team on the field.

Once we'd established our excellence, we were asked if we'd like to work some games in the Catholic League. That was the prestigious "in" league in Chicago. The coaches and players were fiercely competitive, well disciplined, and appreciative of officials. It was a hometown league that made you feel part of a community because you knew everyone and everyone knew you. I was probably the only Jew in Chicago who knew every Catholic League priest by his first name.

We weren't satisfied just working Public League and Catholic League games, so we joined the Indiana High

School Association and attended their meetings until we got assignments there. I was away every weekend for ten weeks with these guys—we became a family. It was like being with my pals at O'Keefe. There was a bonding that, later in my career, would become the trademark of every Jerry Markbreit crew.

Eventually we lined up seventy games a year together—Public League on Thursday and Friday afternoons; Indiana League on Thursday and Friday nights; Public League on Saturday mornings and afternoons; Catholic League on Sundays. We were young and strong and driven to succeed. It was nothing for us to work seven high school varsity games on a weekend. I could make $175 for four days' work, more than twice what I made in a week at *Where*.

I worked seventy-nine games in 1959, earning $719.10. I was climbing the ladder, and people were familiar with my name. I was incurably stricken with this mysterious obsession I call "officialism." Officiating took over my life. I invested myself completely in the pursuit of my Big Ten dream, and I gave whatever was left to my job and my family. It's the same for me today in the NFL. I don't think you can get to the top in officiating at any level without sacrificing almost everything else. Officiating is not a weekend avocation. It's a demanding, seven-day-a-week *vocation*.

Of course, my neighborhood pals didn't take it seriously. After all, who ever heard of a Jewish kid officiating football games? We had a poker club, and every time we sat down to start playing, Don Cole would shout, " 'Turk' (my playground nickname) throws another penalty flag!" And all the guys would toss their handkerchiefs on the table and rib me: "Personal foul, 'Turk.' Wrinkled shirt." "Unsportsmanlike conduct. Wearing the jock *outside* the pants." They rode me like that at every poker game for eight years. The day I made it to the Big Ten, the kidding stopped. They never said another word about it. I think they realized that maybe Markbreit was accomplishing something that *was* important.

It was so important, it began detracting from my

regular job. During the football season, the only thing that mattered was officiating. On game days, I'd knock off at *Where* at two-thirty, get in my car, and go to a football game. For a while, my boss didn't know. He thought I was out making sales calls. Since my boss was Henry Markbreit, I felt too guilty and ashamed to tell him. Finally, he called me into his office. "Cocker!" he boomed. "How come you're not selling any ads?" I confessed on the spot that I was out working ... football games. "I know all about that," he said flatly. "Are you any good *there*?"

I *was* good, and in demand. Public League coaches selected their officials, and I was getting a lot of games. Sometimes I'd have twenty straight days of games: Public League, B'nai B'rith, Catholic League, Indiana High School League. I had ninety-three games in 1960. When I wasn't with "The Four Musketeers," I had some of the legendary officials of my time—Bill Downs, Bill McCue, Ellie Hasan. Guys I'd looked up to for years, and now I was working alongside them. The first game I had with Ellie, I was field judge and he was referee. The second game, he was field judge, I was referee. Here was his protégé actually running the show. He was so proud of that, he was like a father watching his son become president of the United States.

In the early sixties, I learned the lion's share of what it takes to be a great football official. At every turn, I discovered an experienced mentor. Like Dutch Rittmeyer. I recall preparing for a 1960 high school playoff game with Dutch, who was a high school teacher and fine Public League official. He said, "Always know who's blocking on kick plays. If you kick to me—and I'm wearing red—when the ball is kicked you say to yourself, '*Red is blocking.*' " That was so I wouldn't mistakenly call a foul on the wrong team. If the kicking team blocked below the waist, it would be legal. But if the receiving team blocked below the waist, it would be a foul. Dutch wanted me to be able to distinguish constantly between the kicking and the receiving teams. I applied that simple tip on every kickoff in every game I officiated, until

1987, when the rule was changed. (Now *nobody* can block below the waist.)

My favorite Dutch Rittmeyer story is about a famous Chicago high school game where he blew the whistle to kill a fullback plunge into the line when, in fact, the *end* had the ball. It was an extra-point play that kept the team from taking the lead. The quarterback's fake was so beautiful, it faked Dutch out. I observed as the coach ran out to find out what happened. Dutch said squarely, "Coach, I blew the play. Your boy faked me out of my shorts." He was so sincere, the coach just said, "Well, what can I say to that, Dutch?" and walked away.

That team came back to win the game. But the point was, any official can look good and walk with his head high when he does something right. The real test comes when you make a mistake. Not only do you have to own up to it, you also have to live with it. Dutch felt awful about that call, but he was a man about it. He knew he had to admit his mistake and go on with the game. I was so impressed with how Dutch carried on afterward, refereeing a flawless game the rest of the way, that I never forgot the incident. Twenty-two years later, my recollection of that incident would help me survive *my* most humiliating moment on a football field—in my very first Super Bowl.

I was impressed, too, with the respect shown Dutch by the offended coach. It taught me the importance of an official's reputation on the football field. It's built up over time, and when trouble comes it's like credit in the bank. Even though Dutch made a costly mistake, the coach accepted his word. Dutch was so magnificent in defeat that I thought, "If I can ever conduct myself with such grace and earn as much respect as they show Dutch, I'll have achieved something really important in life." And I honestly feel that, today, I have achieved that.

I reached another plateau in 1961, when I was awarded my first Blue Division high school championship. The Chicago Public League was divided into Blue and Red divisions—Blue for smaller schools, Red for larger. I umpired the Englewood-Roosevelt champi-

onship at Soldier Field for $25. It was a tremendous thrill. There were only about a thousand people in Soldier Field for that game, but just being *in* there for a major game was such a mechaieh (great joy), it was unbelievable.

By 1961 I was developing habits that formed the spine of my success. I made it a habit, for example, to study the rules a few days every week during the season, even though I knew them inside out. And I kept reminder books of mistakes and lessons learned. I believed then, like now, that you could *learn* to succeed —that diligence to detail, adopting the best of what you admire in others, and obeying your instincts eventually pay off.

My first big payoff was set in motion in November 1961, when I got my first junior college assignment— Wright vs. Wilson. Junior college games were like high school games, except they played collegiate rules. So I spent a week studying the rules and priming myself to work a perfect game. On a cold, rainy, miserable Saturday, I drove to Eckersall Stadium at Eighty-third and Yates on Chicago's South Side. There I met with the three other officials: Les Dohr, athletic director and coach at the Harvard School for Boys, a private school in Chicago; Harry Pritikin, baseball coach at Bowen High; and Tommy Kosmanoff, a sportswriter for the old *Chicago American.*

They didn't want to be there. In those days, junior college games drew less interest than high school games. To most officials, these games were a pain in the behind. They paid the same as high school games, but they had fifteen-minute instead of twelve-minute quarters. And they were usually played at odd hours, when the fields had already been used and were chopped up pretty good. On top of that, the weather that day deteriorated every sixty seconds. It drizzled steadily; there was literally nobody in the stands; the mud was up to your rear; the field was already a bog. Of course, to me, this was exciting. It was junior college; these were older players; I might learn something.

We went into the locker room—an old, dreary boiler

room—and started getting dressed. They complained about the lousy conditions. Kosmanoff said he had another game that night in Indiana, so he didn't want to get his pants dirty. They didn't even want to go out on the field. Of course, they decided I should be the referee. I knew what they were thinking: "We'll make the kid referee. He'll work the middle of the field, and we'll lay around the sidelines where we won't get dirty."

I didn't care about that. I reminded myself of something Ellie Hasan told me: "To coaches, players, and their families, every game you work is the most important game there that day." So I decided I'd work the game of my life. I'd pretend that this was the Prep Bowl, with seventy thousand people in the stands. I'd go out there in the rain and mud and do everything I'd learned in my five years of officiating.

And that's what I did. I went out in that monsoon, and I pretended the sun was shining and the crowd was roaring and the game hung in the balance on every play. I hustled around like a man possessed, diving in the muck to check fumble recoveries; retrieving balls; stepping off penalties. The other officials snickered to themselves, probably thinking: "Look at this dodo. He's running his fanny off." Even the *players* thought I was nuts. They kept looking at me sideways: "Who *is* this guy?"

The game was sensational; the final score was 7–6. If people had been there, they would've seen a classic. It lasted three hours and felt like it rained fifty inches. I was exhausted and blackened with mud. I looked like walking death. As I dragged toward the boiler room, I noticed a short, cloaked figure with a clipboard making his way down from the top of the stadium. He'd obviously been huddled behind the tiny pseudo-press box where he was shielded from the wind and rain. As he approached me, I recognized him. It was Heine Schultz.

Heine was the Hyde Park High School baseball coach—and Ellie Hasan's best friend. I had known him since I was six. He'd been a Big Ten official for years until an injury ended his career. He came over to me

and said, "Jerry, I'm out here scouting officials for the Big Ten. I watched you work this whole game and you did a fine job. This was a perfect game to do nothing." With that, he turned and walked away. I was stunned. When I turned back to thank him, the gloom had swallowed him up. It was eerie; he disappeared into thin air. An hour later, I wasn't sure it really happened.

I worked a whopping 111 games in 1961 and made an almost whopping $995. Officiating was working out, but my job at the magazine was starting to drag me down. I felt like I was going nowhere there. In the spring of '62, I was so unhappy, I would come home from work and go straight to sleep. Bobbie hounded me to death to see a doctor. "You're twenty-seven years old. You shouldn't be tired all the time." So I got a complete physical and the doctor said, "You weigh 214 pounds, you're about twenty-five pounds overweight, you have high blood pressure. For a guy who does as much physical activity as you do, you're in terrible shape." He gave me a diet and exercise regimen, and I slimmed down to 180 by the fall.

When I got my officiating schedule, I perked up. I had a full schedule in both the Public League and the Catholic League; Indiana High School; as well as small- and junior-college games. At the end of the season, I was scheduled for a semifinal playoff game, with maybe a shot after that at my first Red Division championship. Out of nowhere I got a call from Bill Reed, commissioner of the Big Ten. He said, "Jerry, you've been recommended to us for your excellent work." I thought of Heine Schultz. "We have an assignment for you," he said. "We need a sideline recorder for the Michigan State-Northwestern game at Dyche Stadium on November seventeenth. Are you available?"

I was amazed—then torn. If I worked the Big Ten game, I'd lose the chance at the city championship. But I couldn't pass up the opportunity, so I got permission and then called Bill Reed back. "I'm available," I proclaimed ecstatically. "But what's a sideline recorder?" He explained that the recorder monitored substitutions

from the sidelines. He added that there was a college rule in '62 that allowed a player to enter the game only once in any quarter. If you started the quarter and left, you could not return until the next quarter. A recorder would stand on each sideline with a chart and a horn, checking players in and out. In the event of an illegal substitution, the recorder must blow the horn.

Howard Wirtz was to be referee. He invited me to attend the pregame officials' meeting at the Orrington Hotel in Evanston. At the time, Wirtz was the best-known and most highly regarded referee in the Big Ten. Every time you turned your TV set on and saw a Big Ten game, you saw Howard Wirtz refereeing. He was aloof and dictatorial and magnificent on the field. His signals were stylish and unique; he glided up and down the field; and no one knew the rules better than he. They called him "His Eminence."

We had breakfast and lunch together and went to the pregame meeting. He treated me like I was part of his crew. I met the other five officials, and they were accepting and down-to-earth. I thought, "This is where I want to be: the Big Ten." Wirtz could see how interested I was in the technical aspects of officiating because I bombarded him with questions all day long. I remember saying, "I've got so many things to ask, so many notes at home, I can't even remember half of them." He patiently answered as many as he could. I was in awe. To have even a chance to meet this man was unthinkable and, all of a sudden, I'd just spent a whole day with him!

Dyche Stadium was a full house. Ara Parsegian vs. Duffy Daugherty—an annual classic. When I stepped onto the field, my adrenaline was pumping so hard I thought I was airborne. I took my position on the Michigan State sideline, and everything went smoothly until midway through the second quarter, when Michigan State sneaked a guy into the game for the second time that quarter. I grabbed my horn and blew the hell out if it. It sounded like a *train* horn. Wirtz immediately stopped the game and looked at me. *Everybody* looked

at me. I took two steps onto the field and announced, *"Illegal substitution, number 62, Michigan State. Five yards."* Whew—my first Big Ten call.

Duffy Daugherty thought it should be my last. He ran over and exploded at me: "You stupid jackass! Nobody *ever* calls that here! You'll never work in this league! I *promise* you!" He stormed away, then settled down and approached me again. He said, "I'm really sorry, son. We hate that damn rule. Nobody ever calls it. We've been substituting like that all year and we've never been caught. You made the right call, I shouldn't have teed off on you." Duffy was really a wonderful gentleman, everybody knew that. He always had class.

Something even more exciting happened in the third quarter—a small moment no one else noticed. The head linesman, George Spehn, sprained his ankle. He stayed in the game, but when Wirtz called for a measurement on the other side of the field, Spehn didn't think he could run over there. He turned to me and ordered, "Take in the chains." My eyes popped. I said, *"What?"* He repeated, *"Take in the chains."* Suddenly, it registered. I was going into my first Big Ten game ... *now*!

I grabbed the chains at the yard mark, ran across the field, and kneeled near Wirtz for the measurement. "First down," Wirtz signaled. I ran the chains back to the sideline, and Spehn took over again. My heart was pounding, I was hyperventilating, I couldn't see or hear or think. I had just experienced the biggest thrill of my life to that day. I had actually *done* something in a Big Ten football game. Yet for the life of me, at that instant, I could not remember what it was.

At the end of that spectacular day, I thought: "How much luckier can you get?" I got luckier. Howard Wirtz told me, "I think you have a future in officiating and I'd like to be a part of it. If you have any more questions, write them down and call me. I have a lot of things I can teach you." Unbelievable. The premier referee in the Big Ten was going to be my private *tutor*!

I did call Wirtz a couple of times with questions. Finally he suggested that, after the season, I should visit

him at his home in Cincinnati. So in the spring of 1963, I drove down and we talked for hours about officiating mechanics, technique, and philosophy. I made several more trips that spring and summer just to spend an afternoon talking football with him. That was the start of an unusual mentor-student relationship with Wirtz that molded me into the official I am today. Without him, I would've just been Joe Ordinary as an official.

I was trying to learn anything that would set me apart from everyone else. When Heine Schultz had carried the word about me to Bill Reed, and Reed offered me the recorder's job, I realized I was developing a reputation as a top prospect and that all my dedication was starting to pay off. But I wanted an *extra* edge. I wanted to be somebody special. I knew that I would have to accelerate in order to make the the "big time" at any early age. That was my dream. I desperately wanted to be in the Big Ten by the time I was thirty.

I picked Wirtz's brain, and he gave me that something extra I yearned for. He taught me the basic shell of refereeing—things that weren't written down anywhere, things that could only be passed along from man to man. He gave me the style I needed to supplement my reputation, and a foundation of philosophy to buttress my style—things that have drawn the spotlight to me throughout my career. For much of that, I am certainly indebted to Howard Wirtz. But you still have to be able to *apply* these things. If you're not cut from that kind of cloth to begin with, the lessons are worth nothing.

Before I met Wirtz, I paid little attention to style. I didn't really have a role model yet. Ellie Hasan was predominantly a field judge, not a referee. The prominent referees had excellent reputations but no outstanding styles. I wasn't aware, at the time, that style was important. As long as you did the job, what was the difference? I hadn't realized yet that style was what set the good officials apart from the great ones.

At Wirtz's house we'd go through the entire book of signals, and he'd show me how he did them. Howard

signaled very dramatically; picture George S. Patton conducting the *1812 Overture.* I decided I didn't want to copy him, so I absorbed what he did and developed my own style from that. My style is more powerful. I call it "pointism." Whereas Howard pointed dramatically, with a flourish, I point powerfully, as if I'm hitting a solid dot in the air. I flick my wrist sharply at that dot: "Time out, Seattle"—flick *hard* toward Seattle. "TV, you got it" —flick hard at the TV man on the sideline. It's sharp, it's snappy, it's firm.

When I give holding, I say, "Holding, number forty-five . . ." and I pause. Then I flick that finger hard and— bang—finish up with, "*offense.*" It's not a soft, indifferent gesture, it's a small explosion. I don't know of anyone else in the league who signals that way. And I give a very crisp touchdown signal. I come up with the touch-down signal, then I clench my fists and—bing—I pull my arms halfway down, like I'm chinning myself. Then—boom—I shoot 'em straight out to my sides to signal completion of the play and that time is out. If you were to phrase it verbally, it'd be something like, "I got it—*touchdown!* Okay, it's over—bang—get *out* of it." I don't just float out of the signal, I knock the *daylights* out of it. "This action is *over.*" Boom—get *out* of it!" It's dramatic à la Howard Wirtz but powerful à la Jerry Markbreit.

My real personality comes out in my signals. I have a very firm, strong demeanor. My wife says I frighten people. I come on like gangbusters at home, and that's the way my signals are. Wirtz told me, "You cannot change what you are. Whatever your real personality is, that's what comes out on the football field. Find your strengths and develop your style around them, so peo-ple will know who you are when they see you." He was right. People have continually remarked to me, "We always know it's you. We can tell by your gestures." Of course, Bobbie says, "We always know it's you by the size of your tochis when you turn around!"

Wirtz taught me fascinating nuances, like how to carry my penalty flag. I've always been a side-carrier; I carry

the flag in my side pocket. I started that way, but Wirtz showed me that the flag should be tucked down *deep* in the pocket, with just the tip sticking out. His theory was that if you walk out on the field with that big yellow flag hanging way down out of your pocket, you look like you can't wait to throw it. He believed that could undermine an official's credibility. He said, "Keep it down deep, so they can barely see it. That way, you're no longer the guy looking for *fouls,* you're the guy who's going to see that the game is played *fairly."*

He also taught me the art of whistle-blowing, for which, believe me, there isn't any school. He said the metal whistles were the best because they had more resonant volume—the same thing I'd told Stu Popp. But Howard showed me how to induce a firm, staccato "Teet-teet-teet-teet" instead of a long, shrill screech. He said sound affected people's reactions. "The whistle sound should be dynamic and controlled. It should emphasize not only that a foul is called, but also that you are completely in control of that call."

The first time we covered this, we went outside and he said, "Let me hear you blow the whistle." I blew it long and shrill. He said, "That's one way, but sometimes you should use shorter, firmer blasts to attract more attention." He analyzed it for me. "The short blasts will alert everybody that something's wrong and that you won't tolerate it. It's like a *language."* He demonstrated different tempos you could use, depending on the situation on the field. He emphasized, "The whistle is your most valuable ally on the field because it directs the action." I had never heard that before; I didn't consider it important. It *was* important. When I tried it during games, it *did* direct the action. For example, the louder and sharper the whistle, the quicker the players quit the play, including pileups and fights. It's like a stoplight—or, better yet, Arnold Schwarzenegger standing over them with a tree trunk, asking them *once* to stop.

Wirtz and I talked a lot of philosophy: handling other officials; dealing with players and coaches. He was very formal. He always talked to his crew this way: "Gentle-

men, are we ready to go to breakfast?" That's exactly
the way I talk to my crew. Military bearing appeals to
me. And even if I know a coach well, I never call him
by name. I always say, "Hello, Coach, how are you
today?" They respond positively to that. Howard felt that
you should always treat coaches this way because they
were "the generals of football," the ones who the soldiers on the field looked up to. "Show a leader respect,"
said Wirtz, "and he'll respect you in return. He'll treat
*you* as a leader, too."

Howard said that formality and firmness commanded respect. I've always subscribed to that. People
tell me all the time, "When I watch you work a game,
you're really in charge." They can't see me for most of
the game, so how do they know if I'm really in charge?
They sense it in my manner and my presentation in
those brief instants when the camera is on me. It's a
presentation of strength—something Howard Wirtz proj-
ected every minute he was on the football field.

One other Wirtzian lesson was a simple tip about
making calls. "When you have a call," he always said,
"step out in the clear. And make sure you pause long
enough so that when you give your call, everybody's
eyes are riveted on you." He believed that the more
style you displayed, the more prominent you became
and the more you were recognized. According to Wirtz,
"When people recognize you, they talk about you, and
your reputation grows. That combination," he insisted,
"will push you right to the top in the officiating world."

Because of all the time I spent with Howard Wirtz
and the quality of his information, I was a new man in
1963. I was like a young Thoroughbred prancing to the
starting gate for the Belmont Stakes. I was absolutely
bursting with confidence. In late October, during my
busy Public League and Catholic League schedules,
Dwight Wilkey, commissioner of the Interstate Intercol-
legiate Conference (IIC) hired me to work my first big
college game—Western Illinois versus Peru State (Nebraska) at Macomb, Illinois. He said Bill Reed had recommended me as "Big Ten material." I was thrilled.

Western was a sizable school; the game was under collegiate rules; the players were high-caliber. I felt important because of the three hundred miles I had to travel to get there. They paid me $50 for the game and $16 for travel expenses, but the money wasn't the point. In those days, if they bothered to import you three hundred miles, the message was: You're worth it. That game is now a blur, but I remember standing in the stadium in front of some fifteen thousand fans and exulting: "You're on your way, Jerry. This is a giant step in your career."

During the season, Howard Wirtz was assigned a Northwestern home game, so he decided to come in early and watch me work an Indiana high school game. I picked him up at the airport and we drove to my game together. Wirtz sat in the stands and took notes. I thought: "This is like an audition before the king." I couldn't believe that the biggest referee in the country had taken time to watch me work.

After the game, driving back to Chicago, we discussed Wirtz's critique. He suggested that I taper my pants because they looked too baggy, and he thought my flag still hung too far out of my pocket. Other minor things: "Make your calls more forcefully"; "Work on the whistle technique." He was pleased with everything else. And why not? To date, we'd probably spent a hundred hours discussing officiating at his home or over the phone. I hadn't developed my own style yet; I was using the techniques he taught me. So when he observed me that day, I looked so competent because I was *him!* I was what he taught me—from my staccato whistle bursts to my demonstrative signals. I was practically his clone out on the field.

I didn't know this at the time, but shortly after observing me, Wirtz sent a recommendation to Bill Reed. Wirtz wrote: "As you know, I have become quite interested in the possibilities of Jerry Markbreit as a football referee in general and his potential in our conference in particular. In order to get a fuller picture of his capabilities, I came to Chicago to watch him work a game.

He impressed me tremendously. He has a fine sense of the game, reacts instantly, enforces penalties quickly, has excellent signals and fine poise on the field. I'm enthusiastic and confident in suggesting that he will merit your consideration after about a year or two of solid schedules in Dwight Wilkey's league. If dedication and hard work mean anything, Jerry will make it."

Obviously, Howard Wirtz's influence on my career— as it developed—was even greater than I knew.

By the end of the '63 season, I had seven college games under my belt. I'd also worked the Public League championship game at Soldier Field on the saddest day of my time—Saturday, November 23, the day after President Kennedy was assassinated. The night of the twenty-second, I was so devastated I sat in my basement crying with Bobbie and my two daughters, Kathy and Betsy, who were too young to understand. I couldn't even think about the game.

But the league decided on Saturday that it would be played. We had the flag at half staff; no school bands; no cheerleaders; no halftime fanfare. Soldier Field was empty. It was a dreary, unfocused, 6–0 game. I felt like I was officiating from behind a veil. It showed me how insignificant football could be. I thought this championship was going to be one of the biggest moments of my life, and all of a sudden the president was dead and it didn't mean a thing.

I entered '64 confidently, with high expectations. Bill Reed had recommended me to Brick Young, commissioner of the Collegiate Conference of Illinois and Wisconsin (CCIW)—comprised of small colleges like North Park, Augustana, and Illinois Wesleyan. Young gave me a full schedule to supplement my Public League and Catholic League games in Chicago. This promised to be my finest year of officiating.

On November 14, 1964, I almost quit forever.

I was scheduled to work the Illinois State-Illinois Wesleyan game in Normal, Illinois. Both schools were located in Normal, so this was a rivalry as fierce as Michigan-Michigan State. Wesleyan belonged to the

CCIW, and they played high school rules; State was in the IIC, they played collegiate. The game was at Wesleyan, so high school rules were in effect.

One rule provided that any punt fielded in the end zone was an automatic touchback. You couldn't run it out. Late in the fourth quarter, State was ahead, 14–13, but had to punt. The kick spiraled to the Wesleyan goal line. The Wesleyan receiver tucked it in and dashed a hundred yards for what would have been the winning touchdown. The crowd went wild. But just after the receiver crossed the goal line and got mobbed by his teammates, my field judge raced a hundred yards downfield to tell me the punt had been caught in the end zone. The touchdown would have to be nullified.

Amid unbelievable boos, I marched the ball eighty yards, back to the Wesleyan twenty, and declared a touchback instead of a touchdown. I had just given the ready-for-play signal when a substitute Wesleyan lineman ran onto the field, bumped me, and cursed me out: "You're a *& ↑ %$#@ $% ↑ *@#%, ref. That was the worst *& ↑ %$#@ call I've ever *& ↑ %$#@ seen!"

I immediately ejected him and paced the ball back to the ten. He refused to leave. I escorted him to the Wesleyan coach and said, "Coach, this man's out of the game." The coach dispensed a barrage of the filthiest curses I had ever heard in my life: "Markbreit, you're a *& ↑ %$#% ↑ #$*& and a *&#@$% ↑ !" I threw my flag. "That's fifteen yards, Coach." I walked the ball half the distance, to the five. He charged onto the field in a rage and mouthed me again. Another flag; ball to the two-and-a-half. He came back out and called me a "*& ↑ #$*&@!" Another flag; ball to the one-and-a-quarter. Cursed me *again*; half-yard line. "1& ↑ %$& ↑ %, Markbreit." Nine-inch line. " ↑ *& ↑ %$#!" Tip of the ball a quarter inch from the goal line. I would've set the ball on the goal line *sideways* if he said another word. He didn't.

Needless to say, Wesleyan lost the game, 14–13. Unfortunately for us, the officials' dressing room was in the Wesleyan team locker room. There was no security for

us in those days, so when the game ended we ran quickly for the locker room. When we got inside, we found our dressing room locked. In behind us clomped the Wesleyan team—and they weren't smiling. Suddenly we were pinned between them and the dressing room door. The players started peeling off their equipment and pelting us with shoulder pads, helmets, cleats, even jock straps. The coach stood inches away, screaming and berating us. Players yelled, equipment rebounded off our bodies—it was insanity. We were scared for our lives.

Finally, someone opened the door and we rushed in and shut it again. We were afraid to shower, so we changed clothes, sprinted out of the locker room to our car, and peeled out of that town like nobody's business. On the way out, I realized I'd made only $30 for the game. I said, "Man, who *needs* this! It isn't worth it." In the heat of that moment, I was ready to give it up.

But the next day, I was scheduled to work the Catholic League championship at Soldier Field—and I could never just back out. Even though I was still shaken, I went out there in front of thirty-five thousand people and worked a solid game. I thought: "Well, that wasn't so bad," and I started reconsidering.

A week later, I had my first Prep Bowl, the prestigious Chicago Super Bowl between the Public League and Catholic League champions. Getting that assignment rejuvenated my spirit. The stadium was almost packed with more than ninety thousand fans for what was almost certainly the biggest high school football event in the nation. Before the game, the officials were introduced to Hizzoner, Mayor Richard J. Daley, at his fifty-yard-line seat. With the press box full of sportswriters and dignitaries, and the game carried on local TV, it was every bit as exciting as a major college game. It told my peers—and me—that I had arrived at the pinnacle of high school officiating. Emotionally, in two weeks I had gone from from the dregs to the pinnacle—and I knew I wanted more.

As I climbed in officiating, my job at *Where* maga-

zine began to feel like a twenty-ton ball and chain. I wasn't going anywhere. In football, I was recognized widely in the Chicago high school sports community. When they talked about which referees would work the big games, Jerry Markbreit's name was always mentioned. Players trusted me; coaches selected me; the media and the sports community liked me; officials respected me. I was an *entity* in that world. At the magazine, I was just a shlepper. I wasn't succeeding like in football, I was just making a living.

I would call on a restaurant and they'd throw fish, lettuce, stale bread, and vegetables at me. "Get outta here! We're not interested!" One guy tossed a meat cleaver at me. My dad didn't exactly give me the Gold Coast accounts. I had the shlockers, the places that *nobody* had a chance to sell. They kicked my tochis all over the place. I had no future there. I was just making a living for my family. I never looked any farther than "How much can I make next year on commissions?"

For years, I felt guilty that I didn't love my job the way I loved officiating. At the office, I still felt intimidated by my father. I could never be as good a salesman as he. I was a background figure, a watcher, Hank Markbreit's kid. I felt insignificant, inadequate. But whenever I donned that official's outfit, I transformed into someone else. I was center stage, I had authority, I was a success. I wasn't Hank Markbreit's kid out there, I was Jerry Markbreit, referee. I was the *real* Jerry Markbreit.

During those years, as I started to settle into my football persona, I became the referee *all* the time—on the field, at the job, at home. I was more regimented, more "take-charge." Bobbie, always a free spirit, absolutely hated it. I was away every weekend for months at a time; I was bossy at home; she didn't like being treated like "one of your football crew." We argued about it all the time. I'd say, "Why am I killing myself at a job I really hate? If I could only make a living at officiating." Bobbie'd say, "If you devoted as much time and energy to your job as you do to shlepping around a football field, you'd make a *great* living."

I recall working a high school game on a Friday night when our daughters were babies. I came home and there were Bobbie and a neighbor huddled on the couch in fear, with their feet folded under them. When I walked in, Bobbie burst into tears and told me that a mouse had been running around the house for three hours, and they were afraid to get off the couch. The babies were in the living room and she was worried about them, too. She yelled angrily, "I'm tired of you never being home when I need you in a crisis. Make a decision right now. It's either gonna be me or officiating." Without thinking, I said, "Where are your suitcases?"

I don't know if I was serious or not. I was just getting my feet wet in officiating, and I knew it was something special for me. When she threatened me, I realized how important it really was. I can't remember what Bobbie replied, but we're still married.

My progress was so encouraging in 1964, I could see that down the road, if I really worked hard, I might have a shot at becoming a full-time college official, hopefully in the Big Ten. I never saw farther than that. I thought: "Can you imagine the prestige and excitement of working a Michigan-Ohio State game or a Michigan State-Notre Dame game?" On a Saturday afternoon that year, while packing my gear for a game that night, I was watching the Notre Dame-Michigan State game. My four-year-old, Betsy, who was always fascinated with my official's equipment, helped me pack. An official on TV made an exciting call and I looked at Betsy as she set my striped shirt in my bag and I said, "Betsy, you see that?" She looked at the television with wide eyes. I said, "Someday Daddy will do that game on TV." She said, "When, Daddy?" I gave her my whistle and cap. "I don't know, honey," I said seriously. "Someday *soon*."

That vision was driving me. That's why I worked so obsessively. I believed firmly that the Big Ten was where I would find ultimate contentment and success. The Big Ten, I thought, was my promised land.

# 6. THE PROMISED LAND

I had a tremendous schedule booked for the 1965 season: Public and Catholic leagues; CCIW; IIC. I was all set. In March, I got a call from Bob James, commissioner of the Mid-American Conference. He said Bill Reed had recommended me highly, and would I like three games as a referee in the Mid-American this fall? I accepted eagerly. These were major college games: Louisville at Western Michigan; Marshall at Kent State; Dayton at Toledo. And I could still work all my other games.

I was flying high into summer. On July 11, 1965—out of the blue—came the call of calls. "Daddy," yelled my daughter Kathy, "it's Bill Reed!" I chuckled to myself. Guys in the officiating game always called each other and said, "It's Bill Reed." You'd get on the phone, excited, and the guy would say, "Ha-ha, it's *me*, Joe Dokes!" In fact, Ed Maracich—a longtime Big Ten basketball and football official—did that a lot.

So I picked up the phone and groused, "Yeah, what do you want?" The voice at the other end said, "Jerry, this is Bill Reed." I said, "Okay Ed, cut the baloney." The voice insisted, "Jerry, it *is* Bill Reed." Suddenly I realized it *was* Reed. I said, "Oh, excuse me, Commissioner. I

66

thought it was one of the guys playing a practical joke. They often do that, you know. And your name is the one they usually use." He said with a laugh, "I've heard that before. But are you convinced it's me?" I said, "Absolutely. I hope you're calling with some good news." Reed said, "The best I can think of. We're offering you two games in the Big Ten this fall. We've been interested in you for a long time. Would you like to join our staff?"

Would I *like* to? Would I like a guided tour of Heaven? "When do I start?" I almost hooted. I took down the dates: Northwestern-Indiana on September 25; Iowa-Minnesota on October 16. My heart was pounding so loud, I thought Reed could hear it. Incredible! All of a sudden, I had two Big Ten games, three Mid-American games, and the rest of my regular schedule. I was on the threshold of a dream year.

I hung up and went absolutely crazy. I hugged the girls and danced with Bobbie and ran around the house, screaming, "I'm in the Big Ten! I'm in the Big Ten!" I called my mother and father and elaborated, "I'm in the Big Ten! I'm in the Big Ten!" That was all the elaboration I could muster.

I couldn't sleep that night. I kept envisioning those Big Ten stadiums and the crowds and the national exposure. It was just starting to sink in: "You made your goal. You're going to be in the Big Ten for the rest of your life. How much luckier can you get?" At 4:00 A.M. I was sky high, so I woke Bobbie out of a dead sleep. "What's *wrong*?" she panicked. "What's the matter? Are the kids all right?" I babbled, "I'm gonna work Ohio State-Michigan games! Notre Dame-Michigan State! Southern Cal-Notre Dame! Can you believe that I'll be in those games—on *television*? I can't believe it! Can *you* believe it?" She yawned, "What time is it?"—and went back to sleep. The next morning, I told her again. "Jerry, that's fantastic," she said sincerely. "Do the dishes. I have to feed the kids."

In Chicago officiating circles, however, I was an instant celebrity. I was the first guy in the area to make the Big Ten in many years. Congratulations poured in.

On July 19, I got the best one—a telegram from Ellie Hasan in Livorno, Italy, where he was refereeing on the Globetrotters' European tour. It read: "HEARD NEWS. CONGRATULATIONS. SEAMS BURSTING. SO PROUD OF YOU. ELLIE." What a wonderful message. I cried when I read it then—and I cry every time I read it now.

At first, I wasn't nervous about the Big Ten games. Even though I had to work as a back judge, I knew the position well and had studied the mechanics and rules. My main job was to watch deep passes and kicks. And while the average official had worked maybe two hundred games before making it to the Big Ten, I had worked more than *six hundred* games—about a hundred more in eight seasons than most guys would work in *twenty*. In chronological age, I was young. In number of games, I was Rip Van Winkle. I thought: "I know what I'm doing now. This will be fun."

On September 25, 1965, Bobbie, my mom, and my dad drove down to Bloomington to see my first Big Ten game: Northwestern at Indiana. I was so proud; I had a chance to display my excellence in front of people I loved. I got another bonus that first game: Howard Wirtz was the referee. He made me feel so comfortable that I started thinking of it as just another game. I remember in the pregame meeting we reviewed the rules, including the new fair-catch rule, which stated you could not advance the football after a fair catch, even if the ball hit the ground. Howard emphasized that change, and then we dressed and went out to the field. I was supremely confident. I was a six-hundred-game rookie, I knew everything I needed to know, this was where I belonged. But just before kickoff, I got butterflies. "My God," I realized, "you're about to actually live your *dream*."

On the first punt of the game, the receiver signaled for a fair catch on the twenty. But the ball bounced, so he grabbed it and ran about thirty yards—and I *let* him run. I was in a fog—just like in my first city league game when I almost tackled the halfback. Wirtz blew the whistle and trotted over to me. Our discussion went like this:

WIRTZ: Wasn't there a fair-catch signal on
   that play?
ME: There sure was.
WIRTZ: Didn't we talk about the new rule be-
   fore?
ME: We sure did.
WIRTZ: Well, is he allowed to run the ball?
ME: He sure isn't.

I'd gotten so excited during the play that I forgot the
rule! Wirtz said calmly, "The ball goes back to the twenty,
where he recovered it." That was a relief; I'd expected
a reprimand. As I started back to my position, Wirtz
thundered, "Don't ever miss that rule again on *my* crew!
Understand, Markbreit?" I looked at his stern face. "I
sure do," was what came out.

I got over the blow before my second Big Ten game:
Minnesota-Iowa at Iowa City. I got to town Friday evening and spent an awful night listening to strange noises
echoing through a dilapidated downtown hotel. In the
morning, I dragged down to meet with the crew. The
referee was Ross Dean, who would eventually work thirty
years in the conference. He saw the tightness on my
face, so he tried to put me at ease. "How'd your first
game go?" he asked. I said, "Fine. Except I never had
a penalty." Dean smiled. "Well," he said, "maybe we'll
get your first foul for you today."

The Northwestern-Indiana crowd had been only
about thirty-five thousand, but Iowa had sixty thousand.
Though I'd worked a Prep Bowl in front of more people,
there was something electrifying in a Big Ten crowd. I
had goose bumps out there. This time I wasn't so cocky.
I wanted to prove to everybody that I really *did* belong
there, that I had what it took.

The game was a barn-burner. In the middle of the
second quarter, I saw a Minnesota defender clobber
an Iowa player out of bounds. I ran over and threw my
flag right in front of the Minnesota head coach, Murray
Warmath. My first flag in a Big Ten game! Suddenly Ross
Dean came tearing over from the middle of the field. I

thought: "Oh, my God, what did I do?" Warmath was ready to blast me when Ross rushed up and said, "Great call, Markbreit. Nice going." I understood what he was doing; he wanted Warmath to know that the rookie knew his stuff. I never forgot Ross for that classy gesture. In the pressure of a game, not many people consider the other guy's problems.

My 1966 Big Ten schedule arrived in the mail on April 5. I had six games, all as a back judge: Notre Dame at Northwestern; Minnesota at Indiana; Purdue at Michigan State on national TV; Ohio State at Minnesota on national TV; Purdue at Minnesota; and, on November 19, Notre Dame at Michigan State on national TV. Three TV games—which were expected because almost all of Howard Wirtz's games were televised. This was a heckuva schedule for a second-year official.

I was now a regular member of a Big Ten crew for the first time. There was Wirtz; myself; Bob Hepler from Indiana; Bill Makepeace from Ohio; and Ed Bronson from Chicago. I was the youngest, the pisherkeh. And that's the way they treated me. I was the last guy in the car; the bag-hiker; the meal reservation man; the shlepper they sent sprinting to the airport gate to hold the plane for the rest of the crew—and God forbid it should leave *without* them. It was like college hazing all over again.

Wirtz was our father-figure and captain. He ran a tight ship. We had long meetings and a lot of study groups on the weekends. "What an opportunity," I thought. "For a whole season, I can observe firsthand how Howard Wirtz molds a crew into a unit." He insisted that the crew spend "personal" time together on game weekends. A lot of crews would come in for games the night before and go straight to sleep. They'd meet the next morning at the stadium for the first time—the only time they'd spend together. Howard Wirtz's crew always arrived Friday night to have dinner together, met the next morning for breakfast, and traveled to the stadium together. Through this routine, strangers slowly became

friends—even if they didn't want to. The closeness off the field made it easier to work as a unit on the field. I had this in my high school officiating days with "The Four Musketeers," but I didn't think we'd have that closeness in the Big Ten. We did, because Wirtz drew us together like a family, even though we barely knew each other.

Wirtz was an emperor. He arranged activities, set up timetables, gave orders. Though some guys didn't like his dictatorial manner, he commanded such respect that everyone accepted it. He always called us during the week to kibitz and toss in reminders: "Get yourself prepared for next week. Review that new rule." Or, "What time are you arriving? Remember, we meet at the hotel at five-thirty for dinner." He used to tell me, "Markbreit, when you leave home, leave everything there except your football knowledge. Otherwise, stay home and watch TV." On the field, he kept us on our toes by constantly reminding us, "Concentrate! Don't let *anything* distract you from the game." After enough time with Howard Wirtz, I found myself doing things his way—and enjoying it.

Early in the '66 season, at the Minnesota-Indiana game, I had my second humorous encounter with Murray Warmath. I went into the Minnesota locker room before the game and announced, "Two minutes, Coach. Bring 'em out on the field." Warmath snapped, "We'll come out when we want to." That threw me. It was only my fourth Big Ten game; I had no idea what to do. So I came back out and reported to Wirtz, "He says he'll come out when he wants to." Wirtz gave me the executioner's glare. "Get back in there and get him out on the field!" he ordered. I raced back in and said breathlessly, "Coach, you've got to come out right now!" He said, "Maybe we'll come out, maybe we won't." I didn't want to face Wirtz again, so I continued to badger Warmath. "Coach, you're jeopardizing your team. Let's bring 'em out." Strained silence. Finally he said, "I'll think about it and let you know." I was petrified. I thought: "What if he *stays* in there?"

I stood around, worrying. Suddenly the locker room door opened and out strolled Warmath. He walked leisurely toward the tunnel, followed by his players—one at a time. They walked practically in slow motion all the way up the tunnel and onto the field. It must've taken them five minutes to reach midfield. From there, Warmath glanced over at me, grinned, and shook his head. He'd really tested the rookie. Right after that, I took my position for the kickoff, which happened to be right in front of Warmath. He came over and draped his arm around my shoulders. "Okay rook," he said, "I've given you enough raspberries. Now work a good game." I did—and from then on, whenever I worked one of Murray Warmath's games, his team was always the fastest out of the locker room at the start of a game.

The highlight of 1966, of course, was the controversial "Game of the Century"—undefeated, number one Notre Dame vs. undefeated, number two Michigan State at East Lansing. It was rare that the number one and number two teams would meet—undefeated, yet—at the end of a season. So this was a dream game for all the marbles: the national championship.

All through the season, we knew that this would probably be an important game, but we never imagined it would be of the magnitude it was. The media buildup was tremendous. The game was touted for weeks as a matchup of all-time college football giants. The atmosphere was like that of a Super Bowl game today. And in those days, you didn't have six good college games on TV every Saturday. This was the nation's feature attraction.

When we arrived in East Lansing on Friday, the town was going wild. It was late November, but people were driving around like it was summertime, hanging out their windows and honking their horns; the press was twenty-deep; every hotel room was booked. We stayed at the Kellogg Center on campus and I remember that when we walked in with our bags, people took notice: "Here come the officials." During dinner, people watched us like we were visiting dignitaries. It was the most highly

charged pregame atmosphere I'd ever experienced. But I kept telling myself: "Ignore the hype." This was only my eighth Big Ten game; I couldn't afford to be overawed before I walked onto the field.

The crew knew that the game was something special, but we didn't dwell on it. We went about our business and kept a low profile. We didn't want to draw any attention to ourselves, we just wanted to work the game and get out of there alive. That was on *all* our minds. But we were ready for anything. Howard Wirtz had prepared us for this game with such devotion and care, and gave us so much confidence, we felt we could've officiated the world championship. At our pregame meeting, he gave us an extra pep talk. "Gentlemen," he said, "this is the biggest game of the year. Maybe the biggest game in the next *hundred* years. We must do an outstanding job today because we don't want anyone to remember us. We must work this game so expertly that, later, it will seem as if we weren't even there."

When I marched up the tunnel and onto the field, my first thought was: "This is going to be the biggest game I'll ever work." Of course, that was narrishkeit (nonsense). I've worked many bigger games since then. Yet, in retrospect, I'm still amazed at the talent that was out there. MSU had Gene Washington, who went on to be an All-Pro end for the Vikings; Bubba Smith, all-everything for the Colts; George Webster, probably the first superstar rover back and later a fine pro; running back Clint Jones; and barefoot kicker Dick Kenney. Notre Dame was just as impressive: Alan Page; Jim Seymour; Terry Hanratty; Jim Lynch; Rocky Bleier; Bob Kuechenberg. And Nick Eddy didn't even play because he fell off the train at the East Lansing station and reinjured his shoulder.

Spartan Stadium was stuffed to the gills—seventy-seven thousand-plus. The upper decks almost hang over the playing field there, and they were so loaded that I thought people might actually topple out. MSU fans had a million signs. The best one was a thirty-foot banner

that read "BUBBA FOR POPE." That's how popular he was in East Lansing. And, of course, everyone had those buttons "KILL, BUBBA, KILL." Which he almost did. In the first quarter, he put both the starting quarterback (Hanratty) and starting center (George Goeddeke) out for the game with injuries.

The game was not spectacularly well played. Which didn't surprise me because they were two outstanding teams with fantastic defenses that shut the offenses down. They butted heads all afternoon, trying to scratch out a yard here, a yard there. Notre Dame's defense set a record by holding MSU to minus yardage or no gain for sixteen plays. Jones, MSU's leading rusher, got thirteen yards all day; Seymour, Notre Dame's great receiver, dropped his only chance. The rest of the game, he ran pass patterns with a frustrated scowl on his face.

The hitting was devastating. Ferocious tackling, guys battling for literally inches of turf. It was like concrete walls colliding until a chip or two cracked off. I had never seen a football game where the hitting was harder. We had clips, interference, head-on collisions, five fumbles, four interceptions, and a thousand incomplete passes. Even Notre Dame's touchdown pass skimmed the defender's fingertips into Bob Gladieux's hands. Nothing was free out there. They'd physically punished their opponents all year long, and they were doing the same to each other now. They were so evenly matched, it was hard to see how *anyone* could win.

Late in the third quarter, it looked certain that Notre Dame would score a touchdown and take the lead, 14–10. But the drive stalled, and Ara Parsegian sent in his kicker, Joe Azzaro, to tie it from twenty-eight yards out. The crowd had been roaring continuously all game, but now the noise was deafening. I positioned myself under the goalposts. Azzaro booted the ball and it sailed straight over. I signaled "Good" and the sound immediately died. The "Game of the Century" was now a 10–10 deadlock.

The score didn't concern me; I was busy trying to do my job. One thing people don't understand is that of-

ficials are neither fans nor spectators. I'm out there looking at the game strictly from an official's point of view.
I don't know or care who the stars are, what's at stake,
or what the announcers are saying on TV. I know from
nothing. For years after this game, people asked me
how it felt to be an official in the biggest college game
of our time and I always said, "Which game was that?"
They're consummate fans nudjeling me about what
happened in the game, and I might only say, "Oh, we
had two holds, a roughing the kicker, and a roughing
the passer." To me, *that's* an exciting game.

Late in the fourth quarter, a Notre Dame defender
picked off a Spartan pass and ran it back to the MSU
18. Everybody thought this was it—the Irish would run
a few plays and kick the winning field goal. They ran
two running plays and a pass, and *lost* yardage. In
came Azzaro to try a forty-two-yard field goal. I remember standing right under the goalposts waiting for
the kick that would determine the national champion.
I was scared stiff I'd make a mistake—but I couldn't
wait to make the call. What a sense of *power!*

The ball headed straight toward me . . . kept coming
. . . still looked good . . . then angled off at the last second
and missed by a foot. I waved it off, and the whole
stadium let out a sigh. I thought: "God, I hope I'm right."
I *knew* I was right, but I also knew that, for a split second,
one of the biggest college games ever was in Jerry
Markbreit's hands. That little moment was a tremendous
thrill for me; it's exactly the kind of moment that officials
live for. I used to wonder: "What would've happened if
I had sneezed and missed the play?"

As back judge, I was in the middle of the field all
day, so I didn't hear much conversation. Nobody talked,
nobody complained, nobody swore. But with a minute
to play and Notre Dame on its own thirty, the Spartans
started jabbering. When Notre Dame came to the line
for the first play, the defense dug in like soldiers girding
for an enemy assault. I remember thinking: "Ready for
the long pass, Jerry," and at that exact instant, George
Webster hollered to his linemates, "Watch the pass! Watch

the pass!" It was a dive straight into the line. The clock was ticking away and Parsegian let it tick, even though he had time-outs left to call.

The Spartans couldn't believe it. They were so frustrated, they started taunting the Irish offense, "Going for a tie, 'number one'?" "Chicken$% ↑ &#! Go back to high school!" On the MSU sidelines, the whole team waved and yelled and ridiculed Notre Dame. Most of the Notre Dame players looked humiliated; they *wanted* to go for the win. But Parsegian called line dive after line dive until the clock ran out. His decision to go for a tie heaped criticism on him that's still bandied around in football circles today. It was the stuff of legends, so he will probably never live it down.

My only thought at the end of the game was: "I hope we can make it back to the hotel ahead of the crowd." But as we ran off the field, I noticed the stadium was strangely silent. It was like somebody turned the volume down. I stopped and looked around and there were seventy-seven thousand fans riveted to their seats. Nobody got up, nobody moved, nobody spoke. Total devastation. Nobody expected a tie. They desperately wanted a winner. When the game ended in a standoff, they were so struck with disbelief, they just sat silently and stared. It was the eeriest moment of my career.

The officials were shuttled back to the Kellogg Center, where we showered and dressed. I remember coming out of the shower forty minutes later and turning the radio on. The broadcaster said, "They're finally starting to leave Spartan Stadium." I was amazed; they *still* couldn't believe it was a tie.

I felt terrific about the game. The officiating was absolutely flawless. We didn't have one controversial call or a single complaint from anybody. Nobody mentioned us—not the coaches, players, fans, or press. The game ended in probably the most disappointing tie in history and—just as Howard Wirtz had hoped—it was like we weren't there. I was only thirty-one years old; it showed me that the leadership of an experienced referee was crucial to a crew's performance. In fact, due

to the brilliant choreographing of Howard Wirtz, that was one of the most perfectly officiated college football games of all time. And Jerry Markbreit *was* there.

When the '66 season ended, Wirtz sent a letter to every man on the crew. It said something like, "Gentlemen, we have just completed the most successful officiating year of my Big Ten career. We not only worked an almost perfect season, we also conducted one of the biggest games in conference history without incident. I can't express how proud I am of every man on this crew, including our rookie, Jerry Markbreit."

The incredibly exhilarating ending to my first full year as a Big Ten official whetted my appetite for 1967. When my assignments came in April, I was excited to find I'd gotten eight Big Ten games, seven as a back judge and one—Missouri at Northwestern—as a referee. I couldn't wait for that game. When Ellie Hasan heard the news, he called and congratulated me. And he added, "Let's have lunch. I want to talk." There was something odd in his voice, but I couldn't put my finger on it at the time.

On a Wednesday afternoon, we met at Walgreen's Drug Store—Ellie's favorite luncheonette near Hyde Park High School. His regular lunch was waiting for him: black coffee, peaches, cottage cheese. At sixty, he was still officiating basketball and football, and he was in excellent shape. But I thought he looked pale. He said he had some minor chest pains recently, but he took a complete physical and everything was fine. I was concerned. I'd known Ellie for twenty-seven years, I loved him like family. I suggested that maybe he should see another doctor, but he said no, he'd touched all the bases.

He told me how thrilled he was to hear from Bill Reed that I was scheduled to work a Big Ten game as a referee. We reminisced about the high school games we'd worked together, especially the game when I was referee and he was field judge. He got a big kick out of that—teacher and pupil working together! What he'd

really love, he said, would be a chance to work just one Big Ten game with me. I thought it might be possible to get on the same crew. "In fact," I said, "I have a sneaking feeling that we *will* work together." He lit up, "Wouldn't that be something?"

We talked about everything—how proud he was of my success; the responsibilities of being a referee; the prestige of the Big Ten; my schedule for the year. He advised me not to try to accomplish too much too quickly, and to work very hard even though I might think I knew it all. "It isn't enough to be good," he insisted. "It isn't even enough to be great. You should always strive to be the *best.*" We talked for two hours—our longest conversational visit in all the years we'd known each other. I had the feeling he didn't want it to end.

That Friday night, I attended the Central Officials' Association's annual banquet. Ellie was president and everyone was waiting for him to arrive. While we were kibitzing over cocktails, we got a call: Ellie had passed away. He'd been getting ready that evening when he had a heart attack and died. I was devastated. I couldn't believe it. I had just *seen* him. I recalled the strangeness in his voice that day, and his reluctance to end the conversation—and now I understood. He had sensed he might never see me again.

Ellie Hasan had so many notable friends of such long standing that I felt honored to be selected as one of his pallbearers. I was the only younger person accorded that great honor. At the funeral, I felt like my father had passed away. But I knew that my memories of Ellie's generosity would inspire me throughout my life. That helped cushion my loss. And I told myself that Ellie would want me to go on and become the best official there ever was. Maybe I never will be—maybe *nobody* can be—but that's what I'm still shooting for.

Through the summer of 1967, every time I opened the Big Ten rule book or studied referee mechanics, I thought of Ellie. Only when September rolled around did I start anticipating the Missouri-Northwestern game, my first Big Ten game as a referee. I thought: "I'm ded-

icating that game to Ellie Hassan. He's the one who got
me there."

Finally the day arrived. In interconference games,
we worked split crews. Two Big Eight officials joined
three of us from the Big Ten. The umpire was a big,
hulking Texan named Harold "Moose" Saunders, and
the field judge a leathery, "down home" veteran named
Earl Shostrom. They'd officiated many big games—
Oklahoma-Nebraska; Orange Bowls; Cotton Bowls. I respected their credentials, and I wanted to impress them
with my work. I was nervous that they'd be watching
me closely because I'd told them that this was my first
assignment as a referee.

Things went fine until midway through the second
quarter. I was trailing the quarterback on a bootleg
play when he got hammered out of bounds. Bang, my
flag came out and, in my zeal, I grabbed the ball and
ran off the fifteen yards without getting my bearings. I
ran the wrong way. The other guys were screaming
and waving at me, but I was moving so fast that only
a bullet from a thirty-aught-five could have stopped me.

When I placed the ball on the ground, I was so proud.
But when I looked up and saw everybody else standing
back there, my stomach sank. I looked at Moose and
Earl; they were worried and amused at the same time.
I thought: "Jerry, you shnook. How could you *do* that?"
I was horrified and embarrassed. It was my first big call
as a referee; I was in front of my home crowd; and I
had two veterans from the Big Eight watching me.

I corrected my mistake and finished the game, and
afterward everybody was sympathetic. Moose and Earl
kidded me lightly and were very professional. But when
I went home, I felt like such a horse's behind. A half
hour later, Bill Reed phoned. He said, "Jerry, I was at
your game today." I thought: "Oh, great, the *commissioner* saw it, too." He said, "I wanted to congratulate
you on an excellent job running the game. And listen,
Jerry, there isn't a referee alive who hasn't walked the
wrong way on a penalty." I said, "Thank you, Commissioner. But I *ran* the wrong way." He laughed. "It's not

the first time," he said, "and it probably won't be the last. So forget about it. You really did a fine job. I just wanted to tell you that."

I laid the phone down and, boy, I felt like a million bucks. This important man took time out—probably at a postgame party—to call and tell me I did a fine job. That was the kind of quality person Bill Reed was. Between then and the day he passed away in 1971, we were very good friends. I felt a special fondness for him; he was instrumental in my success.

That game had also marked the start of my friendship with Northwestern's popular coach, Alex Agase. He was a rough, tough, former All-American football player and a highly regarded head coach. The moment I introduced myself to him before the game, he looked at me with such warmth and gave me such a hardy handshake that I somehow knew we would become good friends. And we did. Year after year, we'd discuss the Big Ten and officiating, and he would constantly say, "Jerry, we're losing all the good officials to the pros. But I know *you'll* never desert us." And I always said, "That's right, Coach. They'll have to kill me to get rid of me." Many years later, in a mysterious phone call, Agase would taunt me about that.

In 1967, too, the compliment of compliments was paid our crew when the league gave us the nationally televised Michigan State-Notre Dame game at Notre Dame. We had done such a good job in '66, they gave it to us again—back-to-back. That was rare. I told Bobbie, "Being on Howard Wirtz's crew is like traveling with the president of the United States."

I felt that 1968 was going to be a exceptional year for me because Bill Reed had indicated in late '67 that I would be a full-time referee with my own crew. Then the shocker occurred: In February I got a call from Mark Duncan, supervisor of officials for the National Football League. He said he would be in Chicago the next day, and could I meet him at his airport hotel. I asked what it was all about and he said, "To discuss your future in

the NFL." I was absolutely speechless. I hadn't even *applied*.

The next morning, we had breakfast at his hotel. "We've scouted you for the last two years," he began, "and we like your work. We're prepared to take you into the league for 1968. You'll be on a crew immediately and work a full schedule." I was still speechless. My first thought was: "How did this happen?" Then it occurred to me: "Don't accept."

I had never considered the NFL. After working for three years in the Big Ten, I was about to be promoted to crew chief and referee—my ultimate career dream fulfilled. I was confused. "Mr. Duncan," I said, "I've been told I'm going to be a referee in the Big Ten this year. If I come into the NFL, I'll probably never get a chance to become a referee." He thought it over. I said, "Highly unlikely—true or false?" He said, "Probably true. Your collegiate experience has been at back judge, and that's where we'd use you." I said, "My position is really referee. That's where I want to work. Can I think about this for a couple of days and let you know?" He was shocked that I didn't accept on the spot.

That night, I talked it over with Bobbie. I was tempted to go into the NFL, but I felt unprepared. I was deathly afraid of going too soon and failing. I felt confident and secure in my progress in the Big Ten, and I wanted my chance at referee. I had to prove to myself that I could handle the job. Bobbie and I decided that I should talk to the Big Ten people before making up my mind. We finally agreed on something.

The next day, I met with the Big Ten's new supervisor of officials, Herman Rohrig. Herman was an All-American football star at Nebraska who later played with the Green Bay Packers. He began his officiating career in the Big Eight and then spent ten years in the NFL. At age fifty, he became Big Ten supervisor of officials for basketball and football. I related my dilemma, and we spent two hours reviewing my records. He said, "You're very highly rated. The league has much confidence in you. You'll have seven games as a referee this year,

including the Ohio State-Michigan game. And I think it's unlikely you'll work as an NFL referee without prior college experience at the position." I said, "If I turn them down, will they ever come back to me?" Rohrig replied flatly, "That's the risk you take."

The next day, I phoned Mark Duncan and told him I decided to stay in the Big Ten. "My life's dream is to become a referee," I said. He was surprised. "Are you sure that's your final decision?" I said, "Yes, sir. But thank you very much for asking me. I hope you'll come back to me another time." I knew I made the right decision. Today I'm still convinced that had I gone into the NFL at that time, I would've been a back judge, field judge, side judge, or line judge throughout my whole career. I would've never been a referee.

I had a lot to think about in the spring and summer of 1968. At the tender age of thirty-three, I was going to be my own crew chief for the first time. The Big Ten was taking no chances with me; they assigned me a crew of experienced, older veterans. This was a big challenge—one I would encounter again many years later when I became a rookie crew chief in the NFL. My biggest task was to mold these veterans into a working unit. I wasn't worried about the football games as much as my relationships with the crew. I had to prove to the group that I was worthy of being their chief. I wanted very badly to gain their acceptance; to impress the league; to become a good leader; and to help the crew do excellent work. So instead of adopting the authoritarian approach, I asked for their cooperation. At our first pregame conference I said, "Gentlemen, I hope you will give me as much help as possible in planning our meetings and activities this year, so I can succeed in this position." That attitude quickly won them over.

I started the 1968 season with a Mid-American game—Miami of Ohio at Xavier. The Miami coach was a young man by the name of "Bo" Schembechler. Though Miami won that game, Schembechler was distressed with the officiating. When the game ended, he stormed onto the field and confronted me as I was leaving. He

told me it was the worst officiating he had ever seen in a Mid-American game, and that I was the worst referee he'd seen in many years. Here he'd *won* and he was hotter than hell! He barked, "You'll never work for me again, if I have anything to say about it!" I thought: "Where have I heard *that* before?"

That year also, I got my first look at the finest back in the nation—a graceful, fluid, powerful runner by the name of O. J. Simpson. I had the Northwestern-Southern Cal game in which he ran for over three hundred yards. I felt so important that day because the league had assigned me to a game with the nation's premier running back—even though I was working as crew chief that year for the first time. I remember talking to Howard Wirtz about that game. I was really thrilled that I was starting to get games with great players like Simpson. Surprisingly, he said, "Get out of college football and get into the NFL. The future is there." For the rest of that season, whenever we talked, he hounded me about that: "You've devoted so many years and so much effort to officiating, it's a crime for you not to be in the best football league in the land. You're wasting your time in the Big Ten." There would come a time when I would feel that way, but it wasn't now.

In the Big Ten, I not only had the privilege of officiating games with great young athletes, I also had some of the game's legendary coaches. The most memorable for me was Ohio State's Woody Hayes. When I had him in '68, he'd already developed a reputation for being unpredictable. At the close of the season, we had Michigan-Ohio State at Columbus—the biggest game of the year. At stake were the conference title and the Rose Bowl berth. At OSU, the officials' dressing room was directly above State's dressing room. Hayes had easy access to us, and he had a habit of coming in there under the pretense of asking a question. The league frowned on that. Coaches were not permitted in there before a game. But nobody ever reported him. The scuttlebutt around the league was, "You have a game at Ohio State? Hayes'll be in to diagram for you."

Sure enough, Woody entered smiling. "Oh, hi, fellas. What's the correct time?" I'd given it to him earlier, but I gave it again anyway. He said, "You know, we were noodling a play around downstairs and I wondered what you fellas thought of it." He pulled a piece of chalk from his pocket and started diagraming on a chalkboard. It was a hideout play, and he described it as he drew: "The tailback's over here, see. And the end goes here—"

"Coach," I said, "you know that play is illegal." A surprised look on his face. "Well, I'll be darned," he said innocently. "I thought it was legal." I said, "No, Coach." He looked at me blankly: "Well, I spoke to the commissioner and he—" I cut him off: "Coach, if you run that play today, it's illegal." He put the chalk back in his pocket. "Okay," he said. "Thanks a lot, fellas. I just wanted to know. We won't run it today." Then he walked out.

We all laughed. My crew—Vic Wukovits, Bud Shopbell, Ed Bronson, and Len Heinz—were seasoned vets; they'd seen this tactic many times before. They knew that Woody had no intention of running that play. He thought that the more contact he had with the officials before a big game, the more edge he might have. Vic said to me, "You handled him pretty good. But he's easy to handle in here. Out on the field, he's impossible." I chuckled because I knew I could handle *anybody*—never dreaming that just three years down the road, Woody Hayes and I would tangle in one of the most controversial fiascos in college football history.

In that '68 title game, Woody showed another side to him that I would never understand. Off the field, he was a warm, gentle, wonderful man. But on a football field, he was possessed. His obsession with winning sometimes transformed him into the Wild Man from Borneo. With about a minute left in the Michigan game, Ohio State scored a touchdown to lead, 48–14. Woody sent in Jim Otis—the power fullback who later played pro in St. Louis—for a two-point conversion. The home crowd roared its approval. Bump Elliott, the Michigan

coach, threw a fit on the sideline. This was really rub-
bing salt in his wounds. Otis smashed over right guard
to score the forty-ninth and fiftieth points. When the game
ended, Elliott ran off the field without shaking Hayes'
hand.

A few weeks later, Elliott was replaced as head coach
by Bo Schembechler. Recalling the lashing Schembechler gave me after he beat Xavier, I thought: "Boy,
Schembechler's *perfect* for this league. They *kill* each
other here!"

The next year, 1969, I was to work two Mid-American
and eight Big Ten games as referee. The league decided to pull some of the older veterans off my crew—
a sign that they felt I had arrived as a referee. One of
the new faces was Bill Quinby's. He and I had been
friends since we came into the Big Ten together in '65,
and I'd hoped we would someday be on a crew together. Quinby was a low-key, soft-spoken school teacher
from Cedar Rapids, Iowa, who'd been an outstanding
athlete in high school and at the University of Iowa. The
interesting thing about Quinby was his dual personality.
Off the field, he was a shy, reserved Caspar Milquetoast.
On the field—shazzam!—*King Kong:* intense, hard-driv-
ing, explosive. For seven years, I needled the crap out
of him for that.

Our crew was assigned the Ohio State-Michigan
game for the second year in a row—a very high honor.
Every year, that was the biggest game in the conference. Even Howard Wirtz never had that game two
years in a row. We also got the Michigan State-Notre
Dame game for the third time. My first memory from
that season was a small moment before the opening
game between Vanderbilt and Michigan—Bo Schembechler's first game as Michigan's coach. When I walked
out on the field, Schembechler gestured at me. I walked
over and he said, "Markbreit!" and smiled. I wasn't
surprised he remembered my name, just that he was
smiling. He said, "I guess I don't have too much influence
in the Big Ten, do I?" I said, "That's correct, Coach. Here

you are and here I am." "Well, I hope we can start fresh here," he said good-naturedly. "I've got my hands full just being in this league." I said, "Oh, I don't know, Coach. Somehow I think you'll fit right in." We shook hands—and we never had another bump in our relationship.

The next highlight of '69 was in October, when the league office asked me to fill in on the Michigan State–Iowa game as back judge. I hadn't worked as back judge for a couple of seasons, but I thought it would be fun because my old friend Frank Strocchia was the umpire, and the crew chief was Gene Calhoun, one of the finest referees in the conference. In fact, Calhoun would eventually earn the distinction of being the only referee ever to work the Rose Bowl, Cotton Bowl, Orange Bowl, and Sugar Bowl—a remarkable honor. Today he's supervisor of officials for the Big Ten.

Little did I know that this "fun" game would mark the beginning of a series of personal humiliations for me in Kinnick Stadium. In this first incident, I was positioned under the goalposts for an Iowa field goal. I stood midway between the posts, as I always did, but when the kick drifted right I moved toward it so I would be in perfect position. As I approached the post—bam!— I was sprawled on my back. I'd fallen over a photographer who'd crept to the border of the end zone for a shot of the kick. His camera went flying, broken into a million pieces; he was moaning on the ground; and I was flat on my back as the ball flew *somewhere* over the posts.

I looked at Calhoun, who was looking at me, anxiously awaiting my signal. I gave him the shrugging-hands sign: "Sorry, Gene. I couldn't call that one if my *life* depended on it." He spotted the ball sailing way beyond the posts, turned toward the press box, and signaled that the kick was good. To this day, I don't think he knows—nor do I—whether it was good or not. Gene has been telling people for nineteen years how I blew that kick. He says, "That Markbreit. He was always on his backside when I needed him."

* * *

Something subtle stands out about the 1970 season
—a lesson in relationships. Our second game was the
Texas Christian-Wisconsin game at Wisconsin. It was a
split crew, with two Southwest Conference officials. The
field judge was a bright, witty Texan named Horton
Nesrsta (pronounced "Ne-ses-ta"). He was one of the
top officials in his league and he'd worked a bowl game
every year. We met for the first time at dinner the Friday
evening before the game. We traded officiating phi-
losophies and found we had a lot in common.

We talked more the next day at breakfast, and then
we officiated the game together. Afterward we said,
"Let's keep in touch." And we did. On the basis of that
one football weekend, we remained friends. After Horton had retired from the Southwest Conference, the supervisor of officials for the new United States Football
League asked me if I knew any officials in the Southwest
who might like to work in the league. I recommended
Horton, and he came out of retirement to work three
years in the USFL.

Today we're still friends—even though we haven't
seen each other in eighteen years. He watches me on
my NFL TV games and calls to say, "I saw your game.
You did a great job." It's that mysterious camaraderie
syndrome associated with officiating. When you work
a game with a guy and spend a couple of days with
him, you somehow develop a common bond that can
last a lifetime. I think the key ingredient is the mutual
respect you develop when you're under the gun with
someone. In my experiences outside of officiating, I've
never spent thirty hours with anyone and had it turn
into the kind of lifelong friendship I have with Horton
Nesrsta. That's part of the special magic of "officialism."

On my 1971 schedule were my third Ohio State-
Michigan game; Michigan State-Ohio State; and Southern Cal-Notre Dame—a dynamic season. I didn't know
it then, but 1971 would be the year that all hell broke
loose. I was about to find out if I was tough enough

to withstand the pressures of adversity in Big Ten officiating.

On October 9 I had the Indiana-Wisconsin game in Wisconsin's beautiful Camp Randall Stadium. This was my seventh Big Ten season and I had several of the conference's best games, so I knew I was one of their top-rated referees. But Herman Rohrig was at the game, and I wanted to impress him.

Early in the game, a Wisconsin receiver appeared to haul in a pass in the end zone, and the field judge signaled touchdown. I was watching from forty yards away, and when I saw his arms go up, I turned to the press box and gave the touchdown signal. But when I started downfield for the extra-point play, I caught the end of the field judge's signal for incompleted pass and I realized he'd made a mistake.

I brought the ball back to the forty, feeling annoyed and embarrassed. When you give a touchdown signal and then take it away from the home team—even if they aren't entitled to it—the crowd never forgives you. The booing was ferocious. I started to pout, thinking: "The supervisor's here and I made such a fool out of myself." I was so upset, I sulked like a four-year-old through the whole first half. In my immaturity, I'd forgotten how easy it was to make a mistake by anticipating the outcome of a play. No harm had really been done by giving the touchdown signal—except to my ego and pride.

At halftime, Herman Rohrig came down to our dressing room, and he was absolutely furious with me. He chewed me from top to bottom: "Don't you *ever* show your emotions on the football field. Don't *ever* show anybody you're upset. When the players and coaches see you like that, *they* get upset because they feel you've lost control of the game. No matter how embarrassed or scared or irritated you are at yourself or anyone else, *never* show it on the field. If I ever see you do that again, I'll yank you right off the next game."

I knew he was right. And I never reacted that way again. I've had plenty of embarrassing situations where

I felt like pouting, or where I was furious at myself or somebody else. But I kept it inside. I always imagined Herman sitting up there, thinking: "Don't show how you feel. Stone-face is the name of the game." It was a valuable lesson that would pay off that same season, because the biggest test of Jerry Markbreit's character—maybe of *any* official's character—loomed just ahead.

First, there was the USC-Notre Dame game on October 23. John McKay brought his highly ranked Trojans to South Bend for another pressure-cooker game against Ara Parsegian's Irish. Even though I had worked several Notre Dame games, I never felt that Parsegian liked seeing me. The chemistry wasn't good between us. I knew that the pressure on him was unbelievable, so I always tried to be very polite. But he constantly seemed irritated with me. For whatever reason, he reacted to me as if he thought I was an arrogant young official who didn't show him the proper respect. This certainly wasn't the case, but I could never convince him.

Before the USC game, I went into the Notre Dame locker room to give him the time, and I could see that he was extremely tense. "Coach," I said, "you got five minutes." He jumped right down my throat. "Our films show that Southern Cal does a lot of holding," he said. "I want you and your crew to watch for that." His tone was gruff. I said, "We'll do the best we can, Coach—just like in every other game." Parsegian blew up. "That's not good enough!" he said. "I'm sick and tired of getting those kind of answers from officials!"

He was in an unprovoked frenzy. I said, "Coach, if you have nothing else to say to me, I'll see you out on the field." He hollered, "I'm not through talking to you!" I said, "Well, I'm through talking to you." As I turned to leave, he started coming after me. But one of his assistants stepped between us, and I went out the door knowing it was going to be one rough day.

Southern Cal went ahead, 21–0. They shoved Notre Dame all over the field. The players exchanged a lot of angry chatter, and I had that tinderbox sensation. Then, boom, a fight erupted. Everybody and his brother

were punching, kicking, wrestling; the benches emptied; substitutes limped onto the field and started bashing people with crutches; even the coaches mixed it up. It was one of the worst brawls I'd ever seen.

The fight had broken out so suddenly and spread so fast, the officials could do nothing more than stand back and watch until it burned itself out. I was frustrated because I knew we would probably be blamed for losing control of the game. But this was spontaneous mayhem—*nobody* could've prevented it. Finally, we stopped it and finished the half. And as we ran off the field, I turned to a Southern Cal assistant behind me and said, "That was the most horse$%& ↑ fight I've ever seen in my life." And I kept running for the dressing room.

I was in the dressing room discussing the fight with the two West Coast officials on our split crew when, suddenly, someone kicked the door open. It was John McKay. He stormed in and raged, "Who the #$ ↑ & is the referee?" I said, "I am." He yelled, "How dare you call me horse$%& ↑ !" I said, "I didn't call you horse$%& ↑ , Coach. I said that the fight was the most horse$%& ↑ fight I'd ever seen in my life. But let me ask *you* a question. Why are you in here? Who do you think you are, kicking in the door to the officials' dressing room? You can't intimidate me. You can't keep me from working your games. I work in the Big Ten, and in the Big Ten, coaches don't break into officials' rooms making wild accusations. Number one, you're out of line because I didn't say a thing about you. Number two, you have absolutely no business in here, and I'm going to report you. I want you to leave—right *now!*"

McKay was shocked. He turned to his assistant behind him and said, "*Did* he say I was horse$%& ↑ ?" The assistant looked at him meekly and said, "No, sir. He said the *fight* was horse$%& ↑ ." The blood drained from McKay's face. He grabbed his assistant by the arm and out they went. When they were gone, the West Coast officials applauded. One of them said, "In all the years we've worked our conference, nobody's ever stood up to McKay before." It was the greatest thing they'd ever seen.

We went back out for the second half and out ran McKay, leading his team. Something looked odd—and then I realized that the entire Southern Cal team was heading right for me. I thought: "Oh, my God. This guy's gonna attack me and his team is gonna trample me to death!" But as McKay came running up to me, the team stopped behind him and he extended his hand. "Markbreit," he announced loud enough for them to hear, "I owe you an apology. I'm sincerely sorry for the incident. I hope you can forget it." First I breathed again. Then I shook his hand. McKay and his team peeled to the sideline, and that was it.

I was confused but impressed. He realized he'd made a mistake, and he was man enough to apologize to me in front of everybody. After the Parsegian treatment, this was a welcome dose of graciousness. As far as I was concerned, it was forgotten. In fact, he and I would discover farther down the road that this incident created a mutual bond between us.

My previous clashes with coaches were nothing compared to what came next. On November 20, 1971, the most famous—or infamous—incident of my career, and one of the most bizarre in college football history, happened to me and Woody Hayes. We were in Ann Arbor for the traditional big game between Ohio State and Michigan. Ohio State was not having one of their better seasons. In fact, they had lost at home the previous week to Northwestern—the first time they'd lost to Northwestern in a zillion years. Michigan was 10–0, third-ranked and Rose Bowl-bound. They were playing for pride—and for their first perfect season since 1948. Woody was 6–3; he was out of the Rose Bowl and on the brink of one of the poorest records of his twenty-one-year career. He wanted badly to be the spoiler.

The stadium was loaded with 104,016 people—the largest crowd in modern collegiate football history. With about seven minutes to play, Michigan was down, 7–3, with the ball on their own twenty-eight. Then they engineered a five-minute, seventy-two-yard drive that ended with Billy Taylor scoring on a twenty-one-yard run. Ohio State now trailed, 10–7. After the kickoff, they

passed their way to the Michigan forty-five and, all of a sudden, it looked like they might pull it out. With one twenty-five left, the Buckeye quarterback, Donald Lamka, threw a perfect pass to Dick Wakefield on the Michigan thirty-five. But at the last second, Michigan safety Tom Darden leaped over Wakefield and made a spectacular interception. At least I *heard* it was spectacular. I was forty yards away at the time.

I ran downfield and was told by Bill Quinby that it was an interception, Michigan's ball. I pointed in the proper direction and gave the ready-for-play signal. But when I turned around, I was facing a raging Woody Hayes. He had run forty yards to the far hash mark to dispute the interception. Immediately, I threw my flag for unsportsmanlike conduct because coaches were not allowed on the field. He hollered, "Aren't you gonna call that penalty?" I said, "What penalty?" He said, "That was interference! That's *our* ball!" I said, "Coach, you know I was forty yards away. How can I call it?" He blew his stack. "I was *fifty* yards away," he yelled, "and *I* could've called it!"

I stepped out and gave the unsportsmanlike-conduct signal, and Hayes went crazy. He stormed up behind me and yelled, "You little pip-squeak! You're not gonna walk fifteen yards on *me*! You're gonna reverse that call and we're goin' back and *they're* gonna get fifteen for interference!" I said, "Please leave the field, Coach." He said, "No, dammit! I'm staying here until you make the right call! It's our ball, first down!" I'd never seen a coach so angry or out of control. I just hoped he wouldn't hit me because I didn't know what I would've done.

I walked away, picked up the football, and stepped off the fifteen-yard penalty—which gave Michigan a first down in Ohio State territory. Hayes stalked after me, breathing down my neck. I tried to reason with him, "C'mon, Coach, the call's been made. It's time to get off the field." He refused to leave; he was totally irrational. "You little ?*!&-heel!" he screamed. "You haven't been around long enough to make a dent in the Big Ten! You

have a helluva nerve keeping a team as great as Ohio State and a coach as great as I am from the biggest upset of the year! I'm gonna see that you never work another Ohio State-Michigan game for as long as you live!"

Right then, the head of security, who was standing on the Michigan sideline, stepped onto the field and called to me, "Jerry, do you need any help?" I said, "No, we'll handle it." The last thing I wanted was the police coming out there. I didn't want the embarrassment for Hayes; he'd already embarrassed himself enough. I felt badly for him because I knew the repercussions would go all over the country.

So for five minutes and forty seconds, he yelled and threatened and called me every epithet an official has ever been called in the history of football. Hayes knew I hadn't seen the play. He was trying tactical maneuvers on me, hoping I would lose confidence in my crew and maybe go back and see if we'd made a mistake— which, of course, I would never have done. But he knew that the referee was the only one who could make a change, and he thought that intimidating me was the only way to get it done. I never raised my voice or argued. I kept thinking: "Keep your cool, Jerry. Don't get mad, don't use vulgarity, don't say anything that'll come back to haunt you."

I said, "Coach, you will *have* to leave the field now. The play is over, it will not be reversed." He detonated again, "You pip-squeak! I'll fix you! You'll never work another big game again! How could a little pip-squeak like you keep a great team like Ohio State from the biggest upset of the year?" He must've called me a pip-squeak about a dozen times. Only when his upper bridgework fell into his hand did he stop screaming long enough for his assistant coaches to grab him under the armpits and drag him off the field.

When he reached the sideline, we got the game under way again. The Michigan quarterback fell on the ball two plays in a row and, the second time, I saw Ohio State linebacker Randy Gradishar club the quar-

terback in the head with a forearm. I threw my flag and immediately ejected Gradishar from the ball game. The crowd was jeering, booing, going nuts. In college and the pros, you have to escort an ejected player to the sideline. But I felt if I had walked to the Ohio State sideline, I probably would've been mobbed and murdered. So I had my line judge, Dale Orem—the youngest man on our crew—do it instead.

I then walked off the penalty while, unbeknownst to me, Hayes went berserk on the sideline. He yanked the plastic markers off the first-down pole, ripped them apart, hurled them onto the field, then tossed the pole onto the field. He marched ten yards to the other pole and threw that one onto the field, too. Orem came over to inform me. "Brother," he said, "you should see what's going *on* over there. The guy just ripped the down markers apart and threw 'em at me out on the field!" I said, "Geez, it's a good thing *I* didn't go over there. He'd've probably *brained* me with 'em." Dale walked away, shaking his head. And instead of taking his normal position close to the sideline, he stood way out near the middle of the field for the last few plays of the game.

When I got home, I was down in the dumps about the incident. I knew I'd handled it well, but I was sick at heart that it happened. I felt bad for Ohio State; bad for Michigan because it tainted their victory; bad for myself; bad for Hayes. He never recovered from the call. In interviews, he insisted it was interference. At his team banquet, he said, "It was the worst-called play in the history of college football." The biggest lift I got was from reading a column that Bill Quinby sent me from the *Cedar Rapids Gazette.* Gus Schrader wrote about the controversy and closed his column with: "Incidentally, we were impressed with the restraint and poise shown by all the officials, especially Referee Jerry Markbreit, during Woody's tirade." That made me feel terrific.

A small postscript: When I'd left home to go to that game, I told Bobbie, "This game should be routine. I'll come home early and we'll go out to dinner." But before

I got home, my wife had received about thirty calls about the incident, and she didn't know if I was dead or alive. When I arrived, we went down to a neighborhood drug store and there was a half-page picture in the sports section of the *Chicago Tribune* showing me giving the unsportsmanlike-conduct signal with Woody Hayes stalking behind me. That picture appeared in every major newspaper in the United States. I was not thrilled by the publicity. The incident was so widely publicized that everybody swore they saw it on TV, but it wasn't on nationally.

It was the first time I'd gotten that kind of national notoriety. As a result, I was asked to write a column for the *Chicago Sun-Times.* Because of the column, Doubleday asked me to write a question-answer book, *The Armchair Referee,* and I became one of the best-known collegiate referees in the country. I discussed the controversy with Bobbie. We agreed it was a shame that I was center stage for what a lot of people thought was a mistake. I thought of a funny thing my dad used to say: "Nobody notices you until you step on your pecker."

The 1971 season really put me through the mill. Herman Rohrig chewed my tochis at Wisconsin; John McKay kicked in my door at Notre Dame; Woody Hayes almost murdered me at Michigan. Before the Hayes fiasco, I had high hopes of getting my first Rose Bowl. Afterward, I felt so low about the national controversy, I didn't think the conference would send me. But about two weeks later, Herm Rohrig called and said that despite the publicity and controversy, he and Commissioner Duke decided I should get the Rose Bowl.

Bill Quinby also got the game, so we took our families to Pasadena a week early, rented a cottage, visited Disneyland, and lounged around. I was very relaxed going into the game. It was a seesaw battle between Stanford and Michigan, and I remember only two things: On the opening series, there was an encroachment foul against Stanford, and I walked the wrong way on the penalty. Then, in the third quarter, Quinby made a controversial safety call on Stanford to give Michigan a

one-point lead. But at the end of the game, Stanford marched downfield and kicked a field goal with eight seconds left to win, 13–12.

When I returned home, the only thing my friends said was, "You really blew that penalty!" Nobody said, "You worked a good game"—and I was disappointed. I realized that when you work big games, you can't inflate yourself too much because people remember only the errors. I started to understand that if you could walk away without having made some kind of embarrassing mistake in front of everybody, you could consider the assignment a success.

During the first month of the 1972 season I was center stage in another controversy. I had the September 30 Purdue-Notre Dame game at South Bend. It started off when I went into the Notre Dame locker room to deliver the time, and I ran smack into Ara Parsegian's ice-cold shoulder. He didn't look at me, he didn't acknowledge my presence, he didn't even nod. He was probably still annoyed about the confrontation before the Southern Cal game the previous October. I didn't know what the problem was, I just thought, "Not everybody can like you, Jerry. Work a good game and he'll see what you can do."

The game was close, and Notre Dame was poised to score. They'd had great success running, yet on fourth and one Parsegian called for a pass. It was incomplete. I signaled "First down, Purdue" and Parsegian exploded on the sideline. He was waving and screaming at me, and he had to be restrained from coming onto the field. Then we had a discrepancy among the officials. Two thought it was third down, Notre Dame's ball; three thought fourth down, the ball should go over. Even though we always tracked the downs with rubber bands on our fingers, we couldn't determine *positively* what down it was.

In the meantime, Parsegian was hollering to beat the band on one sideline and Bob DeMoss, the Purdue coach, was hopping up and down on the other sideline. I ran over to DeMoss and said, "Coach, we have a dis-

agreement on the down." He said, "What do you mean? It was *fourth* down." I said, "I'll be right back" and I ran across the field to Parsegian. He immediately unloaded on me, "What the hell are you guys doing?" I said, "Coach, we're trying to determine if it was third down or fourth down." He glared right through me. "Do you think I'd be stupid enough to call a pass on a fourth-down play like *that*? Can't you keep the downs straight? It was *third* down!" I said, "I'll be right back." I went back and forth like a yo-yo. Finally, I decided to call the press box and settle it.

I went to the Notre Dame sideline and asked for the phone to the press box. An assistant coach led me to it and I made the call. I said, "Hello, is this the statistician?" A young voice at the other end replied, "Yes." I said, "What down was the last play?" The voice said, "Definitely third down." I hung up, feeling uneasy. I *knew* it had been fourth down. I ran back onto the field and gathered my crew. "Gentlemen," I said, "I just talked to the statistician. He told me it was third down, but I can't believe it. I can't go ahead with this because it's a major error if we make a mistake. I'm going to call up there again and double-check it."

I went back to the same phone. The Notre Dame players jeered and grabbed at me—they wanted to tear me apart. I called again and the same voice answered. I said, "I want you to identify yourself. Who are you?" Click—he hung up. I got University security to escort me back through the players to the timer's table. It was like running a gauntlet. At the timer's table, I had the timer connect me on his phone to the statistician, and I said, "This is Markbreit, the referee, again." An older voice said, "What do you mean 'again'?" I said, "Didn't you just tell me it was third down?" He said, "You didn't talk to me. I was waiting for you to call, but you never did. It was fourth down. The ball belongs to Purdue." I said, "Nobody in your booth talked to me a minute ago?" He said, "No. What phone did you use?" I told him and he said, "That's connected to the Notre Dame student paper. They probably lied."

I didn't bother to find out who that phone connected

to. I just ran back onto the field and signaled "First down, Purdue." Parsegian had to be restrained again by two assistants. He was berating me for all he was worth. I stayed as far away from that sideline as possible for the rest of the game. One of the hallmarks of good officiating, I decided, is that if a guy is furious at you, go the other way. And stay there.

On October 28, 1972, I suffered my second humiliation at Kinnick Stadium—the scene of my famous "on my tochis" field goal call in 1969. A 4–0 Michigan State team with a fierce defense led by future pros Brad Van Pelt and Bill Simpson came into Iowa City heavily favored against a 1–3–1 Iowa club. But State's offense played poorly; they lost five fumbles and kept getting big penalties.

In the middle of the second quarter, Iowa was backed up on their own five-yard line, leading, 6–3. Quarterback Bobby Ousley fed off to Dave Harris for a left-end run. State's defense swarmed in and forced Harris into the end zone for what looked like a sure safety. I was backpedaling behind Harris, trying to get out of his way, but he was extremely quick. He reversed direction and, bang, he knocked me right on my keester. I took three Spartans with me. It was the best block I'd ever thrown. I couldn't believe it—fifty thousand fans, a big ball game, and here I was on my fanny in the end zone with three big shtarkers sprawled all around me. In the meantime, Harris cut around right end for twenty-three yards to the twenty-eight—Iowa's longest gain of the day.

The crowd gave me a standing ovation while I sat there totally mortified: "Shlemiel! How could you get *caught* like that?" Iowa players patted me on the back and needled me, "Thanks, ref. Great block." I said, "Get away from me. Don't talk to me." I thought: "Where can I hide? What if that safety costs Michigan State the game?"

Sure enough, the safety would have meant an 8–6 victory for State because the game ended in a 6–6 tie. In Iowa, I was a hero. I threw the game-saving block in their homecoming game! But Michigan State wanted to kill me. The following week, I felt terrible about it.

Quinby sent me the *Cedar Rapids Gazette* with se-
quence pictures of the play all over the sports section,
and a small commentary: "Markbreit wore a striped
shirt but, once, he couldn't have thrown a prettier block
at a more opportune time if he had been clad in a
Hawkeye jersey." I thought: "I'll never have anything
more humiliating happen to me for the rest of my career."

Mishegoss.

Saturday, October 6, 1973, Kinnick Stadium, Iowa
City. Iowa quarterback Butch Caldwell handed off to
No. 83, Brian Rollins, on an end-around. An Arizona
lineman was right there, twenty yards into the backfield.
He lunged for Rollins and caught him around the waist.
As Rollins turned the corner, the lineman swung straight
out and his feet clipped me at the knees. I toppled on
top of him, knocking him off Rollins, who ran ten more
yards before being tackled. Even though Iowa lost ten
yards on the play, if it hadn't been for my block, they
would've lost twenty. It didn't influence the ball game,
but it was just another humiliation for me.

After that game, Iowa's coach, Frank Lauterbur, said
to me, "Markbreit, every time I look out on our field, I
see you on your back. Do you fall down on every game
you work, or do you wait till you get to Iowa?" I started
feeling jinxed in Iowa because three times in five years
I fell on my behind out in the open in the same stadium.
"The people here," I thought, "must think I'm the biggest
klutz who ever lived."

I realized later that these little events constituted a
message to me that I wasn't as good as I thought, and
that I was a little too cocky. I'd been positioning myself
too close to the quarterback, and I found out I wasn't
as fast backing out as I used to be. It happens today in
the pros. Recently, Joe Montana dropped back fifteen
yards, bumped into me, and boom, down he went.
Somebody tapped him with one finger and it was a
sack. He looked up at me and said, "You're the biggest
jerk I've ever seen!" and threw the football at me. I said,

"You're absolutely right. I *am* the biggest jerk. I should've been out of your way." He said, "Well, why the hell *weren't* you?" I said, "Damned if I know. Did my best." He said, "Well, it ain't good enough." I said, "Okay, thank you."

Humbling by fire is a recurrent phenomenon in officiating. Every time you start to feel invincible, you get knocked back into your place. Whenever you walk out onto a football field *knowing* that you're too good to make a mistake, you make mistakes. It's an important lesson: Never get overconfident. No matter how good you think you are, you're not that good.

I learned another big lesson in 1973. I refereed the annual grudge match between Michigan and Michigan State in East Lansing. It rained all morning and, at kickoff time, the rain was cascading from the upper decks onto the field. All game, the umpire changed the ball on every play and cradled it in a towel until the next play started. Every time we placed the ball down for MSU's quarterback, Charlie Baggett, he kept hocking me, "The ball is wet. We can't play." He did this repeatedly. One time, we changed the ball twice for him on the same play and he said, "Change it again." I was so aggravated, I snapped, "What do you think this is, *room service*?" Then I spotted the ball and forced him to play with it.

When the offense left the field, Baggett repeated what I said to Duffy Daugherty. The next day, Duffy called Rohrig—and then Rohrig chewed my tochis off again. "Don't *ever* talk like that to a player on the field and act like a big shot!" He taught me an important lesson: Don't needle or talk back to football players during a game because no matter how insignificant your chatter might seem to you, the player might be offended, or lose confidence in your credibility, and tattle on you to the coach. Even though my remark wasn't a serious offense, it upset Baggett, and I shouldn't have said it. Bobbie always said I had a big tochis, but after all that chewing out, there wasn't much of it left.

I also remember an uplifting moment during '73. At

the Southern Cal-Notre Dame game, I was anxious to
see my old friend John McKay, whom I hadn't seen since
the "Horse$%&↑" incident in 1971. I didn't report him
for that, so I wondered how he would greet me. When
I walked over to him prior to the game, he seemed
genuinely happy to see me. He gave me a warm handshake and said with feeling, "Markbreit, I expected to
see you on this game. It's always a pleasure to have
you officiating."

That doesn't sound like much, but officials don't hear
things like that very often. In fact, it was one of the nicest
compliments I ever received from a coach in the college ranks. From then on, McKay and Markbreit were
always glad to see each other at college games and
then, years later, in the pros. One confrontation and a
handshake two years later created another of those
lasting, mutual-respect relationships so common in officiating life. Unlike a lot of "civilian" friendships, these
bonds don't fade away with time, even when you leave
football. Somehow, you remain fraternity brothers forever.

I was involved in one other memorable incident with
a coach that year. Because of the volatility of Woody
Hayes' national tirade back in '71, I was not assigned
another Ohio State game for two seasons. In 1973, I got
the Ohio State-Indiana game. When I walked into the
Ohio State locker room to give the time, I came face-
to-face with Woody Hayes, whom I hadn't seen since
the incident. He was very cordial. "Markbreit," he said
with a smile. "How are you? Nice to see you. I saw a
copy of your book in the bookstore. Would you mind
sending me an autographed copy?" I said, "Absolutely,
Coach. Providing you'll send me a copy of your new
book."

When the season ended, I mailed Woody a copy of
my book, *The Armchair Referee*, with a complimentary
autograph. About a month later, he sent me a copy of
his book, *You Win with People*. Inside, in red letters, he
inscribed: "To Jerry Markbreit: a good official, but not
always. Woody Hayes." Which was exactly like him. To

his dying day, he never forgave me for that Michigan interception call—even though he knew I wasn't the one who made it!

The '73 season had been fantastic. I'd worked eleven Big Ten games as a referee—the maximum. In 1974 I got eleven games again, and I was feeling at the top of my form. I didn't have any major incidents. The one thing I remember is an amusing event during an early-season interconference game—Colorado vs. Michigan at Ann Arbor. Colorado was getting ready to kick a critical extra point, so I positioned myself behind the kicker. As the ball was snapped, I noticed something flying toward us. At first I thought it was a bird, but then I realized it was a bag of Kentucky Fried Chicken. Just as the kicker exploded into the ball with his foot, the bag landed right on the football. I was about to blow my whistle when both the chicken and the ball split the uprights together. I gave the "good" signal and chuckled to myself. If I had a microphone, I would've been tempted to announce to the crowd, "A bag of Kentucky Fried Chicken interfered with the kick. But both the chicken and the kick were very good."

Though I was really enjoying myself in the Big Ten in 1974, the challenge of conference assignments had grown easier. I needed more. Something Howard Wirtz said kept troubling me. "You're an excellent collegiate official," he told me. "But unless you work in the best league there is, the NFL, you'll never find out if you're as good as you think you are, or as good as you can possibly be. *I* didn't. *You* should."

That advice now had some sway. On top of that, I yearned for another bowl game. In those days, the only Big Ten bowl game was the Rose Bowl, which officials shared on a rotating seniority basis. And the Big Ten could send a referee only every other year. I had worked the Rose Bowl in '72, and with five referees in line for the assignment every year, I knew it would be about eight years before I got another one.

I could also see the handwriting on the wall as far

as getting a Notre Dame bowl game. In the Big Ten, coaches were not permitted to scratch officials they didn't like from their bowl games. Selection was up to the league. But since 1970, when Notre Dame changed its policy and accepted bowl bids, Ara Parsegian had the power of selection, and I knew he was scratching me from his bowls. Between '70 and '75, that added up to four or five Cotton, Sugar, and Orange Bowls that somebody else worked. So, year after year, even though I had been told that I was one of the most highly regarded referees in the league, I got no postseason reward.

Something else nagged me, too. I was no longer satisfied to work ten or eleven games a year. The real reason a bowl game mattered was because it was another assignment. The thing I loved to do most was *over* in ten or eleven weeks. It occurred to me: "If I was in the NFL, I could *double* my schedule."

At the end of '74, I was anxious and depressed about all this. Something was missing in my life, and I didn't know what to do about it. For the moment, I shrugged it off by telling myself: "I love the Big Ten. It's the best football around. And I'll have one of the best schedules in the league next year. A bowl is only one game. It's not that big a deal."

In 1975, I *did* have the best schedule in the league —eleven of the best Big Ten games, including Penn State-Ohio State; Iowa-Purdue; Ohio State-Purdue; my fourth Ohio State-Michigan game; and my fifth Michigan State-Notre Dame game. Still, it was an uneventful season, except for a funny incident in the next-to-last game of the year—Purdue-Iowa at West Lafayette, Indiana.

A few years before, our crew had been increased from five to six. Along with myself, Bill Quinby, Russ Kemper, Dale Orem, and Lou Lehman, we now had line judge Art White—a famous Big Ten basketball official from Chicago. We had developed a real closeness and we relished these weekends together. Every time we

had Iowa, Bill Quinby would start feeling the pressure. He was an Iowa graduate and lived in Cedar Rapids, only twenty-five miles from Iowa City. This was a big ball game, so he gave us a pep talk.

He said, "Fellas, nothing bad can happen in this game because I've gotta go home to Iowa after the game. We just can't have any incidents." We kibitzed him and told him, "Don't worry. We guarantee nothing will happen." And for most of the game, nothing did. Late in game, Purdue had the ball on Iowa's one-yard line, first and goal. Scott Dierking, the Purdue fullback who later played with the New York Jets, hit the line three straight times to no avail, although the third-down rush looked like he might've gotten in. It was that close. On fourth down, Dierking plunged into the line again, and Art White came running over with the touchdown signal.

Of course, the Iowa people were certain he never got in, and the dispute erupted into a yelling and shoving match between the players *and* the officials. Iowa players stormed onto the field from the sidelines and started shoving us around because they thought we had blown the ball game for them. With the help of university security, we were finally able to get off the field. The first thing we did when we got inside the locker room and closed the door was fall to the ground in hysterical laughter. We kept kidding Quinby that he had to go back to Iowa and would probably be hounded for the rest of his life. It wasn't funny and the call was made in earnest, but even Quinby was laughing: "You guys *promised* me nothing would happen! How can I go home now?"

When he did go home, everybody and his brother called to give him hell. Quinby kept a low profile that whole off-season, but the local papers wouldn't let it die. It was one of the lowlights of Iowa's 1975 football season—for which, of course, Quinby was partially blamed. And the first time Art White showed up to officiate an Iowa basketball game, he saw himself hanging in effigy from the field house rafters. For all I know, he's still up there.

Years later, I returned to Iowa to give a speech to
the Cedar Rapids Officials' Association. Half-jokingly, I
said, "In reference to that infamous Purdue-Iowa game,
we still don't know if Scott Dierking scored the winning
touchdown." The whole place went up for grabs. Gus
Schrader published it in his column in the *Cedar Rapids
Gazette,* and the town rehashed the game for a week.
When I got back to Chicago, Herman Rohrig called me
up and blasted my kishkas out. "Bigmouth!" he needled
me. "Even though you're not in the league anymore, I
can still bawl the crap out of you! That game was dead
and buried and you had to bring it back to life again!"

I didn't know then that the last game of the '75
season—the nationally televised Ohio State-Michigan
game—was to be the last regular-season college football game of my career. It was at Ann Arbor with a full
house. I also wasn't aware that seated in the stands was
Jack Reader, assistant supervisor of officials for the NFL.
He was scouting Bill Quinby and Dale Orem, who'd both
applied to the league. Reader sat with Fritz Graf, a friend
of mine and one of the premier field judges in the NFL
(he ultimately worked four Super Bowls).

Midway through the second quarter, I was timing
the twenty-five-second huddle count on Michigan. I was
staring at my watch when Michigan rushed in a late
substitute. The man the sub replaced bolted out of the
huddle and ran smack into me. His helmet caught me
flush on the chin and knocked me tochis over teakettle.
The next thing I knew, I woke up on the ground with a
towel on my face. In front of 104,000 fans and a national
TV audience, I had been knocked out cold while waiting for a play to start!

I got up, absolutely out of it. I staggered around; I
had no idea where I was. The crew crowded around:
"What happened? How many times in a career can
you get knocked down?" They were riding me something fierce. I was humiliated *again*—and hurt. But I
finished the ball game.

At the airport after the game, I bumped into Fritz
Graf and he said, "I think you ought to know that Jack

Reader was at the game observing Quinby and Orem for the NFL. It's too bad *you* haven't applied because Reader was very impressed with your work." I said, "You mean, he liked the way I hit the ground when I got knocked on my backside?" Fritz laughed with me. "Fritz," I said, "nobody knows this, but after the Iowa-Purdue game last week, I called the NFL office and asked for an application. I realized that at the end of the season I'd be shut out from bowl games again. I thought: 'Why should I eat my kishkas out every year?' So I called the NFL. They gave me Art McNally (supervisor of NFL officials) and he said, "Are you sure you want to come into the NFL?" I said, "I'm very interested." He said, "It may take a long time to get in." I said, "I'm prepared to wait."

Fritz said, "I'm gonna call Reader and tell him you applied because he asked me several times who you were." That was the end of it. The season ended and, as expected, I didn't get the Rose Bowl or Notre Dame's bowl game. A week later, Herm Rohrig assigned me to a Division II playoff game in Cedar Falls, Iowa. It was, by far, the worst weather conditions I had ever worked in. The morning of the game, they had ten inches of rain. The field was under water when we kicked off. For field goals and extra points, we had to stack three towels on the ground to raise the ball above the water. Nobody was in the stands, and I don't remember who won the game.

When it was over, we threw our uniforms and equipment away because everything was ruined. One of the Division II directors came into our dressing room with a wad of hundred-dollar bills and gave us each $125 for the game and $60 for two days' expenses. He said, "I heard that you had to throw your equipment and uniforms away. I want to pay you for that, too." He paid us for everything but the kitchen sink. When we left there, we each had about $500 in our pockets, which was the biggest payday we ever had for a college game.

Flying home in this torrential downpour, I thought the plane might crash. As soon as I walked into my

house, I told Bobbie, "I'm wasting my time. I've been in the Big Ten for eleven years, I've had one bowl game while other guys have had three or four. I just worked a Division II game in front of absolutely nobody in a total deluge, and I almost got killed in a plane crash coming home. Who needs this?"

In January 1976, the bowl games came and went. About two weeks later, I got a letter from the NFL informing me that I was being considered for the staff for the 1976 season and that I would be interviewed and given a psychological examination. I was shocked because Art McNally had told me it might be a long wait.

Jack Reader came to Chicago, and we sat in the O'Hare Hilton for three hours talking football. He was one of the finest men I'd ever met. He'd worked for many years as a back judge and referee in the NFL, and had decided to continue his career in the league office. He understood exactly why I'd become disenchanted with college football and why I'd previously turned the NFL down. It was a good interview, though he said there were twenty-five applicants, from which the league would select only seven or eight.

Later, I took the psychological examination, which was interesting until the psychologist asked me, "What makes you think you're qualified for the National Football League?" I was a little uptight; I'd been there five hours. I snapped at him, "What gives you the right to ask me a question like that? I don't even think you know what an NFL official *does*. Do you?" He said, "I'm the one asking the questions." I said, "Well, I resent the implication." I settled myself down and finished the test, but I was convinced that I'd just blown my chances of getting into the NFL.

When I got home, I called the league office to tell them I'd completed my test, and they said that on March 30 the league would call all the men who were accepted. On March 30 I waited in my office all day for a call from the league, hoping against hope. I was excited now about the NFL, and I wanted to find out if I could do the job there. But I didn't think I stood a chance.

They'd observed me in only one game and I'd barked at the psychologist—it just didn't add up.

At about three o'clock, the phone rang. It was Art McNally. He said, "Jerry, we're taking you into the National Football League. Congratulations. We're very happy to have you." My heart skipped, just like that day when Bill Reed called to welcome me to the Big Ten. McNally said, "Now the big question: What position do you want to work? We can't start you off at referee." Kiddingly, I said, "Give me the easiest position you've got." He said, "No, we'll make you a line judge. From the line judge's spot, you'll be able to observe the referee to see how he operates—and maybe someday you'll get a chance to be a referee."

I laid the phone down and realized that I'd just taken the biggest step in my career. I'd finally mustered the guts to make a change. I was the guy who never changed anything. Stayed in the same job for twenty years, stayed in the same conference for ten, did everything the same. Always, down deep, afraid to make that one big move—and here I did it. I thought: "Thank you, Ara Parsegian. You finally did something to *help* me." (Five years later, I ran into Parsegian on a plane and he said, "Hello, Jerry, how are you? You're doing terrific in the NFL." I said, "Coach, I want to thank you personally for all you did for me when I worked the Big Ten. In fact, you're the main reason I'm *in* the NFL." He looked puzzled. "That's right," I said. "You drove me out of the league. You didn't mean to, but you made me what I am today." He didn't get it, but it felt good to tell him.)

Now I was finally going to find out if the Rose Bowl and the Notre Dame games and the Ohio State-Michigan games were the best I could do in my officiating life. I thought: "Is it possible that after I'm in the NFL, I'll think of all those incredible games as run-of-the-mill?"

You want to know something? That's exactly the way it is.

# 7. THE NFL: A THOUSAND TIMES MORE INTENSE

The day I got the news, I called my family and then Cal LePore. At the time, Cal was one of the premier referees in the NFL. He'd been the line judge in Super Bowl III and the alternate referee in Super Bowl XII. We'd become friends twenty years earlier as members of the Central Officials' Association, and when we worked high school games together. A stickler for the rules, Cal understood their origination, philosophy, and application.

I said, "Cal, I'm in the NFL. The clinic's in July, so I only have four months to get ready. I don't know one NFL rule, I don't know my tochis from my elbow. I'm scared to death." He said, "Come over to my office tomorrow at lunchtime and I'll start teaching you." I knew it would take years to learn all the rules, so I kept hocking Cal mercilessly: "Can I come over today? Can we study?" He never once said no. He worked for the Chicago Park District, so every day at lunch we pored over the rule book in his office at Soldier Field. Afterward, I'd sometimes look at the deserted playing field and imagine myself out there with Pittsburgh Steelers, Oakland Raiders, Chicago Bears.... I thought: "Could there possibly be a more appropriate setting for learning about the NFL?"

109

Day after day, Cal explained the rules in depth, detailed how they differed from college rules, and tested me until I fixed them in my mind. He was so capable that by the end of the training period, I'd washed all the college rules from my mind. I was ready for pro football—and I hadn't even worked a game.

In May, I was notified that I was to be on Tommy Bell's crew. I was so elated. Tommy Bell, Norm Schachter, and Jim Tunney were the most prominent referees in the NFL. Also on my crew were top-notch veterans Gordon Wells, Ray Dodez, Ed Merrifield, and Tom Kelleher. Kelleher was one of the most famous NFL officials and an idol of mine for years. I remembered him especially from a highly publicized play in a 1960s Baltimore at Chicago game. Lenny Moore caught a pass in the end zone and, an instant after he caught the ball, it was smacked out of his hands. Kelleher signaled "touchdown" and ignited a terrific controversy. Television showed that play a million times, but they could never refute the call.

It was magnificent. Gutsy. I remember pictures of the tall, imposing Kelleher standing almost defiantly with his arms up. In the background, Chicago players and fans were screaming at him. He was undaunted. All week, Jack Brickhouse replayed the call on TV and he kept saying, "It doesn't *look* like a touchdown." But every time I watched it, it *was* a touchdown. Kelleher was always right there in the thick of things, making the gutsy calls. That was his reputation. Back then, I thought: "Wouldn't it be a thrill to meet that guy someday?" And here I was going into the National Football League for the first time and I'd be working right *next* to him! Tom Kelleher, one of the finest sideline officials in history, and the great Tommy Bell—guys I watched on TV for years—and I would be *one* of them, *traveling* with them, *talking* to them! How did that happen?

By the time the clinic began in July, I not only knew all the rules, I'd also conditioned myself physically. Through dieting, I came in at 185 pounds, ten pounds lighter than normal. Bob Rice, whom I knew from the

Mid-American Conference, said, "I've never seen you so thin. You know, that's a big mistake." I said, "Why?" He said, "They're weighing you today and you'll have to weigh that for the rest of your career. If you were smart, you'd've come in a little fat, so you wouldn't have to press every year." He was right; I've never been slim, and I've been pressing every year since then, trying to pare off that extra weight.

At the clinic I met Tom Kelleher, but he barely said hello. He knew I was on his crew and he shook my hand, but he didn't know me from Adam. Tommy Bell was at the other clinic (each year they hold one in the East, one in the West), so I wouldn't see him until the final preseason game—our crew's first game together.

I vividly remember my first preseason game— San Francisco at Seattle—because it was the Seattle Kingdome's inaugural game, and because there were sixty-one thousand fans in the dome, and because I committed my first foulup as an NFL official. I flew to Seattle early Saturday morning, July 31—the only one in first class. The stewardess shmoozed with me and asked who I was, and I told her. I felt so proud to say, "I'm in the NFL." She made a big fuss over me and told the other stewardesses who I was. Of course, they had never heard of me, but I *felt* important.

I arrived at the Red Lion Hotel in Seattle at 11:00 A.M. The referee was Jim Tunney, so I was excited and nervous to meet him. I found him sunning by the pool. I introduced myself and asked if there was anything special I could do before our pregame meeting. He said, "Yes. Get into your bathing suit and come back to the pool. We're going to have a great time today and you'll do fine. So relax and enjoy yourself." He put me right at ease.

That changed in the game. I was so jittery, I couldn't have called a foul if one had hit me on the head. As line judge, my two main jobs were to fire the gun and give the two-minute warning. Simple. With two minutes left in the first quarter, I killed the clock and came running over to Tunney flashing my index finger and pinky,

expertly spread. Tunney said, "What's that?" Breathlessly, I announced, "*Two*, Jim." He looked at me cockeyed and said, "What?" I repeated, "I got *two*." He said, "Come closer." I looked at *him* cockeyed. He insisted, "Come closer, Jerry." I came over and he put his hands on his hips and said, "What's this '*two*'?"

I couldn't understand how this famous, brilliant referee had suddenly become so dense. I explained, "Jim, I'm giving you the two-minute warning." He looked at me solemnly and said, "Excellent whistle, perfect mechanics, your fingers are perfectly spread." I was so proud; I'd done it right. Then he said, "Now, dummy, go back and do the same thing at the end of the *second* quarter, when there *is* a two-minute warning."

The following Saturday, August 7, I worked my second preseason game—Tampa Bay-Green Bay at Milwaukee. Cal LePore was the referee. That was some thrill. He'd spent four months teaching me the rules, and here we were working my second pro game together. The umpire was Pat Harder, a former All-Pro Chicago Cardinal fullback who was a great NFL official and one of the toughest guys you ever met. Anytime a play was killed in the side zone, I had to throw the ball back in to Harder. He had this thing about throwing the ball to him perfectly. If you didn't toss it exactly where his hands were, he blew a fuse. The second time I tossed the ball in, it was low and bounced up off his hands and wobbled away. He looked at me like I'd just dumped horse manure in his lap. "Come on, *rookie!*" he jeered. "Can't you get that ball in *right*? Put it in my *hands!*" He was all over me the whole game. He was so gruff that he scared the daylights out of me. I thought: "Holy cow, all I did was throw one ball in low. This league's rougher than I thought."

Of course, Harder wasn't really mean. He was three-quarters needle, one-quarter serious. But I was nervous, I had no sense of humor. I wanted to do everything right. I had such shpilkes that, for the rest of the game, I practically *handed* him the ball. Cal snickered at me all game.

My third game was Baltimore-Chicago at Soldier Field. I was thrilled beyond belief because I was working a pro football game in my own city in front of my family and friends. I thought of the Prep Bowls I'd worked here, and how incredible it was that this was actually the NFL. The Bears won, 25–14. My fourth game was Washington at Kansas City, with Cal LePore and Pat Harder again. The only thing I remember is that every throw I made to Harder was right on the money. The poor guy didn't have one thing to complain about. The fifth game was Giants at Green Bay, and by then I was starting to feel like a pro.

On August 19, just before the last preseason game, Tommy Bell sent a letter to everyone on his regular-season crew. I kept that letter and I've used it for twelve years as a model for all the letters I write to my crew members at the start of every season. It reads:

"Gentlemen: It is indeed a privilege and a thrill to know that we are all back together again for the 1976 season, except for the loss of Dean Look. I am certainly pleased, and I know that you are, that his replacement is Jerry Markbreit. As you all know, this will be a nationally televised game. And I would like to suggest that we all be in Denver no later than 6:00 P.M. and all have dinner together.

"For our pregame conference, I would like to have Ray Dodez discuss rules and mechanics on running plays; and Jerry Markbreit discuss rules and mechanics of all passing plays; and Ed Merrifield discuss rules and regulations on all scrimmage kicks. I am looking forward to being with each and every one of you for the 1976 season. Sincerely, Tom."

When I read this letter, I knew I was up to my eyebrows in the National Football League. I was petrified that he had selected me to make a presentation before the group. I called Cal; he gave me an outline and I studied everything there was on pass-play mechanics and rules. I was ready. I discovered that this was part of Bell's strategy for developing crew camaraderie. By having me deliver a presentation at our very first meet-

ing, he made me an integral part of the crew right away. No babying, no nantsy-pantsing; strictly "You're part of the crew. You have the same responsibilities as everyone else." That made it much easier for me to feel accepted by such accomplished men.

In that last preseason game—Minnesota at Denver —Tommy Bell's crew came together for the first time. When I spotted Bell at the Denver Hilton, I knew him immediately because I had seen him on TV so many times. He was shorter than I thought, about five-eight. He was a bright, friendly man with a warm southern accent and a perpetual twinkle in his eye. Before I could introduce myself, he came over, shook my hand with both his hands, and said, "Hello, Jerry, how are you?" *He* knew *me*! And he knew all about my college career—when I'd worked, who I'd worked with, how many games. I was so impressed. Here was one of the NFL's best-known referees, and he knew more about me than I knew about him.

Tommy was wonderful to me right from the start. After I gave my presentation at our first meeting, he complimented me in front of the group. "This is the way a new man should come into the league," he said. "I know that the rest of these guys on the crew would've been on the ball because they've been with me. But not every rookie is this prepared. You've proven you're the right guy for this crew." I felt like I'd just been commended by the president. After that, I wanted Bell to think I was the greatest rookie who ever came into the league. Anything he might ask me, I wanted to have the answer ready for him. If he asked about penalty enforcements, I would know them backward, forward, upside down. If he wanted to know the *temperature*, I'd have that, too.

Following the meeting, Bell talked to me again to set the stage for the regular season. He said, "You're going to be a great NFL official. Give it time. Learn all you can about everything you see. If you have questions during the season, ask me. You and I will be traveling a lot together and we'll talk a lot between games, so

think of all the things you want to know and let's discuss 'em during the season." He never intimated that he thought I'd become a referee soon, but he knew that I was a Big Ten referee and that I was working a new position. He gave me this advice: "When they give you an assignment in this league, they expect you to do the best job possible. If you ever want to get another position, like referee, you'll only get there if you excel in the position they start you at." So I knew I had to be an outstanding line judge in order to get a chance at becoming an NFL referee.

Bell also broached a different subject—one that was to affect me deeply as a person and forever alter my professional routine. He said, "Jerry, I know you're Jewish, but this crew goes to Catholic church before every game. I'm a Baptist and I've been going for the last fifteen years. We think of it as something that draws us together. But you're certainly not obligated to go. Everyone will understand." I had no idea how to react. I said, "Does everybody go?" He said, "Yes." I said, "Well, I'm going, too." When we parted, I thought: "Are you *crazy*, Jerry?"

The next morning, when we arrived at church, I felt very awkward. I'd never been in one before. I walked inside and, boy, I had this terrible, almost sacrilegious feeling that maybe the walls would topple down on me for being there. We sat together in the pew and, when the Mass started, they all kneeled on the kneeling boards. I was afraid to do it. I just sat there, thinking: "Is this what it takes to be an NFL official? I can't do this. Why am I here?" Then I realized that not everybody on the crew was Catholic, but they were here, so it must be okay. I decided I would just say my own prayers, like in temple, and God would certainly understand. Even though I was in a Catholic church, I was *praying* Jewish.

After the service, as we filed to the doors, the Catholic crew members dipped their fingers in the holy water and made little signs of the cross on their foreheads. I thought: "What do *I* do? Should I make the sign of the Jewish star?" Then Kelleher came over and grinned

at me and made a sign of the cross on my forehead. It wasn't a religious gesture. It was like he was saying, "Welcome to the crew. You're one of us now." I wasn't offended; I felt honored that he would do it. When we got outside, Kelleher patted me on the back and said, "We know you're Jewish, but this has nothing to do with religion. This is togetherness. We've been doing this for years and we're very proud that you would do it with us."

I had attended church with them because I wanted to fit in. I didn't want these guys to feel burdened with a rookie. I wanted them to be happy that the league put me on their crew. I wanted to be important to them. I didn't want to be the nebechel little shlepperdik who comes on a crew and doesn't know his tochis from a hole in the ground.

I expected my first game with my regular-season crew to be memorable. I was still flying high from my successful debut at the pregame meeting, which made me even more eager to display my wares to Bell and Kelleher. Early in that Minnesota-Denver game, it looked to me like one of the offensive halfbacks jumped before the snap of the ball, so I threw my flag for illegal motion. The halfback was in Tommy Bell's view, but he hadn't flagged it. Bell came over to me and said, "What do you have, kid?" I said, "I've got illegal motion on number forty-two." He said, "You mean, the back right in *front* of me?" I said, "Yes." He walked me out of earshot, like the southern gentleman he was. "We'll penalize it this time, Markbreit," he said pointedly. "But next time you call a foul on *my* man, they'll bury you right here." He stepped away and calmly announced the foul.

I returned to my position, ego bruised. I *thought* I'd seen that halfback move, but Tommy had obviously watched the football and the halfback at the same time. I was such an eager beaver, I had figured that if I jumped in, it would show Bell how alert I was. Instead, it taught me a lesson: If you *think* you saw a foul, you didn't. Never call a foul unless you *know*—especially in Tommy Bell's territory.

When I got home after that game, I told Bobbie, "You'll never guess where I was this morning. I was in Catholic church." Her jaw dropped; she couldn't believe it. She blasted me from one end of the house to the other. "Jerry, how dare you go to church! You're a Jew!" Well, I gave it a lot of thought and I concluded: "I've got to live within the official's family for a whole season. I'm not in a position to change their ritual, and I want to learn why they do it. There are only two Catholics in that group—why are the others in church?"

As it turned out, going to church helped bond me to them. They accepted me immediately, and I had only officiated one game with them. The scene was set for me now. I was with the famous Tommy Bell and the famous Tom Kelleher; we had a ton of terrific games; I would be traveling all over the country with these men. They were becoming my friends. They accepted me onto the crew like I'd been there for ten years. I was on my way.

My NFL regular-season inauguration brought another lesson, one that became my fondest NFL memory. My first game was to be St. Louis at Seattle, so here I was on a plane to Seattle for the second time in seven weeks. I remember thinking, "Boy, is this really *me*?" As a football official, I had never been out of the Midwest. In the Big Ten, I always worked close to home at the Big Ten stadiums. And here I was traveling thousands of miles to work a football game! I was forty-one years old, but I was as excited as a little kid.

I had six games under my belt, yet I kept thinking about what everybody had told me: "Regular-season games don't resemble preseason games. They're a thousand times more intense." Preseason was mostly a tryout period in which as many as eighty players were harvested down to forty-five. By the first regular-season game, the chaff would be gone and there'd only be wheat. At our pregame meeting, I could sense the difference. Tommy Bell was more intense; there was greater concentration and less joshing around; everybody was down to business. I started to get worried. Maybe I had

just breezed through the preseason games and wasn't taking this league as seriously as I should. Maybe regular-season games would be *so* intense I couldn't handle them.

When we got out on the field, I was petrified. I thought the *warm-ups* were intense. I couldn't imagine what the game would be like. Just before the kickoff, Tommy Bell draped his arm over my shoulder and said, "Kid, in a couple of minutes the first regular-season game of your professional career will begin. A few plays into the game, you'll probably get your first foul. Three things to remember: First, be sure it's *your* foul, not mine. Second, be sure it *is* a foul. Third, be sure you get the number." He patted his microphone. "I've got this microphone," he said emphatically, "and everyone in the stadium and everyone watching at home will want to know *who committed the foul.* I have to give 'em the number." I puffed with confidence: "You can count on me, Tom."

The first few plays, the intensity was unbelievable— like everybody said it would be. Each play was so hard-hitting that I just stood there on the line of scrimmage in awe as the play went by. Everything was happening so fast, I could barely register. I had just started settling into it when I caught my first foul. A defensive lineman charged into the neutral zone before the ball was snapped. My flag went thirty feet in the air; the play continued; there was a pile up. I raced in to try to get the number but, for the life of me, I couldn't remember who it was.

Bell saw my flag down, killed the clock, and hollered from the middle of the field, "What do you have, kid?" I said, "I've got defensive offside, Tom." He said, "*And?*" I cringed. "And," I stalled, "I didn't get the number." Bell's smile dissolved to a frown. He stepped out, switched his microphone on, and drawled, "He's got offside, defense." Then, instead of looking up to the press box like he always did, he looked right at me and said, "*AND HE DIDN'T GET THE NUMBER.*"

The crowd broke up. I mean, belly laughs. I dragged despondently past Tom Kelleher. "That'll teach you to

have a number for Tommy Bell," he needled. "Next time, make one up."

Making up a number, of course, is not uncommon. But I learned that if you make one up, be sure it's a logical number. Everybody knew the story about the famous Ohio State-Illinois game when Illinois had a ninety-yard kick return—the winning touchdown—called back on a foul. The referee went over to the field judge who'd thrown the flag and asked what he had. He said, "I've got a clip." The referee said, "What number?" The field judge said, "I couldn't get one." The referee said, "You *better* get one. The Illinois coach is irate. I've gotta go over there and tell him who committed the foul." The field judge pondered his predicament. Finally, he said, "It was seventy-seven." The referee hurried over to the Illinois coach and said, "Coach, the clip was on number seventy-seven." The coach spit on the turf. "Yeah?" he said. "It must've been a helluva clip. Red Grange retired forty years ago—and so did his number!"

More memorable than missing my first number were my developing relationships with Tom Kelleher and Tommy Bell. I didn't know then, of course, how important they would be to my success in the league. I also didn't know that I would lose one of them much too soon and find a sort of older brother for life in the other one. Bell was the leader of the crew; my relationship with him was more like that of a statesman and his aide. But Kelleher was my sideline man. He was seventeen yards downfield from me, so we worked tandem on sideline and goal-line plays. We had to know everything about each other on the field—how we thought, how we made our calls, our strengths and weaknesses under fire.

Early on, I didn't kibitz with him much. He was six-two, 210—an iron-willed, confident man who came across as extremely tough. And he was practically a legend in the league because he'd already worked two Super Bowls (he got his third at the end of that season; today he is the only official in NFL history to have worked

*five* Super Bowls). I had watched this man on TV for years, and here I was working alongside him. I felt I had to show him that I was serious. So, while I actually found him warm, caring, and witty beneath that leathery exterior, I started out all business with him.

Kelleher immediately took me under his wing. I knew he liked me a lot; I could tell by the approval on his face when I made a good call. He'd constantly reassure me with, "Good call!" or "Good positioning!" or "That's the way to look at me when you're not sure!" He taught me nuances: "Never guess at anything. Always do what your eyes tell you." And: "If you're not a hundred percent sure, always look to the nearest official in case he had a better look at it than you."

I knew his reputation, I knew how tough he was. I realized I had to show him that I knew my stuff. Early in the season, we had a couple of tough plays and he looked at me to make the calls, just to see what I would do. He put me on the spot and I made the calls and they were right. He nodded his approval. He knew he was working with someone who could take the heat. After that, we worked in almost perfect synch. We weren't that close the first year because he and Bell had worked together for fifteen years and I was just the new guy on the block. But Kelleher more than accepted me.

Kelleher knew that I had been studying the rules very diligently, so one day, he said, "If you ever see something on the field where you think Bell is not enforcing a penalty properly, or he gets confused, come forward and save the day. It'll be terrific. But only do it if you're sure." A couple of games into the season, we had a head slap on the defense on a scoring play—the defender slapped the offensive man in in the head real hard—and our umpire, Gordon Wells, flagged it. After the touchdown, Bell got the foul from Wells, stepped out, turned his microphone on, and said, "Head slap, number eighty-seven, defense. Penalty declined. Touchdown."

The home team had scored; the crowd went crazy. But I knew a mistake had been made. I walked over

to Kelleher and said, "Tom, that penalty's enforced on the kickoff." He said, "Are you sure?" I said, "I'm sure." He said, "Well, go on out and tell Bell." I was gun-shy; I remembered Bell's first reprimand: "They'll bury you right here." I said, "I'm not going out to tell Bell. He'll *kill* me." Kelleher said, "All right, I'll tell him." He did, and Bell replied, "*I'll* enforce the penalties. Tell Markbreit to mind his own business." The penalty was not enforced on the kickoff.

The next week, the film review came back: "The penalty should have been enforced on the kickoff." At the meeting, Bell said to me, "Why didn't you tell me about that?" I said, "Kelleher told you." He said, "If *you* see something, *you* tell me." I said, "Well, what if you holler and yell at me?" Bell grinned. "If I yell at you, just stand there and I'll know you know what you're talking about." I said, "What if you tell me to mind my own business?" He said, "Tell me it *is* your business." I said, "But what if you *really* get mad?" He smiled: "*Then* send Kelleher out. I'll light into *him*."

It doesn't seem like much of an event now, but it was significant. The easing off, psychologically, and the touch of humor really opened the door for me. I could relax a little. And I felt so proud because he was acknowledging that I was right. Several times afterward, I assisted Bell on enforcements and he always appreciated it. Tommy Bell was a very proud man, and I was just a rookie, but he respected my interest in the intricacies of the rules. Howard Wirtz had recognized the same thing back in my Big Ten days. It was my calling card all along the line. And because of Bell's response, I do the same thing today with the fellas on *my* crew. If they see something I missed, or if I misenforce a penalty or become confused, I encourage them to question me or point out my mistake.

Kelleher played a little game to ensure proper penalty enforcements. He used to draw a pie on paper or a chalkboard, and divide it into the different enforcement categories—penalties on running plays; on kicks; on pass plays; on fumbles. We called it "TK's Pie." He'd

always say, "If you can put a play in the right hopper, you'll always get the correct enforcement." To this day, once a year, my crew studies "TK's Pie" so we all have a solid understanding of penalty enforcements and how to put everything in the right hopper. I still carry his pie in my briefcase.

Like Kelleher, Tommy Bell was a perfectionist. He had everybody on his crew work every week on penalty enforcements so that during a game we could *all* dump 'em into the right hopper. He would test us in the meetings. He would say, "Wells: penalty enforcement on backward pass and fumbles. "Markbreit: penalty enforcements on running plays." And bang, we had to know them. We had a quiz every week and we never knew which hopper he'd call on us to explain. Consequently, everybody had to know all of them. Bell was like Professor Kingsfield in *The Paper Chase*. He demanded that everyone be as informed as he was. If you missed a question, he'd show his disappointment: "You haven't been studying the rules. You're cheating yourself *and* the crew." Embarrassing yourself in front of Tommy Bell, never mind the rest of the crew, was the worst shame imaginable.

Up until then, my life in officiating had been blessed by associations with some of the greatest officials who ever walked on a football field: Ellie Hasan, Howard Wirtz, Herman Rohrig, Cal LePore, Norm Schachter, Art McNally, Jim Tunney, Tom Kelleher. People who really *were* legends in their own time. But Tommy Bell was special; he was a dream come true. I watched him like a hawk that season. I studied his mannerisms: the way he talked to the coaches; the way he handled the sideline people before the game; how he handled the crew. I observed how he functioned as a referee: how he dressed; how he walked; how he announced penalties; how he handled the coaches; his technical nuances. There were so many little lessons that weren't in the book, things that only an experienced referee like Bell could pass along.

Tommy's outstanding quality was his natural ability

to draw people together. His crew worked as a unit. We all liked each other; we were friends. He created the perfect atmosphere for everybody to work together, meet together, dine together, go to church together. He applied many of the same concepts that Howard Wirtz had used so effectively.

That whole season, I loved having Tommy Bell in charge of everything. I had spent eleven years in charge of a crew; this was like a vacation from responsibility. I didn't have to worry about running the crew, arranging travel schedules and meeting times, enforcing rules, announcing the fouls. All I had to do was pack my bags, show up, make my calls, and go home. I didn't have all the tough decisions anymore. I just had to say, "I've got holding, Tom, number sixty-five, offense," and then I could walk away and let Tommy Bell do everything I used to do. It was a relief, it was fun. I was like a kid in a candy store with my choice of Kelleher and Bell. All I had to do was gobble them up.

What was especially interesting about Bell was that he had everything figured out—all the small details that might help you do your job more effectively. For example, he always took me with him when he went to talk to the coaches before the game. He told me, "When you talk to the coaches, always take someone with you. If there's a misunderstanding, like in giving a rule interpretation, you'll have somebody else there to verify what was said."

He even prepared for the weather. I remember the November 28 Bears-Packers game at Green Bay. It was one of those typical blustery, frigid, Green Bay winter days. We went to church that morning and it was five below zero with a wind-chill factor of twenty below. I had never worked a game in that kind of bitter cold. When we came back from church, I said to Kelleher, "I bet you that nobody will be at the game. It's too cold." He said, "You wait and see. They'll *all* be there. But don't worry about the cold. We have all kinds of ways to keep warm." I didn't know what he meant until we got to the stadium.

In the locker room, we laid out our clothes—long underwear, heavy wool socks, gloves, earmuffs, sweaters, windbreakers. Everything six grown men could possibly think of. Bell pulled out six green garbage bags. He cut two holes at the top and two at the bottom of each bag and handed them out. He told us to wear them over our insulated underwear, underneath our striped shirts. He said the bags would keep the last bit of moisture inside our clothes. He then gave us sandwich Baggies and instructed us to put one on each foot and then put on our socks. "If you can keep your feet warm," he said, "your body will be warm." The only things we probably couldn't keep warm, he said, were our faces and lips.

Cal LePore always said that on a bitter-cold day you should rub cocoa butter all over your face. It tastes terrific and it keeps your lips moist enough so they don't chafe. Being a constant whistle-carrier, I'm able to carry the cold metal whistle in my mouth without it sticking to my lips. I have a rubber cover on it, of course, but years ago in a high school game, the rubber cover cracked and the whistle froze to my lip. It was so cold, I didn't notice it until I tugged the whistle out and it took a chunk of my lip with it. These are the hazards.

After we put on all our clothes and the "customized" garbage bags and the foot Baggies, we looked like blimps. Officials are very vain about their appearance; we always want to look trim and fit. And here we were lumpy and thick. I mean, stuffed into about ninety-five thousand pounds of clothes. We were so packed, we couldn't bend over. We broke up laughing. We looked like six fat men who'd just won an elephant-eating contest.

I didn't understand how cold it could be until we went out to the field. The stadium was loaded. It was a rivalry game, the fans didn't know from cold. People's breath was so thick, you couldn't see their faces. It looked like a stadium full of steam radiators. When people ask, "How can you function in weather like that?" I always compare it to the Indian ritual of walking on burning

coals. Somehow they get across those coals. And despite the pain, they don't feel it and they don't get burned.

Well, there was pain throughout this football game, but I got through it. Even though the cold was distracting, it taught me an important lesson: Although the weather will influence the football game, you can't let it affect your officiating. You do a lot of complaining about it and a lot of adjusting, but you can't let it affect what you do. Because no matter how horrible the weather, that game is just as important as every other game. Officiating comes first, personal comfort second.

The fact is that when it's zero or colder, there are no tricks of the trade. No matter what you wear, you're cold. We can't wear jackets; we have to wear our striped shirts on top. The league provides the finest insulated underwear, socks, and gloves, but you still freeze your fanny off. In that kind of cold, the pain numbs your body and then starts to close in on your psyche. Unlike players who can move around a lot, and sit on heated benches and wear electric mittens, officials have to stand out there in position, cocked and poised. No extraneous movement. On Arctic cold days, even the relatively short wait between plays is like a Chinese water torture.

Which is why I absolutely *love* it.

Look at the challenge. You have to shove the elements in the background and remember what you're out there for. Through sheer force of will, you learn to function with the pain—like enduring a toothache. I tell myself: "I know I'll make it through the game. I'm ice-cold now, but when the game is over I'll take off all this stuff, get under a blistering hot shower, and warm up. I'll put my clothes back on and my warm winter coat, I'll have a hot meal, and I'll feel like a million bucks." It always works; I forget how cold I am.

But that day in Green Bay, no matter what I did or what I told myself, I could not get warm. It was so cold that when we came inside for halftime, we found steaming vats of hot soup instead of the traditional soda pop and coffee. After a few cups of soup, I had to pee badly. But Tommy Bell hadn't cut a fifth hole in the garbage

bag, so it required a superhuman effort just to get arranged. I remember how funny and incredibly frustrating that small chore was. One thing about football officials: We can be remarkably ingenious. I won't describe how I finally managed it. Let's just say you can't find it in a manual.

I've worked miserably cold days like that one in Green Bay, and some torrential rain games, but I've never really had my fantasy bad-weather game. I've always fantasized a game in an unbelievable blizzard where *everything* is obliterated—the lines are gone; you can't see the goalposts; you can't see your own feet; you can barely see the football. The most horrendous winter conditions imaginable. I would *love* the challenge of working a game like that. We'd have makeshift sidelines; people constantly running out and sweeping the snow off the lines; it'd be impossible to measure first downs; you wouldn't see handoffs; you wouldn't see who recovered the ball on fumbles; you wouldn't see where a runner was down because he'd continue to slide; passes would literally disappear in midair.

When I was a kid in high school, we went down to St. Louis for a game against University City High School in a freak, early-winter, twenty-inch snowfall. We played the whole game on a field that was absolutely inundated with snow—no sidelines, no yard lines, no goal lines. The game ended in a 0–0 tie, but it was the most fun I ever had playing football. It was pure football; the officials were almost taken out of it. It was like playing in the park before we even had officials. That's how I'd like a pro game to be. It would take me back to a wonderful event in my sports life when everybody was out there for pure love of the game. The best part would be to have officiated a game like that perfectly. After the game, the officials would sit down together, totally exhausted, and review the conditions and everything that happened. Since officials love to complain, we'd start complaining that it was horrible out there. Then I'd chime in, "It *was* horrible, gentlemen. But not horrible *enough!*"

I was disabused of a different fantasy during my first

*Monday Night Football* game, Cincinnati at Oakland
on December 6. I was extremely excited because I was
about to be on national TV as an NFL official for only
the second time. It rained heavily before the game, so
the field was very slick. I wore my ripple-soled shoes,
and the first four times I ran in to get a forward-progress
point, I fell down. I was humiliated; I thought everybody
in the world saw me falling down. Kelleher came over
and said, "The only reason you keep falling is because
you wanna be on television." He was trying to loosen
me up, but I was too tight to laugh. Calmly, he explained, "Jerry, you're so darned excited because of
television, you're moving twice as fast as you normally
move. Slow down when you come into the play or some
guy's gonna break your leg. Hang back a little, take
your time coming in."

When I got home, I was waiting for all my friends to
call and needle me for looking foolish on national TV.
Nobody called. Turned out they never showed me on
TV. The only guy they ever showed was the referee and,
occasionally, a downfield official. They never even
mentioned me. That straightened me out about my van-
ity. I realized that I should never be concerned about
what people see on television. I told myself, "Shmendrick! You're a National Football League official, not
a matinee idol. *Yet.*" At least I regained my sense of
humor.

In fact, after that comedown, I loosened up. In
the beginning of the season, I hadn't joked much with
Tommy Bell. I was very laid-back; I wasn't in my shtikl
mode. I was preoccupied with establishing my position
in the group. But when the right moment finally presented itself, I couldn't resist. We had a game in San
Francisco and the six of us were driving from the hotel
to Candlestick Park. There were people fishing along
the bay and Bell said, "I wonder what they're fishing
for." I said, "Gefilte fish." He said, *"What?"* I said, "Gefilte
fish." Bell didn't know from gefilte fish. He was from Lex-
ington, Kentucky; how many Jewish people live there
—maybe two?

He looked at me like he was on the wrong subway

in New York. "What the heck is *that*?" he asked. I said, "It's a totally round fish. It has no head and no tail." Kelleher started to chuckle—he was from Florida, he had Jewish friends. I milked it for all it was worth. I said, "It comes in a jar, Tom. You eat it with horseradish." Everybody roared, and Bell loved it.

It was that kind of kibitzing that helped accelerate our rapport. By the end of the season, I was secure as a full-fledged member of Tommy Bell's crew. I was happy with my performance. I felt I was good enough to get a playoff game, even though, back then, rookies couldn't get them. Since the last game would bring an end to my season, I wanted to finish up strong. I wanted to work the best game in the league. But we had New England at Tampa Bay. It was Tampa Bay's first year in the NFL; they were 0–13, and New England had clinched a playoff berth. It was a mean-nothing game in the standings.

Beforehand, I renewed my relationship with an old friend. John McKay had left Southern Cal and signed a long-term contract with Tampa Bay as their first head coach. In those days, the line judge announced the time to both coaches, so I walked in and saw McKay sitting there in his hat, puffing his cigar. I said, "Hello again, Coach." He looked up. "Markbreit! Good to see you. Looks like we both made some big changes in our lives." I said, "Yes, Coach. I'm a line judge now, not a referee." He said, "Well, I'm a freshman coach in this league. We're both starting from scratch. I wish us both well." I said, "Do you have anything unusual today?" He turned to Abe Gibron, his assistant coach, and said, "Abe, do we have anything unusual today?" Abe said, "Well, we may be able to get on the field for the kickoff today, if we're lucky. *That'll* be unusual." McKay looked at me, we smiled and shook hands, and out I went.

Before we went onto the field, Tommy Bell gathered the crew under the stands and said, "Gentlemen, I want to let you know how happy I am that we had such fine season. This is a really excellent crew, and I sincerely hope that we'll be working together for many, many years." I was thrilled to hear that.

We went out and worked the game, which could've easily been a rout. It wasn't. New England won by a close margin and, to me, it was more exciting than the most exciting college game I'd ever worked. I remember wondering why I was so exhilarated. It was the intensity and the skill level of the players, and the enthusiasm of a home crowd of seventy thousand that was pulling for their team win its first football game. Both teams played as if it *were* a playoff, and I was so impressed. Walking off the field, I knew I was where I truly belonged, that I'd made the right decision in leaving the Big Ten.

I thought of Tom Kelleher's story about when he first came into the NFL. Back in 1960, he had worked two years in the Eastern Collegiate Athletic Conference, and his dream was to someday work the Army-Navy game, which, in those days, was one of college football's fiercest rivalries and always a thrilling game. Kelleher was a shining star in the collegiate officiating world and was already working big games in his home city, Philadelphia, so he had a tremendous collegiate career ahead of him. Yet after only one talk with Bert Bell, commissioner of the NFL, Kelleher left college for the NFL. Bell told him, "Tom, I want you in the National Football League." Kelleher said, "But, sir, my goal has always been to work the Army-Navy game. I've dreamed about that for years." Bell grinned. "Son," he said, "in our league, *every* game is the Army-Navy game."

The New England-Tampa game confirmed for me that this was true. Every game *was* the Army-Navy game ... *and* the Michigan-Ohio State game; *and* Michigan-Michigan State; *and* USC-Notre Dame. In the NFL, every game was *all* of those.

I knew one person, though, who wasn't too happy that I was in the NFL. Back in October, someone called my house and Bobbie had answered. The caller said, "Is Jerry home?" Bobbie said, "No. He left for his NFL game." The caller said with a groan, "Tell him he's an S.O.B." and hung up. When I got home, Bobbie told me about it and I immediately knew who it was. It would've been just like Alex Agase to leave a message like that

because he was still upset that I left the Big Ten. Out of curiosity, I checked around and found out that the day Agase called, his team, Purdue, had lost its game. He probably called to blame that on me, and to nudjel me for my desertion.

But the college game was out of my blood forever. The 1975 Big Ten season was the finest schedule I'd ever worked, culminating with the Ohio State-Michigan game. At that point, I thought that college football was the epitome, that nothing could be tougher. But in 1976, the pro game made college look like kindergarten. The pros offered higher skill levels, more intensity, even more foul calls. It was possible, for example, for a head linesman or a referee to have as many fouls in one pro game as he might have in half of a college *season*.

At the end of '76, the most significant lesson I'd learned for my life was: Never be too rigid to make a change. I'd fought even thinking about the NFL for many years, convincing myself it wasn't for me. Deep in my heart, I knew I was afraid to try, afraid to change. I was afraid to leave my secure, comfortable position as a highly rated Big Ten referee to go into a position I had never worked before. I knew I would have to prove myself all over again from the beginning. Not only prove my skills to my crew, but also to the corps of NFL officials who didn't know me and couldn't care less what I did on the collegiate level.

For a long time, I was afraid. I thought: "What if I fail? What if I'm not good enough to make it in the NFL?" But I was never going to know unless I tried. That's why, at the end of the season, I was the happiest guy in the world. Because I made the decision, I tried it, and I was successful. I was pleased with what I'd done, with the crew, with the relationships I'd developed, with their acceptance of me. I really felt part of this group and part of the National Football League.

I had gone from a ten-game college schedule to a nineteen-game professional schedule in one year. My only regret was that it didn't last another twenty weeks. I could've kept on officiating the whole year. In fact,

I'd've loved to have a game *every* week. I came into the league a scared rabbit and now I'd emerged as a pretty confident, first-year NFL line judge. I couldn't wait for next year to get back with this crew and be Tommy Bell's line judge again. I had learned so much from him. I thought: "I'm all set. I'll be with this guy for four or five years. By the time he retires, I'll know everything that he knows, and I'll be the best line judge in the NFL." I didn't just hope that, I *knew* it.

Two weeks after the season ended, Tommy Bell called me from O'Hare International Airport on his way to his playoff game in Oakland. He said, "Jerry, I wanted you to know that I have decided that fifteen years is enough to be away every weekend, and I want to spend more time with my family. I've notified Art McNally that after my playoff game, I'm going to retire from the National Football League." I was shocked and hurt and tremendously disappointed. I told him how sad I was that he was retiring but that I'd had the most wonderful experience a man could ever have officiating with him. I said, "Tommy, just to have had the chance to spend one season with you was one of the great thrills of my life." He said, "Thank you, Jerry. You impressed me greatly during the season. I know now why you were such a highly acclaimed collegiate referee. You added a real dimension to our crew as the line judge. With your rules knowledge and your ability to relate to other people, I know you'll become a referee very soon."

Bell's retirement was a big blow. All through January, I kept wondering who his replacement would be and how I'd adjust to the new man in charge. In February, the stunner: Art McNally phoned me and said, "Jerry, how would you feel about being a referee next season?" I said, "Gee, Art, I've only been in the league one year. I really enjoyed being a line judge. If I had my way, I'd like to stay a line judge for a couple more years. I'm having the best time of my life." He said, "Would you do it if we asked you to step in?" I said, "Sure I would. But I'd be scared to death." He said, "Okay, I'll get back to you."

I was astonished. I was only forty-one; I wasn't ready.

I figured McNally would eventually change his mind when he thought about it. Three weeks later, he called back. "You're a referee," he said. "Bell recommended you highly. So did Kelleher. He says you can do it. And he wants to keep the crew together, so you'll be learning from guys you've worked with for a year. Bill Reynolds will replace you as line judge. You'll do fine. Good luck."

After McNally's call, that horrible pang of fear returned. The same fear I had when I made the decision to come into the NFL. I was going through all that emotional upheaval for the second time in a year. First it was: "Am I good enough to be in the NFL?" Then: "Will I be good enough to succeed as a *line judge* in the NFL?" Now, after I'd satisfied those self-doubts: "Will I be good enough to be a *referee* in the NFL?"

All of a sudden, I had a new cartload of tsuris that I didn't know if I could haul. I was going to have to replace one of the top referees in the National Football League—which would be impossible—and I'd have to be in charge of an entire crew of seasoned veterans, including Tom Kelleher, who'd been my *mentor*. How was I going to be the leader of this group? I'd secretly dreamed that maybe four or five years into my NFL career, I'd get a shot at being a referee. But only after I'd established myself so solidly that I would *know* I could do it.

Yet, mixed in with all the fear was also the exultation of knowing I would be back at the position I knew best. That I'd be able to use all those wonderful mechanics I'd developed in eleven years of collegiate refereeing, all the things I'd learned from Wirtz, and everything I'd picked up from watching Tunney and Schachter and Bell. I would now have a chance to emulate all these famous guys. I was anxious and thrilled at the same time. I knew my NFL career lay before me. All I had to do now was follow the best of my dad's advice: "Take the risk and don't give up" and "Find out about yourself." And, of course: "Don't step on your own pecker."

As a Temple
boxer, age
ten

High school
jock

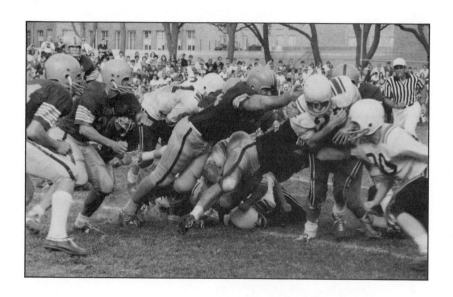

Chicago Catholic League game, 1961.
Was I ever that young?

Chicago Public League Championship, November 23, 1963.
The fans were not in the mood for football.

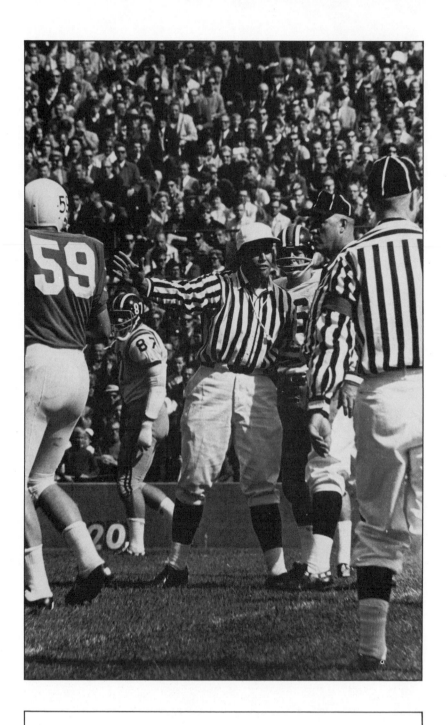

First game as a referee in the Big Ten,
September 30, 1967
STEVE LASKER

Woody Hayes incident.
UPI/BETTMANN

Ref goes down at Iowa/Arizona

JOHN H. MCIVOR

Ref goes down again in end zone at Iowa
(Michigan State)
JOHN H. MCIVOR

Last Big Ten crew: left to right, Kemper, Markbreit,
Quinby, Orem, Lehman, and White.
One of the best crews ever.

First game as an NFL referee, August 6, 1977:
left to right, Dodez, Connell, Markbreit,
Javie, Graf, and Reynolds

Tom Kellehen and me

The "toss of the coin," Super Bowl XVII

Holding
FOCUS ON SPORTS

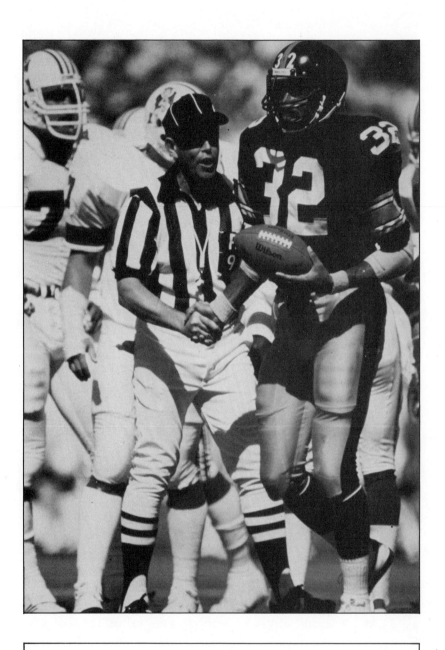

Franco Harris breaks the rushing record.
RONALD C. MODRA/*SPORTS ILLUSTRATED*

Me, Dad, and Gayle Sayers at a dinner in Dad's honor

Lawrence Taylor knocks down the ref.

Roulon Jones and Ref (Mutt and Jeff)
PETER READ MILLER/*SPORTS ILLUSTRATED*

Charles Martin incident
AP/WIDE WORLD PHOTO

Joe Montana, are you all right?
AP/WIDE WORLD PHOTO

Safety! Pay no attention to my hands. It's the
Giants' safety in Super Bowl XXI.
JERRY WACHTER/*SPORTS ILLUSTRATED*

Denver, a
battle to
break up a
scuffle
between the
Broncos'
Ken Lanier
and the
Oilers'
William
Fuller.
AP/WIDE
WORLD PHOTO

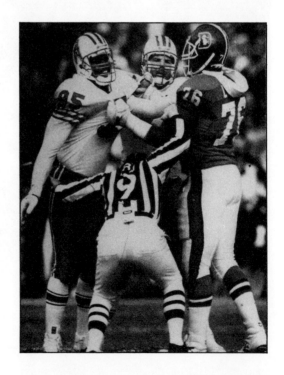

## PART TWO
# JERRY MARKBREIT, NFL REFEREE

# 8. INTRODUCTION

**E**ven after twelve seasons and 234 games as a National Football League official, I am still discovering nuances in the game, in my refereeing, and in my on-field personality that make me wonder: "Will I ever know enough? Will I ever be the consummate football official?" The answer is: *absolutely not.*

Officiating is like life. You can never master it, you can only strive to improve. The most exciting challenge of this profession, the one that continually surprises me, is its complexity. There's always something to discover —a foul you never called before; a test of your knowledge of the rules; an unexpected crisis or success; another lesson to learn.

What intrigues me also is that the complexity of the job is not always obvious or even noticeable. I do a lot of public speaking around the country and, year after year, I answer hundreds of questions about football officiating. People are curious about us because they rarely read or hear about officiating from the official's point of view. In fact, not many people in the lay world of sport understand the intricacies of what NFL officials do, how we do it, and what it means to us.

So let me peel away some of the layers.

# 9. KNOWING YOUR TAIL FROM YOUR HEAD

**M**ost people consider officiating a very straightforward task: either you know the rules or you don't. It's much more complicated. Officials are the epitome of the old saying "Think on your feet." You're always under pressure—especially when you work almost every week before a nationwide television audience. And when you get a playoff, or if you reach the pinnacle—the Super Bowl—the pressure intensifies. You realize that your peers, your friends, and the entire National Football League are watching along with much of the civilized world, and you have that fear of screwing up and looking like a shlemiel. You're always aware that because your work is so demanding and complex, *anything* can stick its foot out and trip you up.

My best example is the most embarrassing, humiliating, horrifying moment of my career. It's also pretty amusing, but I'll never be able to laugh about it. Even though it happened almost six years ago, I still can't watch the tape of that game. It's disturbing for me even to *think* about, never mind relive. If that sounds silly, consider this: I committed my screwup before anybody ever touched the football!

At the end of the strike-shortened 1982 season, at age

forty-seven, I reached the top of my profession. I was rated number one among my peers and, after only seven seasons in the NFL, I was selected to referee my first Super Bowl. When I arrived at the Rose Bowl in Pasadena on Friday, January 28, 1983, for Super Bowl XVII, the place was completely empty. I walked onto the field and looked around and realized that in forty-eight hours, almost to the minute, I'd be standing here in front of a hundred thousand screaming fans, with another hundred million watching on TV. I visualized the crowd, the players, the officials, the TV crews. I felt the adrenaline pumping already; the shpilkes was unbelievable. I didn't know if I could handle the anticipation. I remember thinking: "Can I *wait* forty-eight hours? I'll go *crazy* waiting."

That afternoon, our crew rehearsed the pregame amenities. We reviewed the inspection of the field; how we'd make our entrance for the ceremonies; where we'd stand for the toss of the coin. I was more worried about the toss than I was about the game. I don't know why, but that whole previous week I half-kidded Bobbie that when I got out there for the ceremony, I would probably screw something up. We had a running joke about that.

On Saturday the twenty-ninth, I felt this foreboding even stronger. I nudjeled Bobbie relentlessly about it. I told her, "Boy, I am so excited and so nervous about this game tomorrow, I don't know what to do. Do you realize that this is the biggest game of my entire life? I have a feeling I'm going to screw up the script." We had a choreographed script for the coin toss. I was supposed to say, "Gentlemen, we will now conduct the toss of the coin." I kept telling Bobbie, "I'll probably get out there in front of millions of people watching on national television and say, 'Gentlemen, we will now conduct the *coss* of the *toin.*'" She laughed and reassured me, "Stop worrying, Jerry. You won't say, 'coss of the toin.'" But the more I heard the phrase, the more I worried that it would accidently slip out, even though I was on guard for it.

As always, my biggest fear was that I'd make a fool

of myself. In this game, with this kind of massive exposure, I didn't think I could face that. Everything had to be absolutely perfect. I wanted to prove that I was worthy of working this game. I knew that all the league officials would be watching, and I wanted them to know that the league made the right choice in giving Jerry Markbreit the Super Bowl in only his seventh year as a referee. This was my proving ground, the biggest test of my career—the whole megillah.

I barely ate my dinner Saturday night because my stomach was doing the Olympics. I was afraid even to drink a drop of water. I never had shpilkes like that before. It was a perfect example of talking yourself into a problem. I was already *looking* like a shlemiel just by *worrying* about looking like a shlemiel. And over something that had nothing to do with the football game!

That night, I couldn't sleep. I woke up every twenty minutes, tormenting myself that this might go wrong or that might go wrong. At one-thirty, I woke up thinking my knee had slipped out. I sat on the edge of the bed, mumbling until Bobbie woke up. I said, "I can't believe it. My knee went out. I can't work the game." She said, "Jerry, relax. You're acting like a meshuggener." I said, "C'mon, I'm *serious!* Look at my knee!" She said, "Jerry, nobody sneaked in and wrenched your knee while you were sleeping." I said, "Roberta, my knee is out. I know it's out." She said, "Show me." So I got up and walked around, and it was fine. She said, "It's not your knee, it's your head. I've never seen you so nervous. This is just another football game. You'll do fine."

I walked around some more and the knee was still okay. I thought: "Did I *dream* it went out? What am I doing to myself?" I tried to settle down and fall asleep again, but I must've gone to the toilet twenty times. Each time, I'd take two steps and think my knee was slipping out again and that I definitely wouldn't be able to work the game. At two-thirty I woke Bobbie up and complained, "My knee went out. This time, I'm sure of it." She was so wasted from all the tsimmes that she pulled the covers over her head and said, "So have an op-

eration. I'll *wheel* you to breakfast. Meantime, good night!" And she went back to sleep.

I finally relaxed and fell asleep. But I woke up again at three-thirty, repeating the phrase "*coss* of the *toin*." I got up to find the script, and I was absolutely certain that my knee locked up. I was totally off the wall—my mind was bouncing back and forth *between* catastrophes! I got the script, *limped* back to bed, and started practicing aloud: "Captain Kuechenberg, call the *toss* of the *coin* . . . *toss* of the *coin* . . . *toss* of the *coin*." I wanted to memorize how that should sound. There was no way I was going to humiliate myself in front of a hundred million people and all my peers.

Bobbie woke up again. "Jerry, you're nuts," she said. "The game's twelve hours away. Go back to sleep. You're driving me crazy!" I said, "You're right. This is ridiculous. I'm driving us *both* crazy." Then I got irrational again. I said, "You know something, Roberta? I wish I hadn't brought you. You're bringing me bad luck."

I slept maybe an hour the whole night. I was up before dawn reviewing my notes and my usual game reminders—eleven pages of in-the-grasp calls; roughing the kicker; television time-out procedures and so on. I wanted to keep my pregame ritual exactly the same as always. But I couldn't get my mind off the ceremonies. I couldn't figure out why I was so worried. Then it occurred to me that I'd never *had* pregame ceremonies on TV before. Normally, the toss of the coin was conducted *before* the telecast began.

On Sunday morning the butterflies were so big they were wrestling to get out of my stomach. The crew had breakfast together, but I couldn't even consider eating. I felt like a kid getting ready to go to kindergarten for the first time. It was the same feeling I had before walking onto the field for the first time in the NFL. Except that now I had seven years in the NFL.

After the breakfast, we drove in two vans to the Marriott and dropped off the wives. I went inside and picked up Art McNally and the supervisory staff and, at ten-thirty, we were ready to go to the Rose Bowl. Even though

kickoff wasn't until 3:30 P.M., the league wanted us there in plenty of time—no chance of getting caught in traffic or having a flat tire. When I kissed Bobbie good-bye, I said, "I want to have the best game of my career. I want to prove to myself that I'm worthy of working a Super Bowl game." She gave me a big hug and said, "Everything will go fine. Don't worry." That started me worrying again.

In the van were three supervisors—Nick Skorich, Jack Reader, and Art McNally—along with myself; umpire Art Demmas; head linesman Dale Hamer; line judge Bill Reynolds; back judge Dick Hantak; side judge Dave Parry; field judge Don Orr; and the two alternates, Bob McElwee and Burl Toler. Here we were on the way to the game and everything else was finally behind us. When we hit Pasadena, we picked up a police escort, and the tension escalated. We talked about it: "Boy, we're nervous *now*. What's it gonna be like when we have to kill four hours in the stadium?" I laughed along, but I was so anxious for the game to get going, I was ready to jump out of my skin.

We arrived in the stadium as planned, and we did some reviewing, kibitzing, studying. We dressed in silence. Shortly before going out to the field, one of Commissioner Pete Rozelle's assistants called to inform me, "We're using a special commemorative coin. It's sterling silver. Elroy Hirsch will bring it to the middle of the field and give it to you there. The two helmets are tails." I said, "What's on the other side?" He said, "We haven't seen it. But it'll be fine. Just remember, the two helmets are tails."

Thirty minutes before game time, we inspected the field. I did a microphone check, and then we went back inside for the last twelve minutes. We just sat quietly, reading by ourselves until it was time to go out for the game. Then we all put our hands on the football, and Art Demmas gave a brief prayer that everything would go well, and out we went.

The officials who had to deliver the time went to the team locker rooms, and I started out for the field with

the umpire and head linesman. My security man, a young shtarker, was waiting as I opened the door. I said, "I appreciate you giving me all this attention." He said, "That's my job today. I'll make sure you're protected from now until the game is over and you're in your car." We started for the tunnel. I said, "What do you do?" He said, "I'm a college student. This is the biggest thrill of my life, just being involved in this." I said, "You want to know something? I feel the same way."

He walked me down the runway, and it was a pretty long walk under the stands in a very old section of the Rose Bowl. I listened to my own footsteps and the roaring of the crowd. I thought: "This is what the *gladiators* must've felt like on their way to fight the lions." The closer I came to the end of the tunnel, the louder the crowd roared. They knew the game was about to start. Boy, my heart was pounding so hard and I was so excited, I could hardly breathe.

I hit the sunshine at exactly three-fifteen, and it was gorgeous. The crowd was at a fever pitch—105,000-strong. They were screaming and yelling in anticipation of the biggest football game of the year. My security man dropped me off at the sidelines and I looked around at the blazing lights and the manicured grass and the beautiful flowers. I took a deep breath, thinking: "Brother, I have really made it. This is the Super Bowl. All I have to do now is get past the preliminaries and I'm home free. I can't wait."

The next thing I knew, I heard my name over the loudspeakers: "Referee Jerry Markbreit will now come to the middle of the field to conduct the toss of the coin." Knees wobbling, heart pounding, I marched out to the fifty-yard line. I was joined by the other officials and the team captains. I scanned the crowd, realizing that in a few minutes the biggest thrill of my sports life would begin. Then Elroy Hirsch came over with the coin in his hand. I looked at the Miami captains on my left and the Washington captains on my right and I said to Miami captain Bob Kuechenberg, "Captain Kuechenberg, call the *toss* of the *coin* in the air. The two helmets are tails."

I thought: "Thank God. You got it right. You're home free."

Hirsch handed me the coin and I flipped it. As it spun in the air, I remember slowing it down in my mind so it was going end over end in slow motion. Kuechenberg called, "Tails!" and down it came. I looked in the grass and saw those two helmets and I said to myself: "Heads." I turned to Joe Theismann and said, "Heads. You win the toss." Hirsch tugged my shirt: "Jerry, I think the two helmets are tails." Suddenly Dick Enberg ordered his cameraman, "Pull away from the coin. There's a problem." I reached down and turned my microphone off, realizing that I had just screwed up the toss of the coin in front of a hundred million people in the biggest event of my life—just by saying "Heads."

I was horrified, totally in the ozone. I picked up the coin and looked at both sides. One side had the two helmets and the other side had two players *holding* helmets. They looked identical. I said to Kuechenberg, "What did you call?" He said, "I called tails." I said, "What do you see on this side?" He said, "That looks like heads." I turned the coin over and said, "What do you see on this side?" He said, "That looks like heads, too." So I looked over at Theismann and I said, "It's heads. You *still* win the toss." Theismann shook his head and said, "Where the hell did they find *you*?"

I'd gotten myself so confused and embarrassed at that point that I drew a complete blank. When I'd looked at both sides of the coin, I couldn't register because they were almost exactly the same. But I knew the two helmets were tails and I knew he had called tails. Why I told Theismann it was heads, I don't know. And I probably asked Kuechenberg what he saw because I was trying to collect myself. Finally, Dale Hamer came in to straighten it out. He said, "What is tails?" I said, "The two helmets." Dale said, "Okay, Miami wins the toss." Suddenly it struck me how simple that was.

I felt like crawling out of the stadium. If I could've disappeared and never officiated another game, I'd've done it. I was selected to work the biggest football game there is and I couldn't get by the toss of the coin! That

taught me one of the great lessons of my life. Refereeing the Super Bowl at just forty-seven, I thought I was infallible. Sure, part of me was worried and insecure—that came with the territory. But deep inside, the *real* me thought that I must be the best there ever was, and nothing could happen that I couldn't handle. I was so cocky, so confident, I knew nothing could stymie me. But something did: *me.*

The mistake I made in that ceremony made me ten times stronger as a person. I thought of Dutch Rittmeyer's grace under fire and Herman Rohrig's lecture on pouting, and I told myself, "You just looked like the biggest jerk in the history of professional football. But stone-face is the name of the game. And don't pout. Be professional. Push it out of your mind and do your job." Somehow, although I was devastated, I was able to officiate the ball game and not let it affect my work.

The game flew by, and I was pleased with my performance. The officiating was excellent, and it was one of the closest Super Bowls in ten years. But when it ended, I couldn't shake the nauseous feeling of humiliation. I hid in the shower, knowing that the needling would be unmerciful. I was still in the shower when Art McNally came in. He shook everybody's hand and said, "Gentlemen, that was some of the finest officiating in the seventeen-year history of the Super Bowl." Then he came over to the shower, parted the curtain, and said, "Once we got by the toss of the coin."

To illustrate the psychological carryover of these things, there was a follow-up incident four years later when I was selected to referee Super Bowl XXI—the New York Giants-Denver Broncos game in 1987. Three days before the game, after fifteen practices of the toss of the coin, Bob Stenner, the executive producer for CBS, said to me, "Jerry, by consensus vote, the television crew and the press people have decided that you should take the coin back to your hotel for the next two days, so you can study which side is heads and which side is tails." And I did. I took it back with me and I must've studied both sides five hundred times.

Nobody would let me forget the '83 fiasco. Guys on

my crew were all over me. They said, "Got that coin all memorized, Jer? Want us to review it for you? One side is heads. The other side is tails." They were kidding, but I was dead serious. The tension was tremendous because I considered this my chance for redemption. I felt I needed to wipe the slate clean. I practiced the toss a million times. And I kept thinking: "Please don't make another mistake. Don't miss a word. Don't mispronounce anyone's name. Do the toss exactly the way it's supposed to be done. *Make sure you know your tail from your head.*"

Once again, even though it was a different coin, the helmets were tails. One side had the faces of John Madden and Al Davis, and the other side had the Super Bowl trophy with a large helmet on either side of it. I repeated to myself: "The two faces are heads. The two faces are heads."

In the locker room just before the game, Jim Poole, the back judge and a great needle artist, said, "Jerry, how about one more toss of the coin before we go out?" They weren't going to let me forget it. I was feeling kind of cocky now, so I figured: "Okay, I'll play along." I took out an imaginary coin, looked at Jim squarely, and said, "Captain Jackson, you'll call this in the air. The two faces are tails." I couldn't believe it. The two faces were *heads!* I'd screwed up in the *locker room!* "That was great," Poole said. "If you make that mistake on the field, we'll hang you on worldwide TV." I said, "I *know* the two faces are heads. Don't worry about it." The crew looked at me sideways all the way out to the field.

We walked along the sideline, and the crowd was electrifying. It was the most beautiful day—high seventies, sun shining, flowers everywhere. I kibitzed with John Elway and Tom Jackson while waiting for the pregame entertainment to end. I looked around and thought: "My second Super Bowl. Why should I be worried? I've been through this before. I'm a fifty-one-year-old man, I've handled the biggest personal crises in any normal man's life. This is nothing. Don't look at the coin anymore, forget about the damn thing. Go out there

and do the job. It'll go right." Then I heard Pat Summerall's voice over the loudspeaker: "Referee Jerry Markbreit and his crew will now conduct the toss of the coin."

Out we went to the middle of the field. I waited for Packers Hall of Famer Willie Davis to come out with the coin. He and I had joked around for a couple of days before the game, so he knew how nervous I was about the toss. Willie handed me the coin, shook my hand, patted me on the back, gave me a big smile, and said, "Give 'em hell." That made me feel great. I had the coin in my hand and I looked at Tom Jackson, Denver's captain, and I said, "Captain Jackson, Denver has been designated visiting team. You'll call the toss of the coin in the air." I showed him the coin and I said, "The two *faces* are heads. The *helmets* are tails." They nodded. I said, "Let me repeat. The two *faces* are heads. The *helmets* are tails." They thought I was nuts—but at least I got it right.

I felt so good, I added a little shtik. I handed the coin to Willie and said, "Flip it, Willie." He smiled and gave it a flip. Jackson called, "Heads!" and the coin landed in the thick grass. I looked down and saw the two helmets and said to myself: "The two helmets. *Tails*." I said to Jackson, "*Tails*. New York Giants win the toss. Captain Carson?" Harry Carson of the Giants said, "We'll receive"—and I was ecstatic. Now I knew for *sure* that I was home free.

Bang, wheeled the captains around, tapped them on the shoulders, made the signals. They all shook hands and I hustled downfield to await the kick. There I was, standing alone on the goal line, looking into the sun, and letting it warm my face. Heart pounding, perspiration pouring off me, I told myself: "You finally made it, kid." In that one little moment, I felt euphoric. My bugaboo and nemesis for the past four years had been laid to rest forever. I couldn't wait to see that ball in the air.

Suddenly I thought of my dad, who'd recently passed away. I remembered that whenever we had fun to-

gether, he used to say to me, "Well, son, what do you think?" I glanced upfield and there was the kicker jogging toward the ball. I smiled, looked straight up to the sky, and said to my dad, "Well, H.M., *what do you think?"*

# 10. REGIMENTED INDEPENDENCE

**I**'ve been asked many times what it takes to succeed as an official in the National Football League. I think the most interesting ingredient is a paradoxical personality. You need a sort of regimented independence—stubborn independence to get here, and regimentation to stay.

Everything about an NFL official is a paradox. We come from different walks of life and different professions, yet we're all cut from the same cloth. We're successful, willful, take-charge types with powerful egos and the need to make our own decisions. But we're also reserved, disciplined, follow-orders men who are willing to place ourselves in a strictly regimented environment. All of a sudden, for a few days at a time over twenty weeks, we have to follow rules we didn't make—and we *like* it. In fact, despite our independence, we almost relish it when we hear, "The clinic will be at three o'clock, gentlemen. *No one* will be late."

# ONE MINUTE LATE

The rules and regulations for professional football officials are rigid, and it takes a lot of concentrated work to stay within the boundaries. I think strict rules of decorum are necessary because even though we're individualists, we have to be molded into one skilled unit. It's like being in the service. It's that tough, regimented, "All horses pulling in the same direction" psychology. The players have it, too. For the team to succeed, every player has to do his job. Each must perform according to a set of rules to be part of a close-knit team. The same applies to officiating.

One rule is that we're not allowed to be interviewed by the media during the football season unless it's approved by the league office. It protects us from saying something that might be misconstrued in print. That's a diversion from our normal lives where, if someone wants to talk to us, we can talk. From the time we leave home for a game until we board the plane to return, we're not permitted an alcoholic drink. The reason is obvious: That, too, can be misconstrued. If an official has a cocktail at dinner the night before a game, someone might see the liquor on the table and, bang, the rumor spreads that so-and-so was drunk last night and that's why he made a bad call in the game. I don't drink anyway, but some of the fellas like to have an occasional cocktail in their outside lives—so, again, here's enforced regimentation they're not used to.

We're required to be at clinics and meetings at specific times. You may be coming from anywhere in the country, in any kind of weather, but woe to the guy who walks in a minute late—unless he phoned ahead to explain: "My plane was hijacked to Tochisville!" You don't miss meetings and, unless the earth slips off its axis, you never miss a game. It's as much your own expectation as the league's, and it's very powerful.

Here's an example. The Thursday night prior to the

first preseason game of 1987—St. Louis at Cleveland—
we had a torrential rainstorm in Chicago. On Friday
morning the water was so deep on the expressway that
truck drivers were diving off their semis and swimming
to the shoulder. I was so worried about not being able
to fly to Cleveland, I called the league office and arranged for another referee to take my place in that
event. But I didn't feel right about it. I had never missed
a game in eleven years. I felt it was my duty to be there.

Starting at 5:00 A.M. on Saturday, it took me over two
hours to cover a twenty-minute drive to O'Hare International. I had to find streets that weren't closed or sub-
merged. I arrived at 7:30 A.M. to find that my flight had
been canceled and that the only other available flight
to Cleveland was a delayed 6:30 A.M. flight that was still
in the airport. So I sprinted frantically to the gate. When
I got there, it was wall-to-wall humanity. There must've
been three-hundred people trying to get on a plane
that seated 120. I was desperate: What should I do? I
had the phone number of the official who was ready
to take my place; it was a simple matter of placing the
call, avoiding the hassle, and going home.

Then I had an idea. I'm recognized a lot in public
places, particularly airports, though I don't take advantage of it. It embarrasses me; I just can't do it. But I
felt I had to make this game, so I picked out a supervisor
behind the counter, walked to the front of the line, and
introduced myself. "Sir," I said, "I'm Jerry Markbreit. I'm
a National Football League referee." A guy behind me
immediately asked for my autograph. The supervisor
said, "Yes, Mr. Markbreit"—he recognized me, too. I
said, "I am the referee on the St. Louis-Cleveland game
tonight. If I don't make this flight, they're not going to
have a referee for the game." It sounded like, "I am the
commander of the United States Army, and if I don't get
to Cleveland, you will personally be held responsible
for World War Three!"

The supervisor took my ticket, gave it to a counter
attendant, and said, "Put this gentleman in first class,
please." She punched in my ticket and handed it back

to me. I shook the supervisor's hand, thanked him sincerely, and walked straight onto the plane. That supervisor didn't have to help me out, but he saw how important it was to me. I made Cleveland in time, and I was so relieved. But I was slightly later than normal. When I walked into the hotel, just as I expected, one of my fellow officials greeted me with the needle: "You're one minute late, Markbreit. You'll never be an *NFL* referee."

# "THE TATUM RULE"

Composure is a key ingredient in the regimented decorum of an NFL official. We're expected to conduct ourselves with dignity and professionalism at all times. Profanity is frowned upon. I'm an occasional swearer at home. It helps relieve my tension. But at football games, I control myself. When a player or coach chews me out, I think back to a Big Ten game when I made a controversial call against Michigan State and then had to face Duffy Daugherty. When I approached him, he let me have it with both barrels. Finally he stopped and waited for my response. I just looked at him, and that got him angrier. "Dammit, Markbreit," he fumed, "why the hell don't you say something? I can't have argument with you if I'm the only one arguing!" I said, "Exactly my point, Coach. Now, can I go back to the football game?" He sort of smiled at me, and away I went. The point was: Don't argue, don't swear. *Never lose control.*

Players occasionally lose control, and they like to swear. Funny thing about player profanity: You hate to hear it, but when it's absent, you miss it. During the '87 players' strike, I noticed that one big difference in the games was that, unlike the veterans, the replacement players never swore. They were so intent on what they had to do, so busy *playing*, that they didn't have time to unload. And they didn't want to jeopardize their one

chance of playing in the big time. So, for a couple of games, it was very pleasant. I didn't really notice it, though, until game 5—Denver at Kansas City.

The Chiefs had only a few regulars back, but Denver used ten. It was like old times—the veterans swore and complained bitterly about everything: "Are you blind? That $↑$%# is holding me!" ... "That was a %↑$&* call, ref!" Every time they swore, I turned to my umpire, Bob Wagner, with a big smile on my face. Finally Bob came over and said, "What the hell are you smiling about?" I said, "Boy, that stuff is just music to my ears. It feels so good to hear professional bitching again."

There was another funny incident in that game. With a few minutes left and Denver leading, 19–17, the Denver quarterback ran out of bounds at the KC bench. An assistant coach was standing right there, and he read that poor kid the riot act: "You little ↑&%$#@&! You can't do $%↑&!" He ate that kid alive. It wasn't really malicious; he was frustrated, he wanted to win. My job is to follow the quarterback, so I was there, too. I ran up and scolded the coach, "Don't you *dare* call him all those names!" He was shocked. He said, "What the hell are *you* talking about? You can't control what I say!" I said, "Well, I don't like it. Just cut it out. Don't do it anymore."

I was so regimented to control my own swearing, I became a swearing warden! But I sounded ridiculous. I thought: "Brother, Jerry. Don't be dictatorial."

Of course, losing your *own* cool is the cardinal sin. Players can lose their cool, coaches can lose their cool, but God forbid an official should lose his cool. Every time it happens, the coach calls the league office and says, "Your man lost his poise." And that's remembered. You not only lose your professional demeanor, you can also lose the players' respect. When a player accuses you of something, you feel vulnerable—even when you know he's wrong. But once you defend yourself, you topple from your plateau of respect down to his argumentative level, and you lose your credibility. Now you're just an arguer and complainer like him.

One time, years ago, I tried so hard to exert all my

poise and rationale on an angry defensive lineman who kept saying, "How much did you bet on this game, ref?" The first few times, I ignored it. Finally I gave him a warning. I said, "I'd be very careful who I accuse of something like that. You're insinuating that I gambled on this game. I don't gamble on *anything*. That's a completely unfair accusation, just because you're upset about some call." He said, "I bet you one thing, ref." I said, "What's that?" He said, "I bet you can go %$# ↑ yourself."

Then there was the *classic* case of losing my cool. Atlanta was losing to the Oakland Raiders, 51–20, in the closing minutes when I had a holding foul on Atlanta. I called for the Raiders' captain. Jack Tatum and the middle linebacker were co-captains, but only the middle linebacker came over. I said, "Captain, what do you want to do? Take the penalty for third down, or decline for fourth?" He said, "Decline the penalty." Which was smart because now Atlanta had to punt, though it wouldn't affect the outcome anyway.

After I'd waved off the penalty and announced, "Fourth down," Tatum ran up to me and demanded, "I want to *accept* the penalty!" I said, "It's too late. The other captain turned it down." He said, "I'm a captain, too, and I'm telling you I *want* the penalty." I said, "I'm sorry, Captain." He exploded, "You rotten &* ↑ %$#-@#$% ↑ &!" I was stunned. I said, "*What* did you say?" That gave him a chance to back off. But he looked me in the eye and said, "You heard me, rotten &* ↑ %$#-@#$% ↑ &!" That did it. I snapped, "And you get the @#$% off this field."

When the game ended a few minutes later and I started for the locker room, Raiders coach Tom Flores —a respected, decent man—grabbed me and said, "My man says you told him to get the @#$% off the field." I said, "I did, Coach. And I apologize. I lost my cool. But your guy called me a rotten &* ↑ %$#-@#$% ↑ & *twice* out there." Flores turned to Tatum and said, "Is that true?" I thought Tatum would take this opportunity to apologize. Instead, he glared at me and said, "Rotten

&* ↑ %$#-@#$% ↑ &!" Now Flores was stunned. We both shook our heads and that was the end of it.

I called my supervisor, Art McNally, immediately after the game because I wanted to tell him myself before he heard it from Flores. I was very upset because I *never* use profanity on the field. I told Art how badly I felt about the incident and we agreed that I was wrong, and I accepted his reprimand. Flores never reported it, and nothing more was said. But I told myself, "Okay, Jerry, now you have 'The Tatum Rule' to guide you. The rule is: 'Never throw a @#$%#&* fit, throw a @#$% ↑ &* flag!' "

# THE INTRIGUING TWIST

One thing I like about regimentation is that it's a great equalizer. There's the old saying that you could take twenty-five millionaires and twenty-five ditch-diggers and put them all in the shower, and you couldn't tell who did what if your life depended on it. It's the same with officials. Walking into a stadium, this guy's a bank president; this guy's a lawyer; this guy's a trade and barter manager. But in the locker room, you put on your striped shirts and suddenly you're all football officials, you're all the same. It's that sameness that draws you together and makes you a team. And I love being part of a team.

An NFL officiating team is like a highly trained Army platoon. Art McNally is our commander. He has a cadre of lieutenants working for him and, together, they run the platoon. They conduct a very intricate, ongoing program of meetings, film reviews, and grading sessions so that we can stay on top of things throughout the season. Every week they send us our game film together with videotapes of unique or unusual plays from the previous week. It's an amazing amount of work, but it

takes this type of meticulous administration to produce the high-quality results they get.

It's like you need the guidance and technical schooling to function properly on the field. But there's an intriguing twist. On the field, while you work coolly and by the book as part of a team, when it comes to judgment, you're on our own. You've been taught what to look for and how to make the call *mechanically,* but the *decision* to make the call is instinctive. That's where your individuality comes into play. In that regimented world of "everyone's the same," your instinct—which cannot be regimented—makes the calls *for* you.

Instinct is what helped me make the Charles Martin-Jim McMahon "stuffing the quarterback" call in 1986. Another example: In my second game of 1987, a Dallas-Giants game, there was a tricky play in the second quarter. Dallas quarterback Danny White passed the ball. A split second after he released it, Lawrence Taylor flew in from the back side and, as he landed, his arm hit the back of White's head. It happened so fast that if I had blinked, I'd've missed it. And it wasn't intentional, so it looked perfectly legal. But I knew *instinctively* that it was a foul. I flagged Taylor for roughing the passer.

Taylor bounced up off the ground and protested, "It wasn't a foul." I said, "Lawrence, it wasn't a late hit, but you got him in the head." He said, "But it wasn't on purpose." I said, "I know you didn't do it on purpose, but it's still a foul." He said, "Yeah, I know. I'm sorry." And he turned and walked away. He was truly upset that he'd hit White in the head because he's a perfectionist, not because I flagged him for a foul. And he accepted my call—no screaming, no berating. I took it as a compliment, like he was telling me, "I respect your judgment. If you saw a foul, it must've been a foul."

At the next officials' meeting, they showed a highlight film of about twenty unusual plays from the first two weeks of the season. They showed the Taylor hit and said, "This was a good call. The hit was not late, it was too high." I was correct all the way. Even though it happened in a split second, my mind's eye caught it on instinct.

This is a phenomenon of officiating. I'm convinced that, as plays develop, officials have the ability to slow the action down in their mind's eye. When the quarterback's dropping back with the ball and I'm glancing from him to the tackle to the guard to make sure there's no holding on the pass blocking, I see things that are sometimes difficult to see in the film. And they're there: a grab, a hold, a slight manipulation. On running plays, a pull or a tug just before the ball's handed off that allows the back to slip through the hole. And my flag comes out automatically because I know I've got number fifty-four for pulling his man out of the hole. Two days later, I look at the film and it's not there. Then comes the end-zone shot and there it is. How did I see it on the field?

I probably do it on every play. I'll see a guard come up on a pass play and he's blocking, blocking, blocking. Then, all of a sudden, he gives the defender one little shot to the face—and I see it. It's like his hand is suspended there for that instant. And I tell myself: "Number sixty-three has his hand in that guy's face." Bang, out comes my flag and I'm back watching the rest of the play. It's as if someone's showing the play on a projector and I've said, "Stop it right there for a second, would you, please? Thank you very much. Okay, let's continue with the play."

On November 8, 1987, in the Washington-Buffalo game, it happened again so vividly I could hardly believe what I saw. Washington quarterback Jay Schroeder dropped back to pass and started to deliver the ball. He completed the throwing motion but, for a split second, the ball stayed suspended in air by his ear. Then it dropped to the ground and Schroeder recovered it. Because he finished his throwing motion, everybody in the stadium thought it was an incompleted forward pass. But from my position directly behind him, I was riveted on the ball and, when his hand left it, I saw it frozen in midair as if he were still holding it. It was like a freeze-frame. I had successfully stopped the action in my mind's eye long enough to see the ball fall to the ground *without moving forward*. Fumble, not forward pass. But how

could I possibly register, in less than an instant, the *non-movement of the ball* on the throwing motion?

It's amazing to watch the film after the game. You see the play in *real* slow motion for the first time, and you marvel at the details you saw when you made the call. You think: "That's exactly how I saw it on the field! How did I see, in a tenth of a second on the field, what takes twenty seconds to review on film?"

We watch game films every week, and ninety-nine times out of a hundred the officials are right. How do we do it? The answer—at least for me—is that out on the football field, I *am* the film, I *am* the projector. Both are running constantly in my mind's eye. That's a hallmark of top-flight officiating that people never hear about. And I'm not sure they'll believe it when they do.

# "NO NUMBER, NO FOUL!"

Another part of instinct is ingenuity, and there's nothing in the rule book about that either. But you need it. Years ago, in a Seahawk game in the Kingdome, the visiting team was on the two-yard line, fourth and goal. Suddenly a miniature football flew out of the stands and landed next to the center before he could get off the snap. The entire offensive line jumped, and both wing officials flagged the offense for false start. That would've brought them all the way back to the seven. Instantly, I blew the whistle, killed the play, turned the microphone on, and announced, "No play. A toy football was thrown from the stands, disrupting the line of scrimmage. We'll play it over."

There was absolutely no basis to negate that penalty. There's nothing in the rule book that says you can play anything over in football. But I did it anyway. A few days later, the league office said, "Under unusual circumstances, you did exactly what you should have done." I was a young referee at the time, and that call con-

firmed two important things: Trust your instincts; and the league respects common sense. There is no credo of commonsense officiating in the NFL, no list of rules to cover all the bizarre situations that can arise. They're relying on you as head of a crew to exercise your best commonsense judgment, tempered with your knowledge of the rules and mechanics of the game. They expect you to use your regimentation, instinct, *and* ingenuity.

In some games, we'll miss a number, say, on a defensive offside. In that case, I'll announce, "We have offside, defense." One time, many years ago, when a famous referee missed a number, he turned the microphone on and said, "Holding ..." then shut the microphone off, silently mouthed a number, turned the microphone on again, and added, "... offense." It appeared as if he'd given the number but that technical interference prevented everyone from hearing it.

I can't bring myself to do that. Occasionally I have to rely on my ingenuity to get the *players* to give me the number. But they love to play dumb. At one game, I said, "All right, which of you guys was offside?" They all looked at me with wide eyes, like innocents. They shrugged to each other, like, "*I* didn't see anything. Did *you* see anything?" I said, "C'mon, you *know* the film will show us who it was. Who was it?" A wise guy said, "It was ninety-nine." There was no ninety-nine. I said, "Why is it that when we ask you guys who committed the foul—after it's recorded *indelibly* on film—everybody looks like *Our Gang*?" Another wise guy said, "Hey, ref. What's 'indelibly' mean?"

They'll never give you a number voluntarily. They won't incriminate themselves. They pretend the film won't show it, and they clam up. "All right," I'll say, "who grabbed the face mask?" They'll go, "Gee, ref, nobody on *this* team grabbed a face mask." Then, as you walk away to announce the foul, they'll ride you unmercifully, "No number, no foul!" You start walking it off and they'll holler, "Don't let him walk that penalty off! He might forget the yardage!"

The next time, I'll try to trick them into giving me the

number. I'll know it was one of the linebackers, but I won't know which one. "All right," I'll say, "who was holding?" Nothing. I'll yell to Paul Weidner, my head linesman, "Put *fifty-seven* down on the blue card, Paul!" And fifty-seven will yell, "*I* didn't grab the shirt! It was *sixty-three!*" I'll turn to Paul: "Put *sixty-three* down." They still fall for that.

# OLD RADIO DAYS

One of the best examples of the fusing of training, experience, and instinct occurred in the 1987 Miami-Dallas game, which Miami won, 20–14. It was a routinely exciting game, except for one event—maybe one of the best calls made all year. Miami had the ball on the Dallas forty-five, third down. Miami quarterback Dan Marino threw a forty-yard bomb. His receiver, Mark Clayton, went up to make the catch. The defensive halfback went up with him, trying to grab the ball. As they bumped in midair, the defender snatched the ball. But when he hit the ground, the ball bounced off his chest and rolled down his leg. Clayton, who was also on the ground, grabbed the ball off the defender's leg. Bill Quinby, the side judge, was right there, and I could see him from forty yards away, signaling "Miami ball."

I ran downfield to Quinby, who was still hovering over these two guys. I said, "Bill, what do you have?" He looked up; his face was all red with excitement. He said, "I don't know what I have. But it's Miami's football!" We both chuckled and then Wagner hollered, "They're looking at it on replay!" I said to Quinby, "Okay, what *did* you have?" And he explained it to me precisely. He said, "The defender hit the ground, he never had possession. The ball was rolling loose on his chest when the offensive man recaptured it." I was thrilled for him. I said, "Bill, good for you. That was a terrific

call." About a minute later, I got the message from Wagner: "Continue play." I turned my microphone on and I said, "After further review, the play stands. First down, Miami."

After the game, Quinby told me he was just lucky on that call. I said, "Bill, you don't realize how great that call was, do you? (The next week, the league would inform Bill he got a 7 on the call—the highest possible grade.) You weren't lucky. That was a lifetime of officiating coming together to give you the poise and concentration and instinct to see that whole play exactly as it happened. You knew how to do it because it was all there, waiting to come out."

That night at the hotel, Wagner and I were turning in but we were too keyed up to sleep. So we talked to relax. He said, "You remember any old-time radio shows?" I said, "Sure," and we dredged up the memories: "The Jack Benny Show"; "Inner Sanctum"; "The Shadow"; "Tennessee Jed"; "Fibber McGee and Molly"; "The Answer Man"; "The Green Hornet." For over an hour, we discussed every old-time radio show there ever was: the years they were on, theme songs, names of the entertainers. We shared the funniest memories of shows we heard forty-five years ago, and we remembered them in *detail*! We were so hysterical, we were crying.

I said to Bob, "They talk about how the mind stores everything you ever thought, said, or did in your whole life, and it's there somewhere if you need it. After a conversation like this, is it surprising that when you're out on the football field, all the things you've learned about officiating pop out at just the right moment, when the stimulus arrives? Is it any wonder that after all the years Quinby's put into football, they came out tonight and helped him make the right call?"

As Wagner and I drifted off to sleep at 1:15 A.M., I thought: "These really tie together. Quinby's call *was* like remembering the details of all those old radio shows. Put a mature, experienced official on the field—a guy who's old enough to remember radio shows from forty-

five years ago—and when he needs something to help him make a major call, it'll *be* there."

## "AM I SOMEWHERE ELSE?"

Even if the officiating world were perfectly balanced, there'd still be the unexpected situations where nothing works—rules, regimentation, judgment, instinct, ingenuity, luck. Under the stress of orchestrating a professional football game, some calls just don't get through. Of course, that doesn't matter because you'll always be held accountable, even by your own crew.

Early in my career as a referee, I had a Denver-Dallas game. Dallas quarterback Danny White punted the ball and ran downfield, and I trailed him because he was my man. A defensive player caught him from the blind side and knocked him ass over teakettle—and I flagged it. Meanwhile, Denver returned the kick and then a fight erupted. Flags flew everywhere. As I hurried downfield, I reviewed to myself: "I've got a foul way up here and we've got two flags down there. What the heck do we have?"

The circumstances were bizarre because one foul was a postpossession foul that occurred *before* physical possession but is considered *after* physical possession. I thought of "TK's Pie," but I just could not put it in the right hopper. No problem, though. If I had trouble with a rule, I could always ask Kelleher himself. But as I approached Tom, he stepped in to break up the fight and he got cold-cocked. Boom, out like a light.

So there I was, standing over Kelleher, screaming, "Wake up! I don't know what to do with this penalty!" The players looked at me like I was nuts; the crew laughed so hard, they practically peed in their pants; and Kelleher was still out cold. They carried him to the sideline, where a trainer attended to him. Meantime, I

tried to figure everything out, but I absolutely did not know what I had. I looked at my crew and they all gave me the "Don't ask *me!*" shrug. So I misenforced the penalty—the only misenforcement of my entire career to date. Which still bugs me.

There wasn't supposed to be a walk-off, but I walked off yardage because I just couldn't register "double foul after possession." I was uncomfortable about it, but I was also concerned about Kelleher. I hurried to the sideline just in time to catch him coming to. The doctor, a tall, thin gentleman with a long, speckled beard, was kneeling over Tom. As Kelleher woke up, he was looking at this doctor who, I'm sure in Tom's stupor, looked exactly like Jesus Christ. The doctor said, "Are you all right?" Kelleher was lost. He said, "Where am I, Father? Am I still on the football field? Or am I somewhere else?" Tom's a devout Catholic; I'm sure he thought he was in Heaven with Jesus. Then he saw me and he said, "Oh, thank God."

He got up and I put my arm around him and we started walking. I wanted so badly to ask him about the call, but he looked too woozy to sort it out. I thought he wouldn't even remember it. So I said nothing. All of a sudden, he got this cockeyed look on his face and he said, "Well, you screwed *that* play up, didn't you, kid?"

# 11. A MATURE MAN'S PROFESSION

**I** became a referee in the National Football League at the young age of forty-one. I say "young" because seldom does anyone get in under age forty. NFL officiating is a mature man's profession. The game needs men who have the self-confidence to make split-second decisions; who can make equitable judgments in pressure situations; who can handle the stress of making mistakes; who enjoy the challenge of the unexpected. Only a mature, experienced individual can handle all that.

The coin-toss fiasco at my first Super Bowl was a classic example of immaturity. Even at forty-seven, I had trouble with the pregame stress, and it ruined forever the most wonderful day of my life to that point. If I had been as mature then as I was four years later, at my second Super Bowl, I wouldn't have flubbed the toss. Fortunately, because I had so much experience to draw on, I recovered and worked a good game. I endured enough humiliations to realize it could have been worse; I could have made a horrible call to cost someone the football game.

That perspective comes only with time on the field. There are constant pressures from everywhere—your peers, your friends, the fans, the players, yourself. You're onstage out there, in front of large, excited crowds, enormous television audiences, and very emotional players.

And even though you're part of a seven-man crew, you're all alone. You can help each other in meetings and you can share philosophy in the locker room, but once you walk onto the field, whether it's your first year or your twenty-first, you're responsible for one seventh of the action, and nobody else can do it for you. You're the only guy who sees the back leaning forward as the ball is snapped. If the play turns into a sixty-yard touchdown pass that wins the game, and you fail to drop the flag for that guy leaning forward, it's all yours—you've cost that team the game. Maybe if you had a little more maturity and experience, you would have called it.

During my first eleven years in the NFL, I worked on the same crew with Tom Kelleher—"Mr. Pressure." He *liked* pressure situations. Before every game, he would say, "Let's go out and have the best time of our lives today." At first, I thought: "My God, I'm so nervous, I'm ready to throw up. How can I have a good time?" He explained to me, "This job is so demanding that if you don't learn how to have fun, you're wasting your time. This can be the most fun you'll ever have in your life. For three hours, you're working a football game in front of a big audience with the best football players in the land. What could be more fun than that?"

He knew that if you went out there with ulcers, you couldn't do your best. So I learned how to channel the stress and have fun. But I'm a natural-born worrier. After every game, my mother still asks me, "So how did your game go?" I always say, "It went fine. Except I'm worried about a couple of calls." And I worry for a few days until I get the game report. As soon as I'm clear on the report, I figure: "Great. Now I can I start worrying about next week's game."

## STRESS SALAD

To me, the biggest challenge of officiating in the NFL is handling the pressure. At this level, it's a mixed salad

of different stress ingredients. During a game, you're constantly under a microscope. You're on film, replays, and TV, and you're making instant decisions that can be the difference between winning and losing. You *must* be right. The league expects you to be right; the coaches, players, and fans expect you to be right; you expect yourself to be right.

Every call is critical to me; I want them all to be correct. For one thing, even a call that seems insignificant can affect a player's career. You miss a defensive man grabbing a tight end, throwing him off-stride just enough so he can't catch the pass thrown his way, and he never gets credit for the catch. At the end of his career, he missed the record for pass receptions by one. You can tell yourself: "It's only a record"—but it might have been the most important thing in that man's life.

The league rates us on every play, so any mistake can cost *me* something, too: a postseason game in January. That's what every official strives for: the honor of being awarded a playoff game at the end of the season. The worst punishment—outside of being fired—is *not* getting a playoff game. The ultimate judge of how accurate I am on any given call is me, but the practical judge is the league supervisor who grades what I do. He grades every call of every game, and his evaluation is extremely thorough. It's based on the stress factors, the score of the game, the time, where you are on the field—everything. That's what makes for great officiating; you're always striving to get the highest grade possible. If you miss a call, a supervisor will catch it later on film and give you a downgrade (a "ding"). At the end of the regular season, all your grades are tallied. Only nine out of fifteen officials at each position will work on the field in the playoffs. Forty-four out of 107 NFL officials will have to wait until next year, and they're all excellent officials. You take the fifteen referees in the NFL—their ratings are so close at the end of a season, you couldn't put a credit card between them. Any one of us could work the Super Bowl. The competition is so severe that if you finish the regular season with just one

"ding" more than the guy ahead of you, it could shut
you out of a playoff.

There's also the pressure you put on yourself to gain
the respect and admiration of your peers. The only way
you know how you are perceived by those who judge
you are the postseason games you're awarded. If you
don't get one, your fellow officials sympathize because
they know how important it is. But you're devastated,
you're embarrassed. It's like believing you're the best
candidate in an election, then running and losing. And
all your peers know that you're not the best because
you lost. It dents your pride because you want their
esteem and acknowledgment that "You're a terrific official. We're proud to work with you."

Then there's the subtle pressure from your outside
friends. All year they constantly ask, "Where's your game
next week?" When I have my off-week every year, I tell
them, "I'm off this week," and they're always shocked.
They say, "What? Were you *fired*?" They're personally
upset because you're not working that week. They wonder: "How could that be?" Well, magnify that. The season's over: "Which playoff game did you get?" "I didn't
get one." That's the worst feeling in the world.

I've been fortunate; in my twelve years in the NFL
I've had twelve playoff assignments, including two Super
Bowls (to date, no referee has worked more than three
Super Bowls. I would like to be the first). But the pressure
returns every year. I still judge my whole season by that
yardstick: "If you don't get a postseason game, you had
a feckucteh year."


## FOOTBALL ISN'T A GAME


Football isn't a game to me. I'm not out there to win or
score points or root for a team or become famous. I'm
there to accept the toughest challenge I know: to ad-

minister the rules of a complicated game and see that it's played absolutely fairly. The ball is snapped and all hell breaks loose. When the play is over, any infractions perpetrated by either team in order to gain an unfair advantage *must* be penalized. Otherwise, you have chaos. The experienced official uses a simple rule of thumb: Did he gain an unfair advantage? If so, it's a foul. If not, the play stands.

Many fans don't understand our professional philosophy. They assume that we see the same game they do, and that we respond to the same emotional impulses they get when they're rooting for their favorite team. Not true. We don't root for anyone. We're too busy concentrating. To us, each play is a whole game in itself—the final score is meaningless. After a speech once, a guy said to me, "When an official makes a bad call, you can't tell me he doesn't try to make up for it by faking something on the next call." I wanted to strangle him. We don't care *who* wins a ball game. We have only the one credo: fair play. As a matter of fact, most of the time we try *too* hard to be fair.

That's why, for example, I've always had a problem with running-into-the-kicker calls. In college, there was leeway on the call: Did the defender *try* to hit the kicker? In the pros, there is no leeway. But, for some reason, my personal rule of fairness always intervenes. I saw a play in 1986 that looked like a classic running-into-the-kicker, except that the defender glided right under the kicker's foot and barely brushed him. But the kicker was so extended that he fell, so it looked like the defender knocked him flying. I knew that the guy wasn't trying to hit the kicker after the ball was kicked, so I didn't call it. Sure enough, when the game film came back, it was a good "no call." I did the right thing. And I was more than fair.

As referee, my main job is to protect the quarterback. If something happens to him, it's my fault, I'm the one who hangs. I can't prevent most fouls but, if I do my job, the defender might not take that *extra* shot. So I do a lot of yelling on pass plays after the quarterback releases the ball: "It's *over*!" "Stay *away* from him!" "Lay

*off* him!" Some defensive players get angry. They complain, "That's not fair! Why do you say that?" I tell them, "It *is* fair. I say it so *he* doesn't get hurt and *you* don't get a fifteen-yard penalty." Actually, I'm thinking more about preventing an injury to the quarterback than saving the defender a penalty. I bet most fans aren't aware of that.

There are a host of aggravating misconceptions about how officials operate. When I tell people that my crew watches films every Saturday afternoon before a game, they always assume that we're looking at the teams we're scheduled to have the next day. *Absolutely not.* The film we watch is the game we officiated *last* week. We review all our calls and answer all the questions the league office asks us about those calls in the game report. We don't care which teams are playing our next game, or where they rank in the standings.

People have asked me, "Doesn't your personal feeling for a certain player or team influence what you do?" The answer is *no.* The mature, forty-year-old-plus official doesn't have favorites. We act according to rules, not emotion. Every game is officiated exactly the same way—by the rules, fairly—and that's the end of it. We don't care who's coaching a team or who's playing. We don't watch individuals, we watch what individuals *do.*

Of course, some players will test you, hoping that you'll occasionally be a little *more* than fair. Former L.A. Rams star Jack Youngblood used to try that on me. He was one of the all-time great defensive tackles. He was also very charming and very personable, so he could easily ingratiate himself with people he didn't know. He was a master at it; he had his own psychological tactic, which most guys would never use. Whenever I had the Rams, Youngblood would say my first name constantly in the hope that it would influence a call or two. He was dreaming; I knew exactly what he was doing.

Before a game, he'd greet me with, "*Jerry,* how you doin'?" Or "Good to see you again, *Jerry.*" At first, I was flattered. I thought: "Gee, he knows my first name. He must really think I'm good." Later, I discovered he pulled

the same shtik on every referee. It was, "Hi Red"; "Hi Jim"; "Hi Ben." From that moment on, he'd bellyache the whole game that he was being held. "*Jerry*! Are you watching number eighty-nine? He's holding me like he *loves* me!" "Hey *Jerry*! Eighty-three wants to *marry* me! He's grabbing me all *over* the place!" Jerry this; Jerry that. He drove me crazy using my first name.

And his teammates noticed it. They had to be thinking: "Hey, he knows this ref personally." One game, Youngblood said to me, "For God's sake, *Jerry*! This guy's holding me left and right!" I said, "Jack, there isn't any one guy in this league who can hold you. It would take at least two—one to hold *you* and the other to hold your *mouth*." He just grinned and strolled back to the huddle. It didn't faze him. A few plays later: "*Jerry*! They're holding me *openly* now. They think you're *mad* at me!"

After a few years of this, I had the 1979 Rams-Cowboys divisional playoff game at Dallas. We were staying at the the same hotel as the Rams. The night before the game, I was down in the lobby when Youngblood walked right past me without recognizing me. Later, he passed me again and didn't say a word. The next day, early in the game, he tried his routine again: "*Jerry*! The guy's got me like an *octopus*!" I went up to him and said, "You know something, Jack. You're full of it. You passed me twice in the hotel lobby last night and you didn't know me from Adam. What'd you do, read my name in the program and write it down on a card?" He chuckled, "*Jerry*, I've known you a long time." I said, "Bupkes! Using my first name will get you absolutely *nowhere*."

He returned to the huddle and I thought I had him. Two plays later, I was returning to my position when I heard Youngblood's voice again: "*Mr. Markbreit! Mr. Markbreit!* This guy's *strangling* me!"

The point is, as an official I am completely unbiased. I've said many times that if my mother were out there playing and she committed the foul that would cost her team the game—bang, my flag would drop at her feet. Step out, flick on the mike: "We've got unsportsmanlike conduct on number one, Rena Markbreit. Roughing her son, the referee."

And it doesn't matter to us if a game is for the world championship or last place, or whether there's a hundred thousand in the stands or a thousand. A recent example was our first "replacement game" at the start of the 1987 strike—Tampa Bay at Detroit. At 12:30 P.M., we went to check the field. We walked into the Silverdome, which seats over eighty thousand, and the place was empty. It wasn't a small crowd, it was *no* crowd. Just before gametime they announced the crowd at forty-nine hundred, but it looked more like four hundred.

We'd never worked a regular-season game in front of practically no one. We had to respond like the stage performer who peeks through the curtain before he goes on and sees the empty seats. When that curtain goes up, he still has to give his best performance. Our crew agreed that, regardless of the size of the crowd and the fact that replacement players were taking over for the regulars, they were still the Detroit Lions and the Tampa Bay Buccaneers. And we knew we would be graded like we always were.

The only major difference I noticed in that game was the crowd noise. We didn't get the terrific volume we're used to from those huge NFL crowds. It was like playing in a studio with fake crowd noise on a tape. But that didn't affect our officiating. When I had a penalty, I stepped out, looked up to the booth, and gave my report the same as in any other game. I didn't say, "'*Replacement*' foul, unsportsmanlike conduct, number sixty-six, offense. But we'll give him another chance because he's new." It was fifteen yards because it's *always* fifteen yards.

# CONCENTRATION

If fairness is a hallmark of professionalism in officiating, so is the ability to concentrate. Nobody can teach it. I work as hard on this as I do on studying the rules be-

cause I know that, once the ball is in play, if I'm distracted for just an instant, I could miss something major
in a football game. I could walk off too many yards and
misenforce a penalty and maybe cost a team a field
goal that might've won the game. I might not hear one
of my crew reporting a foul to me. Or the quarterback
can throw a pass and, instead of staying with him, I
might daydream and watch the flight of the ball. Total
concentration is absolutely necessary.

I've learned to discipline myself in a game. I never
think about anything else. I don't allow my mind to drift
to the weather, the teams, what time my plane leaves,
what our meeting will cover next week, or what the
announcers are saying up in the booth. In fact, I have
learned to maintain complete concentration no matter
what happens to me physically. I demonstrated that
most recently in the second strike game of 1987—San
Francisco at Atlanta.

The Falcons had the ball on their own four when the
quarterback rolled right and dropped back into the
end-zone. Back I went with him, until I was almost on
the end-line. He cocked his arm, ready to throw, and
someone dove at him. I took a half-step forward to watch
closely for a safety or maybe an in-the-grasp. I was
watching only the quarterback and the diving player
when another Atlanta player came flying in from my
blind side. He cut me hard and knocked my legs from
under me. My hat went flying and I went down like a
bowling pin.

There I was, dazed on my fanny in the end-zone,
pain shooting through my neck and head from the concussion. But I watched the quarterback get dragged
down for a safety and I gave the safety signal, while
still watching the quarterback to make sure nobody
gave him a late hit. When the play ended, the other
officials came over and helped me up. The TV people
went to commercial and I stayed right there for the
kickoff. I thought I was fine, but I was really shaken. Bill
Quinby came over and said, "Jerry, it was a safety.
You're down in the *other* end-zone." I had lost touch for

a second; I was hit much harder than I thought. I trotted a hundred yards to the other end-zone and awaited the kick. I was still half in the ozone, but I was thrilled about my concentration. I had been so honed in on the quarterback that nothing—not even getting the day-lights knocked out of me—could break me away from the play. So even though I got hurt (it took me about a month to lose the soreness in my neck, shoulder, hip, and ankle), it was worth the pain. I found out that my concentration is almost instinctive now. I can block out humiliation and pain, and still do the job.

Only one thing can break my concentration: *animals*. Since I view my life as a series of connected lessons, it's no wonder that my love for animals has seeped into my football career. There's a little history to this. In 1963, my dad got me Lady, a German shorthaired pointer, to take hunting with us. As a puppy, Lady could point at *flies* in the backyard. At six months, she was hunting pheasant and duck with us in the woods. It was all she cared about.

But after six years of hunting, Lady was so stiff with arthritis she could barely walk. I'd open the door to leave and I could see her disappointment. Pretty soon, I didn't have the heart to leave her behind. As much as I loved being with my dad in the woods, and the thrill of seeing birds fly from the bush, I quit hunting and sold my guns. My dad was very upset. He thought I didn't want to be with him anymore, which wasn't true.

When Lady passed away, my dad asked me to resume hunting with him, but I couldn't do it. By then, I'd realized that killing wasn't for me. Bobbie and I had accumulated cats, and I used to see them mauling birds and mice. It struck me one day: "That's what *I* used to do. How could I have done that?" I decided I'd never kill anything again. I even stopped fishing because I didn't want to take the chance of injuring a fish. Today, I'm so sensitive to animals, I am shattered when I see a dead possum or bird on the road. When my cat Fletcher was sick recently, I would've given up officiating to save him. So if I see an animal on the football field, it's difficult

to concentrate on anything else. Here are my two best animal distraction stories:

## SALUTE TO A MOUSE

During a Michigan-Michigan State game in the early 1970s, some unkind person brought a mouse into the stadium and set it loose. With a few minutes left in the second quarter, and the marching band waiting on the rim of the field to start the halftime extravaganza, the mouse scurried onto the field and froze in fear. I had given the ready-to-play signal and was looking downfield when I spotted the mouse about forty yards away, petrified in front of a hundred thousand fans.

The teams came up to the line of scrimmage and I envisioned that mouse getting crushed, so I immediately stopped the game. But I had no idea what to do. I looked over at the fifty-yard line and I saw the Michigan drum major in his tall hat watching the mouse. He caught my glance and took off his hat, and I knew what he wanted to do. So I gestured to him and he high-stepped out to the mouse, scooped him into his big hat, pranced to an exit area, and released the mouse to safety. He then looked at me and gave me a proud salute.

I don't know how many people in the stadium saw that brief salute, but the band did. The drummers started clicking their sticks on the sides of their drums in applause—clickety-click, clickety-click, clickety-click. The whole episode only lasted about thirty seconds. I don't even think the guys on my crew knew what had happened. I never mentioned it to anybody and I never got a chance to thank that drum major. It was a mystical, Disney-esque moment I never forgot, and if I hadn't been distracted by that mouse, it never would've happened.

## THE PITTSBURGH PIGEON

It was Baltimore versus Pittsburgh in the waning days of the Baltimore Colts, before they moved to Indianap-

olis. Pittsburgh brought about fifteen thousand fans with them; it was probably the last sellout Baltimore ever had. We were ready to start the game when a big, plump pigeon landed on the fifty-yard line. The field was in bad shape; you could see where they had sprinkled seed for new grass. So I figured the pigeon had dropped in for lunch.

When the teams lined up and TV was ready to go, the pigeon was still in the middle of the field. I hollered to one of the other officials to get the bird out of there. He tried to shoo him away, but he flew to the forty, then to the thirty-five, and finally stood stubbornly on the thirty, unwilling to budge. So I walked over and tried to spook him myself, but he wouldn't fly. I chased him back to the fifty where he just waddled away from me. Television was screaming now, so I ran back to the goal line and blew the whistle for the opening kickoff.

The teams charged each other on the kickoff and, I swear, feathers were flying. They blitzed right past this meshuggeh bird and somebody nicked his tail feathers, and somebody else bumped him, but he refused to fly. When the play ended, he was standing on the forty like a bum looking for a handout. I was scared for him; I was more upset than I'd ever been in a football game. I didn't have the confidence at the time that I have today or I'd've insisted they stop the game and get that pigeon out of the danger zone.

The other guys on my crew laughed about it: "Don't worry, Jerry. He'll be okay." The teams ran a few more plays, but I couldn't take my eyes off the pigeon. He was standing right over the center on the line of scrimmage, like he was taking a poll. His feathers were practically touching the football, yet nobody else seemed to notice him. I thought maybe he was sick; I wanted to try to pick him up, but he kept avoiding me.

Pittsburgh ran three running plays and the pigeon stayed right there, dodging cleats as these monsters thundered past. You'd think he'd be smart enough to get away from the action. On fourth down, Pittsburgh lined up to punt. Just before the snap, the pigeon stepped between the Baltimore nose tackle and the Pittsburgh

center, and his fantail covered one end of the football. Neither the center nor the nose tackle paid any attention. When the ball was snapped, I was in my usual position for a punt—about five yards from the kicker. As the ball spiraled back to him, I was mesmerized by this feckucteh pigeon, who was now staring the center right in the face.

The snap was low and it bounced into the kicker's hands. As he punted, two defensive men wiped him out. Normally, that's running into the kicker. But any time a snapped ball hits the ground and bounces into the kicker's hands, it negates the foul. If a defender hits him then, it's no foul. Well, it would've been a great no-call. The problem was that I was watching the pigeon, so I never saw the ball hit the ground. When they buried the kicker, I threw my flag. Everybody in the stadium saw the ball hit the ground—except me. Baltimore's coach, Frank Kush, called me every name under the sun. He really blistered me. The foul gave Pittsburgh an automatic first down, and they went on to score. They eventually won by a touchdown, so Kush was incensed with me.

The next day, the sports page headline in the Pittsburgh paper read: "Steelers Come Home to Roost." The article gave Steeler Coach Chuck Noll's comments after the game. He said something like yes, the pigeon was there again in Baltimore, and they had planned their offensive attack around him. I learned later that Pittsburgh knew about the bird because they'd seen him in the Baltimore game films. They joked about it, but the pigeon *was* a distraction and, in this case, he *did* help them win a game. In fact, that was the most I'd ever been distracted in a football game.

The following week, Art McNally called me and said, "The call you made on the running-into-the-kicker play was a poor call. We looked at all the angles and it was close, but the ball hit the ground. We had to downgrade you on the call." I didn't tell him why I called the foul. What could I say: "I was watching a *pigeon*?" That week I wrote in my notebook: "The Pittsburgh Pigeon taught

me a great lesson about myself. Life and living things are more important than football. But next time you go to Pittsburgh, bring the pigeon a helmet and pads."

## "IT COMES WITH THE TERRITORY"

When the hometown fans don't appreciate a call against their team, they try to pressure the official. You need maturity and self-control to be able to handle it. Even then, it can be so intense it still can unnerve you.

I worked the 1987 Washington-Buffalo game in front of seventy-one thousand people. In the second quarter, Washington quarterback Jay Schroeder faded back to pass, cocked his arm, and was ready to throw when a defender charged in, encircled him in his arms, and started driving him back. That's an in-the-grasp call—the most difficult call a referee has. The rule is: When the quarterback is in the grasp and control of a defender, you blow the whistle before he's thrown to the ground. The problem is that the referee's position is behind the quarterback, where it is almost impossible to see the ball. Normally, if you don't see the ball, you don't blow the whistle. But on this call, when you feel that the quarterback is in the grasp, you *have* to blow the whistle.

Just as Schroeder was in the grasp and I blew my whistle, I saw the ball squirt free. A Buffalo player recovered it and ran fifty yards for a touchdown. Since I'd blown the play dead, it didn't count. Everybody heard the whistle, but the crowd saw a touchdown and got very upset. The half ended shortly thereafter, and I got a tremendous barrage of boos as I left the field. When I came back onto the field for the second half, I got an even more strenuous barrage of boos and chants: "Markbreit! Markbreit! Lousy call! Lousy call!" They did that throughout the half; it was organized booing and

hostility. Every time I stepped out to announce a call, they booed so loud nobody could hear my announcement.

When the game ended and we were walking up the runway, they were still booing me. Later, when I emerged to get to the car, there were hundreds of fans waiting for the players, and they booed and cursed me some more: "You ↑ %$&*#@ bum! You robbed us! Don't show your face around here anymore!" Unnerving threats like that. We got in the car and turned on the radio and we heard some players criticizing my in-the-grasp call. I turned to Nick Skorich, our supervisor, and I said, "Oh, brother. I've been around a long time, but I have never been treated like this before." Nick said flatly, "It comes with the territory."

He was right. It's just that you never relate that kind of hostility to yourself. I know I'm out there doing the best I can and here are seventy-one thousand people who think I'm the worst referee who ever lived. You have to stand out there and take it like a man. The only thing you can do is ignore it and do your job, knowing that after the game it will all die down.

This time, though, the stress followed me onto the airplane home. I dragged into the plane and sat down and there was Terry Bradshaw, who was the color commentator on the game for CBS, and his director, Bob Fishman. They looked at me and simultaneously said, "It was definitely a fumble." When we started discussing it, Bradshaw told me, "I raked you over the coals pretty good for that one." I said, "Don't you understand the in-the-grasp call?" He said, "I don't wanna hear that. I'm tellin' you it was a fumble." I said, "You, above all people, ought to understand the call because *you're* one of the reasons it was instituted." (Late in his career, while in the act of throwing, Bradshaw was lifted up by a defender and slammed to the ground on his shoulder, and he had to leave the field in an ambulance. That play stimulated the development of a call specifically designed to protect the quarterback.) We spent most of the flight debating the in-the-grasp call and its philoso-

phy. By the time we reached Chicago, Bradshaw was sorry he'd blasted me on TV. When we parted, he said, "I guarantee you, next time I see that call, I'll be lookin' at it differently." That's fine, but it won't take the constant pressure off me to get it right.

# WORSE THAN DEATH

The stress of professional football officiating is so pervasive, you don't even recognize it. I remember how I first saw the stress almost written on my face. In 1977, when I was selected to replace Tommy Bell on my crew, I was set for my first preseason game as an NFL referee. The game was Buffalo at Pittsburgh, and since you didn't work with your own crew until the last preseason game, the league assigned me a crew of mostly twenty-year veterans. Fritz Graf was field judge and Stan Javie, the dean of NFL officials in years of service, was back judge. That should have helped me relax, but it didn't.

In that game, my mechanics went South. Even though I had been away from refereeing for only one year, I couldn't summon all the little nuances and the sharpness that had made me a spiffy signaler. That annoyed me, though I didn't really feel it. I just told myself: "In time, it'll all come back." I managed to struggle through the first half without a major crisis and I thought: "Hey, I did okay. That wasn't so bad." As we came off the field at halftime, Stan Javie stopped me and said, "I've got a photographer that's gonna take a picture of us before we go inside. It'll be a photo of your first crew as a referee. You'll want to keep it for posterity."

The photographer took the picture and I finished the game and I felt pretty good about myself. That week, I couldn't wait to see the developed photo. When I finally got it, I was horrified. I looked like death. *Worse* than death. The strain on my face practically crinkled

the paper. I realized: "It's going to be *tough* to be a referee in the NFL."

But that's the challenge that produces greatness. It's how you handle stress that determines, eventually, how good you will be. I think every official in the NFL believes he's the best at his position. Otherwise, he wouldn't be worth his salt. If you don't have absolute confidence in yourself, you'll fall flat on your face. If all fifteen NFL referees were on *To Tell the Truth* and the host said, "Will the best referee in the National Football League please stand up"—we would *all* stand.

But each of us handles his mistakes differently. I want to be the best referee ever, so I believe that every one of my mistakes provides an important lesson. Of course, the first lesson is the fact that, no matter how mature and experienced you are, you *will* make mistakes. The best halfbacks in the game will fumble the ball several times a season; All-Pro defensive backs will drop easy interceptions; the most reliable kickers will miss field goals; the top quarterbacks will almost certainly complete less than 60 percent of their passes. The difference is that unless a player commits a mistake at a critical moment in a critical game, he'll take some flak for a few days and it will probably pass. He can still end up in the Super Bowl. But officials never make minor mistakes. For us, *all* mistakes are huge. Any one can cost us not only a playoff game or the Super Bowl, but also self-esteem, peer-esteem, confidence, and pride. And, in order to live with this job, you accept that people rarely remember the good things you do. They only remember mistakes. And if you're serious about your work, your mistakes will haunt you forever.

Here are some of my old ghosts and some of my lessons in maturity:

## "FORGET WHAT I SAID"

In my first year in the league as referee, I did fairly well until the third preseason game—New England at Philadelphia. The Eagles had a middle linebacker and

captain named Bill Bergy. In the first five plays of the
game, we had three offside and false-start penalties
and, on all three, I walked in the wrong direction. I just
got confused, and the more confused I got, the worse I
looked. After the third time, Bergy walked up to me and
said, "You're the worst referee I've ever seen in the National Football League. How many years have you been
doing this?" I said, "This is my third game." He said,
"That figures." I was hurt and humiliated, but I understood why he felt that way. I said, "I agree with you. I
*am* the worst referee in the league. But I won't be for
long." And I meant it.

I don't know why I was such a shlemiel that day, but
I got over it. On October 30, well into the regular season,
I had the Philadelphia-at-Washington game. About
midway into the second quarter, Bergy walked up to
me and said seriously, "Boy, have you improved. You
look like a real NFL referee. I can't believe you're the
same guy that walked the wrong way three times. Keep
up the good work." I thanked him and went back to
my position.

The next play was a blitz. When Bergy rushed the
quarterback, someone grabbed his shirt and yanked
him to the ground right in front of me. But my eyes were
on the quarterback, so I caught only a peripheral glance
of Bergy going down. I reminded myself: "Don't call
anything you don't actually see." When I didn't throw
my flag, Bergy jumped up off the ground, ran over, and
screamed at me, "*Forget* what I said! You're *still* the
worst referee in the National Football League!"

## WATCH WHAT YOU SAY . . .

Talk about pressure in officiating. You're out there conducting the game and, after a foul, the other officials
have to give you the information and you have to sort
it out in your mind before you announce anything. Then,
while they relax and return to their positions to fill out
their foul cards, you have to turn your microphone on
and pray that what you say will explain what's hap-

pened in as few words as possible; that it won't embarrass anyone; and that you haven't made a shmendrick out of yourself.

A tiny bungle can be the "The Shot Heard 'Round the World." I was the referee for the first football game the Raiders played after they moved from Oakland to Los Angeles. It was opening day and the Raiders called a time-out, so I announced, "First charged time-out: Oakland." The crowd went wild. Immediately I said, "Correction: *Los Angeles*." Only one second elapsed, but it was already too late. The next day, every paper in the United States carried a variation of this little note: "Jerry Markbreit, announcing the first time-out of the game, referred to the Los Angeles Raiders as 'Oakland.'" One little word and it was like I'd *murdered* somebody!

A thoughtless slip of the tongue can also ruin a perfectly good call. One time, Buffalo was playing Tampa Bay, and both were having horrendous seasons. The place was filled—there were seventy thousand people in the stands. Just before the snap, the entire Buffalo line moved—an obvious false start. But *everybody* moved, so rather than give the number of a single player, as I normally did, I stepped out, turned my microphone on, and announced, "False start, offense. The *entire line* jumped." The crowd roared; even the guys on the field were laughing. I thought I was very creative.

The Buffalo coach, Chuck Knox, stomped onto the field and read me the riot act. Boy, was he hot. He thought I was trying to humiliate his team. I should've selected one or two players and given their numbers. The lesson: Never embarrass a team. I never said anything like that again.

## . . . AND WATCH WHEN YOU SAY IT

A good way to compound a mistake is to advertise it. For a referee, the most common way is by accidentally leaving the microphone on. Some referees get excited

when they have to use the microphone. I see it in college a lot. They get a call and they try to sort it out too quickly and they step out and make the call. But they forget to turn the microphone on. So to prevent that from happening to me, I trained myself to turn it on all the time, no matter where I am. I probably flick that imaginary switch five hundred times a day when I'm at home. It drives Bobbie crazy. She'll say, "Jerry, you don't have to turn your microphone on to take out the garbage."

But it's habitual, especially in a ball game. I do it for two reasons. Number one: to make sure my hand always knows where it is because I don't want to look down. It's clumsy; you know, "Where the heck's my microphone?" Number two: to make sure it's off. The microphone is dangerous. You're walking around lethal on that field. It gets knocked off your belt a couple of times a game and, when you put it back on, you think it's off but it's not. Or somebody bumps you and the microphone switches on and a player runs by and says something profane. That's so embarrassing it's unbelievable. If you don't keep flicking that switch, somewhere along the line you'll humiliate yourself.

In 1979, Pittsburgh was playing Cleveland in a critical game. Brian Sipe was the Cleveland quarterback and it was a crucial third-down play on a drive that could've put them ahead. Sipe was over the ball, calling signals, when he jerked his head to the left and drew the defensive line across the neutral zone. My wing officials threw their flags for defensive offside. But my flag went for false start, quarterback—a difficult technical call for a referee which is really called a head bob.

I made the call and marked off a five-yard penalty and they didn't make the first down, so they had to punt. After the punt, we went to a TV commercial. I was standing there and my umpire, Bud Fiffick, came over to me and said, "Jerry, what did you have on that play with Sipe?" I told him, "Head bob." Bud said, "Head bob? I was lookin' right at him and I didn't see anything. Are you sure you had a head bob?" I said, "I had a head bob. I *think*." Immediately I heard the word "think"

resounding around the stadium over the PA system. I
looked over to the sideline and there was one of the
communications guys from the league office gesturing
wildly and yelling, "Your microphone's on! Your microphone's on!"

I looked down and realized my microphone *was* on
and the whole place had just heard me say, "I think."
Unpardonable sin! An official who wasn't positive, calling back a key play like that? I was mortified. Then I
wondered, "Were they in commercial or out of commercial? Did it go over the network? Did the entire *country* hear it?"

Pittsburgh wound up winning by one point on the
last play of the game. I was absolutely beside myself. I
*knew* Brian Sipe had head-bobbed. Why I blurted "I
think," I'll never know. But the head bob is an unfair
trick that a quarterback perpetrates, and it takes an
experienced referee to detect it. It's just a slight jerk of
the head or shoulder, but you *know* it's drawing the
defense across.

Sipe didn't say a word to me about it, yet here I'd
broadcast to everyone in the stadium that I *thought* he'd
head-bobbed. Well, after the game, Art McNally came
into our dressing room, and I was waiting for him to
mention the head bob. But he didn't. *Nobody* did. It
turned out they were still in commercial when I said it.
And it came out over the stadium PA system when there
was so much noise, apparently nobody heard it. I *thought*.

Two days later, a friend sent me an article about the
game in the *Liverpool* (Ohio) *Gazette*. The sports editor
wrote something like: "Even the officials aren't sure about
their calls." Apparently he had been seated right under
a stadium speaker and heard exactly what I said. Until
that moment, he and whoever read his article were
probably the only other people alive who knew about
that call. At the time I prayed that none of the clipping
services in the United States would send it to the league
office. Fortunately, none did.

When the game film came back the following week,
the head bob showed up. It was an excellent call. It
taught me two more great lessons. One: Don't doubt

yourself to anyone but yourself, because what *appears* to be a mistake may *not* be a mistake. And two: Keep shutting the microphone off when you take the garbage out at home.

## A SNAKE ON THE GRASS

A referee suffers the worst tsuris over the "either way" plays—the weird calls that could be interpreted either way. The fallout from a split-second decision can be unbelievable. In these rough seas, maturity is your only lifeboat. A major case in point: the September 10, 1978, Oakland Raiders at San Diego Chargers game—sarcastically dubbed the "Immaculate Deception" game. That's a reference to yours truly. I remember it well because it was my first nationally televised game as an NFL referee and because what started out as an ordinary early-season game ended on one of the most bizarre plays in the history of pro football.

With ten seconds left in the game and San Diego ahead, 20–14, the Raiders had the ball on the Chargers' thirty-three. The crowd was going crazy. Their team was beating the Raiders, and they were savoring every second of it. There was time for only one or two more plays. As I looked up at the clock, I thought: "We've done a great job of officiating this game. I've established myself, they're watching me all over the country, my family's watching, ten seconds left. What could possibly go wrong?"

Raiders quarterback Kenny Stabler—whose nickname was "The Snake"—rolled right, got sandwiched from both sides, and coughed up the ball. From my position behind him, it looked like a fumble. The ball was then batted, muffed, and kicked until it wound up in the end zone, where one of the Raiders fell on it. I looked to the goal line and saw two of my fellow officials signaling "touchdown." I stepped out, faced the broadcast booth, and gave my touchdown signal. Before anyone could absorb what had happened, the Raiders kicked the extra point and won, 21–20.

John Madden ran onto the field waving his arms

and screaming, "Did we *win*? Did we *win*? Don't penalize us!" He was going wild. I said, "Who's going to penalize you? The game's over, Coach." The crowd was shell-shocked; the Chargers had just snatched defeat from the jaws of victory, and they couldn't comprehend it. We had to have security surround us as we left the field. Running off, I noticed that the fans were staying in the stands, like they did after the MSU-Notre Dame game in '66. They were stunned.

When we reached the locker room, I suddenly had that sick feeling that maybe I had done the wrong thing. I felt weak; I looked like a ghost. Tom Kelleher, one of the toughest guys I know, grabbed me and hugged me. He said, "Jerry, that'll go down as one of the strangest plays in football history. It was a *great* call. But they'll never know whether we were right or wrong." He was excited. He always loved a bizarre play. And he could see that I needed some reassurance. He was really saying: "Don't worry about it. The league will back that call."

Everybody and his brother tried to get in to interview us, but security wouldn't let anyone in. We stayed in the locker room for more than a hour. Because the crowd outside had grown unruly, security finally had to escort us from the stadium to our cars. I felt like a spy on the lam. As we hurried to the cars, San Diego fans jeered me ferociously. Kelleher threw his arm around my shoulder and said proudly, "They may not have known who Jerry Markbreit was yesterday, but they sure will tomorrow. Your name will be in every paper in the United States."

After the game, Kenny Stabler announced to the press that he'd intentionally fumbled the ball forward. I didn't believe him. I felt he was hotdogging for the press. Gloating, as in: "I made the smartest play of all time and we won the game because of it." If he *did* fumble the ball intentionally, it wouldn't have been ruled a fumble. It would have been an incompleted forward pass and the touchdown would have been nullified.

That evening I was supposed to meet a business

associate in San Diego and stay overnight, which was not my normal routine. The atmosphere in town was so charged that Norm Schachter suggested I change my name at the hotel where I was registered. I did. I felt so depressed about the controversy, I signed in as "Joe Shmuckmeyer."

The next day, just as Kelleher predicted, I was infamous. My name was used in vain in every newspaper, coast to coast: "Referee Jerry Markbreit made the worst call in the history of the National Football League." In San Diego, they immediately produced fifty thousand T-shirts with a fat, blindfolded, cartoon referee giving a cockeyed touchdown signal. Odder than that was the fact that there were scary repercussions back in Skokie. For a few days, my wife received threatening phone calls and letters—almost all from the Chicagoland area. I began to reflect on the pressures of the job. I was a young man, I had just gotten into the most exciting facet of my athletic life, and my family was getting threats. I thought the risk to them might warrant my quitting.

The next week, the league looked at the film and supported my call. One thing about the NFL league office: They're unbiased in evaluating calls. They're constantly tightening their standards. They don't wink at us under their hats and defend bad calls in public. If the films show that you blew it, they downgrade you, and you take your lumps.

Although the league supported me, I never got over that play. I reviewed the film many times. Sometimes it looked like I was right, but other times it looked like Stabler *might* have intentionally fumbled the ball forward. The play taught me a memorable lesson: Never take your eyes off a "Snake" on the grass.

A small postscript: Almost three months later, on Sunday, November 26, 1978, in Seattle, I had Oakland for the second time. Kenny Stabler couldn't look me in the eye. Twice in the first quarter he went back to pass and got nailed as he was about to throw. Both times I ruled fumble and both times Seattle recovered. Each time, Stabler bounced up complaining bitterly that his arm

had come forward. The first time, I said nothing. The next time, he yelled, "Dammit, that's the second one! My hand came forward again! It was a *pass*, not a fumble!" I approached him, looked him in the eye, and said, "Yeah? Was it *intentional* or *unintentional*?" He looked at me with a half smile, said "Touché," and trotted off the field.

The following year, because of the "Immaculate Deception" play, the league changed its rule on fumbles. Now, any time you have a fourth-down fumble or a fumble in the last two minutes of either half, only the *fumbler* can recover the ball for a gain. If anyone else recovers on the fumbling team, the ball is returned to the spot of the fumble—a ruling that would have nullified the Raiders' winning touchdown. Insiders refer to the fumble rule as the "Markbreit Rule." I like to call it the "Shmuckmeyer Rule."

# 12. THE VIOLENT ENVIRONMENT

**W**hen I was a kid, I saw a newsreel about oddities. One vignette showed a guy who claimed he had the strongest stomach muscles in the world. He stood in front of a cannon, and they shot a cannonball into his stomach. It knocked the living daylights out of him —blew him twenty feet into a wall. I was horrified and impressed; the guy almost got killed.

To me, officiating in the NFL resembles that vignette. Like the guy standing in front of that cannon, I want to be somebody important. In order to be important, I have to be where important things are happening: out on the football field. I want to know that I'm tough enough to work the biggest game there is, in the biggest stadium, in front of the biggest crowd, for the biggest prize in the sport. If I have to get blown into a wall a few times to find that out—fine. Fire away.

## THE PENALTY OF PAIN

The worst part of officiating isn't getting to the game; it isn't the pregame meetings, the film work, and all the

concentrated preparation once you're there; and it isn't the physical strain of running around with thoroughbred athletes for three and a half hours during the game. The worst part is going home after it's over. If you could step into a time capsule and press a button and be back at your front door, it would be the greatest thing that ever happened.

No matter where I am for a game, I almost always get home on Sunday night, usually before midnight. If I'm in Tampa, maybe I can get home by 11:00 P.M. On West Coast trips, the game ends at 4:00 P.M., the flight leaves at midnight, and I won't get home before 4:00 A.M. I fly first class because then I'm not stuffed into a narrow seat, and nobody's elbowing me on either side. In fact, on the red-eye flight, I'm usually alone. I don't have to talk to anyone, the lights are turned out, and they try to make it as comfortable as possible. But it's difficult to sleep. The thought of a four-hour plane ride at midnight, after I've worked a football game and I'm weary and sore and stiff as a board, is aggravating. I figure: "If I sleep on the plane, I'll be so tired when I wake up, I won't be able to function in the airport." So I don't really sleep.

The red-eye always seems like a ten-hour flight. I write up my game report, I review every call on the game sheets, and I add notes to my "Reminders" diary. I even read some rules just to stay awake. When we finally land, I'm absolutely starving. Somehow, I end up napping through the snack. Brother, am I tired. My legs are so stiff, I can barely get out of my seat. When I grab my duffel bag out of the rack, it feels like it weighs a ton. I wonder: "Did somebody put a couple of gallons of water in it after I stuck it up there?"

When I get into the terminal, it's almost 4:00 A.M.; the place is a tomb. I don't think I can take another step. I tell myself: "Maybe I'll just sit in the waiting area and fall asleep and go straight to the office tomorrow from here." I'm always tempted, but I always keep walking. There are no luggage carts, so I have to carry my briefcase and my forty-pound bag, which now feels like forty

tons. I can walk only about a hundred steps at a time before I have to stop and sit on a bench and recuperate. At the first bench, it always hits me: "Where the heck did I park my car?" I've parked at O'Hare a thousand times, but I never remember to jot down the parking spot before I leave. So two days later, at four in the morning, feeling like death warmed over, how am I supposed to remember which elevator to which floor to which spot?

I drag from bench to bench a hundred agonizing steps at a time. My legs don't feel like they belong to me anymore. My whole body is begging to collapse. It's unbelievable; when I leave Chicago every Saturday, I'm middle-aged. When I return the next night, I'm ancient. It's murderous; I don't understand why I put myself through it. The game itself gives me so much pleasure, so much fulfillment, I hate for it to end. I dread the day I won't be doing it anymore. But what comes afterward, and what's in store before I can get myself in bed, is such torture that I have to question my sanity.

With about two hundred yards to go before I reach the end of the concourse, I have to drop the bags and rest on the last bench. A ten-minute walk has taken me *thirty* minutes. I have to pee like a racehorse. I should've gone to the bathroom as soon as I got off the plane, but I didn't have the energy to put my bags down, do my business, and pick the bags up again. And I don't have the stamina to walk back to find a bathroom *now.* So I trudge to the elevators and, somehow, I remember: "The car's on the fifth floor."

I find the car and I think: "Thank God" because I know I couldn't have survived even a five-minute search. I put the duffel bag on the backseat so I don't have to lift it out of the trunk when I get home and maybe wrench my back. At this point, I *have* to pee. It isn't my way, but I'm so weary I could care less if anyone is watching me. Anyway, who's in an airport at four-thirty in the morning? Only shmecks like me.

Boy, what a relief. I get in the car gingerly and check the time: four-thirty. It feels so good to be seated and

relieved of that bag. I could easily fall asleep in the parking garage. But I don't. I drive out to the expressway and head home. The best thing about driving at four-thirty in the morning is I can get to Skokie in twenty minutes instead of the usual forty. But I'm so hungry, I start looking for a hot dog stand along the way. The thing is, who's serving hot dogs at this hour? I figure: "Bobbie will have something good for me to eat when I get home."

I pull into the driveway and I'm so drained, I can't get out. If I could yell to Bobbie and have her come down and help me get out, I would. I could honk the horn, but I don't want to scare her. I consider sleeping in the car because my legs feel like cement blocks. Somehow, I coax myself out of the car, grab the bags, and get to the door. I'm thinking: "I'll bet a thousand dollars the storm door's locked and I'll have to ring the bell and scare Bobbie anyway." I'm right; it's always locked. Now I have to ring the bell forty-seven times before she wakes up. "It's *me*! Yes, Roberta, I *know* it's almost five in the morning. I *know* I'm crazy. Open the *door*, already!" I get inside and I'm absolutely dead. But I'm home; I got another trip out of the way. "Honey, is there anything to eat?"

"Jerry, are you crazy? It's almost dawn. What am I, an all-night chef?"

"Bobbie, I gotta have *something*. What'd you have for dinner? There's nothing in the refrigerator! There isn't even a lousy piece of *bread*!"

"So order Chinese. I'm going back to sleep."

She goes back to the bedroom. I'm so starved, I'm tempted to open a can of cat food. But I'm too tired to eat now anyway. I decide to unpack. It'll take me fifteen minutes, but I have to do it; I have wet clothes in my bag. So I go downstairs to my "Officiating Room," open my bag, and pull out everything I wore: pants, shirt, jockstrap, underwear, T-shirt, sanitary hose, striped socks, hat. I put my equipment away; hang the wet clothes in the laundry room; prepare my shoes for Mike the shoemaker to clean and polish in the morning. The last thing

I always do is put my hat on my owl decoy, where it will dry out. That's a sentimental ritual for me. The owl is the only thing my dad gave me that I've kept forever. I've had it for twenty-five years. My dad got a kick out of seeing my hat on the owl, and I loved needling him in his later years, "Dad, you're starting to *look* like an owl—a *Jewish* owl."

Finally, I get upstairs to the bedroom and dump my throbbing bones into bed. It feels so good to be on my back. I try to fall asleep, but every muscle in my body aches. I get up and take two Tylenol to kill the pain. At about five-fifteen, I fall asleep. At six-thirty, the alarm goes off. My legs are so stiff, it takes me ten minutes to get off the bed. I get into a hot shower and stand there for fifteen minutes until my muscles loosen up. Then I inch downstairs to feed the cats, just to move around a little. Eventually I feel semihuman again.

Boy, I dread Mondays. I drive an hour and fifteen minutes to work and, when I arrive, I can't get out of my car. I feel like I have steel braces on my knees. When I get out, I walk in slow motion. I get to the office and I start to work, but when I have to get out of my chair for the first time, it's like that nightmare you have where you're running in place but not *getting* anywhere. I'm *trying* to get up, but I can't. At about two in the afternoon, I fall asleep at my desk. It's embarrassing, but I can't stay awake. I leave work early and I'm looking forward to watching my fellow officials on the *Monday Night Football* game. It's the only chance I have to see other referees at work. Of course, by the middle of the second quarter, I'm sound asleep.

Every football season, I ask myself: "Why do you put yourself through this torture? Who needs this anymore?" I know the answer: *I* need it. It's an incredible ordeal, but it's also the most exciting, exhilarating thing that I do in my life. The price I pay for the rewards is the agony of the after-game. Because at fifty-two, I'm not young anymore; the pain gets worse every year, not better. But the thrill of the challenge gets better, too. The greater the risk on the field, the more demanding the

work, the greater the challenge to succeed. So even if I *do* come home Sunday nights 105 years old, I still have to call it an offset. The incredible fulfillment offsets the penalty of pain.

# WHISTLE-ITIS

The physical demands on pro football officials are mostly overlooked. It starts with a little-known ailment I call whistle-itis. I stay in condition in the off-season, but there isn't any way to condition for blowing the whistle. I have to blow the whistle more often than other officials. I get through the first game and then, the next morning, I can barely move my jaw. For the next three days, my lips, jawbone, and cheek muscles are so sore, I have a charley horse of the face.

How can you get your lips in shape? You can't blow a whistle in a health club because it would drive people up the walls. You can't blow it outside because it will frighten people or make them think you're in trouble. Or else fifty dogs will show up. I once practiced a few blasts in a park and, ten minutes later, the police arrived. They had a report that a lady was being mugged.

# FRITZ GRAF'S ACHING FEET

Here's another paradox of the job: You have to be an older, mature man to do this work, yet you're expected to keep up with a bunch of young stallions running around on a field. At my position, I've got a twenty-five-year-old quarterback who decides to sprint out to the sideline thirty yards away. I'm a middle-aged man with

the responsibility of sticking with this kid to make sure nobody hits him illegally or hurts him. If Wade Wilson runs forty-five yards upfield, Jerry Markbreit runs forty-five yards, too. If John Elway gains ninety yards scrambling, so does Jerry Markbreit. I'm right on his tochis every step of the way. I know I absolutely have to cover that ground. If I lag behind and somebody hits him, I won't see it. But the *film* will. So if I have to push myself to the limits of my body to cover a play, I do it. Even if I hurt for two weeks because of the strain.

Of course, you'll never hear a TV announcer remark, "Great move by the official. He's some kind of athlete." But I think we *are* athletes. I consider myself an officiating athlete. I don't block and tackle, but I'm straining my body, taking some lumps, giving every ounce of energy I have on every play. I'm right inside the action of the football game, doing a physically strenuous, athletic job.

In almost every game, you either get kicked or shoved or bumped. Occasionally you get knocked on your behind. Or you reach into a pile for the ball and somebody's helmet cracks you on the jaw. Or you break up a fight between two huge bruisers and you get accidentally clipped in the head. I got knocked down in a recent game and I landed right on the tip of my shoulder. That shoulder throbbed every day for the rest of the season. The same thing happened in 1986; somebody hit my arm and it took me almost the whole season to recover. One time, my umpire, Bob Wagner —a big guy—got hit so hard on his arm that he had a four-inch bruise for about a month. That was from a *pad* hitting him.

There's lots of pain, but we get through it on adrenaline. I've seen officials twist ankles early in a ball game and go to the sideline and have a trainer wrap it and then come back for the next play. An hour after the game, they're on crutches. The entire next week, they can't walk. But by the next game, they're ready to go again. It's interesting: When was the last time you saw an NFL official leave a game voluntarily because of an

injury? In all my years as crew chief, I've never lost an official during a game. And knock on wood, in twelve years I've never missed a football game myself. I've worked with 102-degree fevers, sprained ankles, pulled muscles, stiff necks—you name it. Players are out regularly for all kinds of injuries. They can rest on the bench and recuperate, or the coach can send in a replacement. But for officials, there *are* no replacements during regular season games.

The first things to go on athletes are their legs, and it's the same for officials. I've been running on football fields for thirty-two years; my legs aren't in great condition. I've had arthroscopic surgery, just like players, but I'm afraid to tamper with weights. All I do is jog in the off-season because I just want to be able to stay on my feet for three and a half hours. How many jobs require that? How many people stand up that long every day to do *anything*? Everybody sits down, including football players.

A recent study showed that professional football players actually play only ten to fifteen minutes out of every game. The rest is dead time between plays, some of which the players spend sitting on the bench. Officials don't have a bench. We're out there the whole time. We go out to the field about ten minutes before gametime. From that moment until the game ends, we're on our feet for all but maybe five minutes at halftime. We're not only standing, we're also running and dodging and jogging. And we have these 285-pound monsters stepping on our feet all day—it's like a bulls' parade out there. After some games, my feet ache so much that I fantasize about finding a "foot exchange" and making a trade-in: "New pair of twenty-five-year-olds, please."

Which brings to mind something that Fritz Graf told me just after he retired. He'd been an NFL field judge for over twenty years, including four Super Bowls (he's now an NFL replay man); the pain in his feet made him miserable. I bumped into him at a meeting and I said, "Fritz, how does it feel to be retired?" The first thing he

said was, "My *feet* don't hurt anymore. Until I retired, I thought *everybody* had sore feet."

If you watched a carful of middle-aged officials pull up at the airport after a short drive from the stadium and you saw us get out and drag through the terminal, you'd think we were seven lame old men escaping from a nursing home. For three and a half hours we worked our fannies off, and it shows. We're so pooped and sore, we can barely crawl to the plane. Officials don't complain to each other about their aches and pains. Nobody really wants to hear about anyone else's tsuris. But we've all got it. You walk into the Chicago Bears' locker room and the average age might be twenty-seven—they don't really have these problems yet. Add twenty-five years to them and they'll have every ailment we have: arthritis, bursitis—and Fritz Graf's aching feet.

# RISKY BUSINESS

Along with regular doses of pain, there's the occasional unexpected physical risk in refereeing. For example, a couple of years ago, before a Green Bay-Minnesota game in Green Bay, the security chief came in and said, "Jerry, we just got a call that there's a shooter in the stands. He's threatening to shoot (Packers quarterback) Lynn Dickey." I said, "What're you telling me this for? Go find the guy." He said, "Well, you're the referee and we know you stand near the quarterback." I said, "*And?*" He said, "Well, we thought maybe you'd change your position today." I said, "You go find the guy with the gun. I can't change what I do."

When I walked out on the field, Lynn Dickey was standing there in a thick flak-jacket. He said, "Hi, Jerry, how are ya?" I decided to needle him. I said, "Fine, Lynn. You hurt your ribs?" He laughed and said, "No.

Where's *your* jacket?" I said, "All we can wear is this striped shirt, Lynn." He said, "Well, what're you gonna do if they start shooting?" I said, "I'll be where I always am. *Right behind you.*"

In a recent Rams-Browns game in Cleveland, I had to contend with those fanatic Cleveland fans in the end-zone seats who call themselves "The Dawgs." Whenever the Browns did well, "The Dawgs" hollered and barked. They did one other thing that was potentially danger-ous: They threw milk bones onto the field. Every time the Rams got close to Cleveland's goal line, the bones rained down like a hailstorm. They landed everywhere—a few times they hit the players *and* the officials. Security tried to prevent it, but there were too many "Dawgs."

During the game, I had this fantasy: The Rams' quar-terback drops back to pass and throws to a receiver wide open in the end zone. But as the ball spirals toward the receiver, a bone flies from the stands and deflects it out of his grasp. I blow the whistle and announce to the crowd, "We have 'Dawg' bone interference. The ball will be refetched and the down replayed." But the league says later, "Sorry, Markbreit. After reviewing the film, we don't think the bone changed the flight of the football. We're downgrading you on the call."

I decided to put a stop to the bone-throwing before my fantasy came true. I asked the Browns' head coach, Marty Schottenheimer, to have an announcement made at halftime asking people to stop throwing bones. They made the announcement and the bone barrage stopped. A couple of nights later, there was a news item on CNN sports: The Cleveland management publicly requested their fans to refrain permanently from throw-ing bones onto the field. I was gratified. I helped get management to address a potentially dangerous situ-ation, and I avoided what could have been a bizarre downgrade.

For all my trouble, a few days later I received a package from Cleveland. It contained a large, grubby "Dawg" bone and a note to me that read: "Even a dog has to eat."

# A MILLION VOLTS

Some years ago, a free-lance sportswriter requested that he be allowed to work part of an NFL preseason game so he would know what it felt like to officiate. He thought it would be fun: blow the whistle a few times, retrieve the ball, throw a flag; a breeze. The league told him that if he got in shape, they'd let him do it. So he lost weight, got in condition, and studied the rules, and he worked a whole half. He was absolutely petrified. The players were huge; the plays went off so fast; the bodies were flying all around him. I saw him after the game and he was trembling. He said, "That's not the game I see on TV. That's a *war*! I was scared I was gonna be *killed*!"

Most men wouldn't have the guts to walk out on a football field for one play because it's a violent environment. I *love* being out there. Once that ball is snapped, it's like a million volts of electricity. I start looking around: "Okay, what's the tackle doing? Check the quarterback. Is the guard holding? Here comes a blitz." It's five or six seconds of hyperactivity, then thirty seconds of rest, then it happens all over again. In an average game, there might be 140 offensive plays, so on 140 occasions I'm supercharged out there.

I'm never afraid of anything that might happen to me, physically. The only thing I fear is that I might make a mistake and hurt a team's chances of winning. But it's not a "frightened" kind of fear; it's that exciting fear of the unknown, that stimulating fear of taking the risk so I can find out: "Will I be good enough today?"

I love that rough, tough, violent environment because I can control it. It's not a vicarious thing—I don't have the desire to be hitting somebody. It just gives me great satisfaction to know that I am capable of standing inside this very violent world, in the middle of all this swirling activity, feeling safe and secure. I'm out there with the biggest, toughest guys in the country, and even though I do get bumped and bruised from time to time,

I feel comfortable. It's like dropping into a den of lions sensing that you won't get eaten. Or walking into a beehive believing you won't get stung.

I love it and I hate it; I relish it and I'm afraid of it at the same time. On every play, there's a risk. Yet the thrill of the unknown and of finding out how I will handle it is so much fun. It's like being whisked away to another planet for three and a half hours. It's total removal from everything in my outside life. I always feel like I've got a plastic shield around me. All that violence comes very close, but most of it bounces off me. I'm small, but I'm not afraid to be hit or kicked or trampled by nine thousand pounds of humanity. I just feel like I'm floating out there, like I know instinctively where to be next. Nothing in my outside life makes me feel that way.

# I HAVE THE POWER

I'm often asked, "How do you handle yourself out there with all those behemoths?" I always say, "I have the power." The football field is a controlled environment where it's acceptable for people with defined authority to be tough and firm. And I like that feeling. For three and a half hours I know I'm running a big-time activity. Television comes to *me* and says, "Jerry, we need this many commercials today." Off the field, I'm just a little guy from Skokie. But during the Giants-Broncos Super Bowl, I was the guy inserting *$32 million* worth of TV commercials. I like it when a producer making $400,000 a year says to me, "Jerry, please take care of this." I tell myself: "This guy's making more in one year than I make in ten years of officiating, but he knows I've got the power today." How many professions allow you to be as tough and powerful as I can be on the football field without someone eventually saying, "Let's get *rid* of this guy. Let's punch him in the nose"?

The rules provide most of our power, but some of it comes from within. For instance, our "zebra" shirts. One year, during my off-week, I visited Northwestern University to watch a football game. Before the game, I went out to shmooz with the fellas I knew on the Big Ten crew of officials. Of course, they were wearing their officiating shirts with the one-and-a-quarter-inch stripes. I started talking about the power concept. I said, "Gentlemen, I'm convinced that the power of the stripe makes a great difference in the amount of authority you wield on the football field. That's probably why the NFL's founding fathers saw fit to make their stripes two inches. They knew that the two-inch stripe was a power stripe. To my knowledge, it's the widest one in sport. The narrower stripe looks more like a jail stripe. It doesn't convey the same power."

The fact is, when I put on that wide-striped shirt and those white pants, I *feel* the power, I feel like Superman. I'm only five-ten and I'm not exceptionally strong, but when I wear that shirt I feel like Clark Kent stepping out of a phone booth in his magnificent outfit. The zebra-striped shirt with the two-inch stripe is my Superman outfit. When I'm out on the field with those enormous hulks all around me, they never have that enormous, hulking effect on me. They don't *seem* big to me. I always feel as big as they are.

There was a *Sports Illustrated* picture from a Broncos-Raiders game a couple of years ago showing Rulon Jones asking me a question. My head barely came up to the middle of the number on his chest. When I first saw the photo, I couldn't believe my eyes. I remembered the situation and, at the time, I was absolutely certain I stood eye-to-eye with him. I've *always* felt that way on the field. Yet here was this picture and I looked like a midget standing in a hole! *Something* made me feel big and strong out there.

In fact, when I'm on the football field, I think I'm the biggest, toughest guy I know. When I refereed the 1987 Houston-Denver playoff game, I tried to prevent a fight among three big players, and an AP photo of that scene

ran in over three hundred newspapers nationwide. There I was, wedged among these three shtarkers, and I looked like a pisherkeh crossing guard! Yet, in my own mind, I was looking at these guys eye-to-eye, letting them know who was boss. The picture shows the *reality:* I'm actually bending my head to avoid getting clobbered. I'm either looking at the ground or at their navels. But when I was doing it, the reality in my mind was: "Okay, gentlemen, the *big* guy is here now."

That sense of power gets in your blood; you can't give it up. That's why guys stay in the game for years after they retire. They become supervisors or observers or replay men. These are men in their sixties and seventies—they can't get it out of their system. I understand that. When I'm on that field, I feel as powerful as any great athlete, and just as important. That will be very hard to give up.

# MY BODYGUARD

Power is important on the football field, but in order to really control these players, you must also gain their respect. The interesting thing is, if you *feel* tough out there, eventually you're perceived as tough—and that can earn you respect. Here's my best example—something I regard as almost a football parable:

Four years ago, during a Raiders game, I had a strange confrontation with one of the toughest guys you've ever seen on a football field: Howie Long. He kept complaining, "I'm being held! This guy's holding me!" I watched him for several plays and he complained again, "I don't believe you, ref. They're holding me all over the place!" I said, "Howie, nobody's holding you." His face bulged with anger. He said, "Are you calling me a *liar*?" I said, "I'm telling you nobody's holding you." He said, "Man, I'd like to punch you in

the mouth!" I said, "Are you serious?" He said, "Damn right I'm serious."

Suddenly I got hot. I said, "Okay, big shot. Go ahead. Take a crack at me right here. We'll see how tough you are." He was shocked. So was I. He said, "I'm not gonna *touch* you here. I'll get kicked out of football for the rest of my life. I'll meet you outside the stadium after the game." I said, "Howie, I wouldn't meet you outside this stadium for a million bucks. Take your shot now or forget about it." Most of the Raiders heard this, and they were amazed. They looked at me like: "Markbreit's a dead man."

Long didn't say another word to me the rest of the game. About four months after the season ended, there was a big story in *Sports Illustrated* about Matt Millen, the Raiders' middle linebacker. At the close, Millen discussed NFL referees. He said he liked Gene Barth, Ben Dreith, and Jim Tunney. Then he described my confrontation with Long and concluded, "Jerry Markbreit is the wackiest"—obviously because I was crazy enough to actually pick a fight with Howie Long. I thought: "Does Millen respect me for my courage, or does he really think I'm out of my mind?" I wondered what Howie Long thought, too.

Long let me know in every Raiders game I worked for the next three years by arguing with me over everything. He made things miserable for me. Then things changed suddenly in a 1987 Green Bay-Oakland preseason game. We were well into the fourth quarter when Long complained to me about being held. I approached him and said, "Howie, you and I have been arguing for three years. This year, we're not going to be adversaries. There'll be no more arguments. No matter what you say to me, I'm going to be a perfect gentleman."

He just scowled. I said casually, "By the way, are you still doing your HBO show (*Inside the NFL*)?" He said, "No, I dropped it this year. It was so time-consuming, I decided not to do it." Suddenly we were having a normal conversation. I said, "That's too bad. I thought you

did a terrific job with it. You were excellent." He lit up;
he was obviously pleased. He said, "Thank you very
much"—and I was surprised by his sincerity. It was the
first pleasant thing he'd said to me in three years. Then
I gave the ready-for-play signal and the game re-
sumed.

During the rest of the game he complained a little
bit, but nothing excessive. I didn't say another word to
him. After the game, the crew and I rushed to the Green
Bay airport, which is very small. We had about twenty
minutes before our flight left, so we started walking through
the bar to get to the restaurant for some sandwiches.
As we marched through, there were all the Oakland
Raiders.

I passed Tom Flores and he said something to me,
so I stopped to kibitz with him. Then I noticed Howie
Long seated right next to Flores with his back to us.
Without turning his head, Long said, "Is that you, Markbreit? We're going out in the hall and settle this three-
year argument right now. You picked a fight with me
for the last time." I said, "I'm not going out in the hall
with you, Howie. You had your shot on the field and you
blew it. You don't get a second chance."

He turned to Flores and said, "That Markbreit's gotta
be the toughest referee in the National Football League.
He tried to pick a fight with me right on the field. And
the guy has to be at least forty years old." I said good-
bye to Flores, patted Long on the back, and headed
toward the restaurant, feeling flattered that he thought I
was only forty. I felt good also because I knew we'd just
buried the hatchet. He was trying to tell me that he
respected me. I knew that nobody bullied Howie Long
on the football field, and he found out that nobody bullied *me* around either. In this case, respect was the
equalizer, and *that* conferred the power.

There's a "moral" to the story. Raiders at Seattle,
*Monday Night Football* game, 1987. During the first
quarter, I stepped in to break up a fight and somebody
knocked my hat off. As I stepped back out of the melee,
I tripped over someone's foot and went down. I was

sitting on my fanny when somebody lifted me up from behind and gently placed my hat back on my head. Of course, this mystery savior was big number seventy-five—Howie Long. He looked at me and said, "Little guys like you should stay out of fights. I don't want to see you get hurt." Then he walked away. I thought: "Boy, have *we* come full circle. For years he wanted to murder me. Now he wants to be my bodyguard!"

## CHAOS IS OUR CUP OF TEA

More than the supercharge, or being under the imaginary plastic "shield," or even the sense of power, I love controlling the chaos on a football field.

Occasionally, at one of our officials' clinics, I feel like I'm back in college. And it feels good. In college you knew the rules: You had to go to class; you had to be there on time; you had to do your assignments to get a decent grade. I sometimes miss that in everyday life. I tend to think that since my job as trade and barter manager for the 3M Company is so freewheeling, I'm unregimented in my outside life. Then I get back to my football environment and everything makes sense again. I like that feeling. All officials do. Because we all crave order.

It's another irony of this job that men who crave order will deliberately place themselves in the middle of a small field where a bunch of Goliath shtarkers in helmets and pads are wreaking mayhem on each other in front of eighty thousand screaming fans. What could be more chaotic than that? Yet chaos is our cup of tea. It's the beauty of what we do. Without us it *would* be chaos. But because we're there to control it and to see that the game is played fairly, there's a great semblance of order to it. That's the mystique from my intramural days; a referee has the power to restore order from chaos.

This need exists in my daily life. If I want our cats to be back in the house, I can't concentrate until they're inside and I know they're safe. The instant Bobbie comes home, I expect her to get them in (they refuse to come in for me; I obviously have *no* special power at home). If she doesn't do it immediately, it aggravates me. I require total order in everything I do. I clean the dishes the second we're finished eating. I go into my office in the morning, and the phone calls and papers are piled to the ceiling. But throughout the day, I push and shovel all those papers around and, as the day runs down, they get organized. By the end of the day, every call has been made; every paper filed; every note written; every memo answered. When I leave there, everything has been completed.

That's exactly how I feel after almost every football game. When the game ends and I walk away from it, I know it's completed. All the fouls have been called; everything's been walked off properly; except for the occasional tie, somebody has won and somebody has lost. Everything has been done, from an official's standpoint, to put that game in its proper order so the team that played better won the game.

Having a profession that could be chaotic but that ends in perfect order when the the final whistle blows gives me a feeling of fulfillment that I get nowhere else in my life. It's a wonderful completeness that's over. Unfortunately, nothing else in my life is ever over. My job at 3M is never completed; my relationship with my wife is never done; my relationships with my daughters never end; my social responsibilities never end; nothing ends until you die. But a football game is over when it's over. After that final gun goes off, no matter how hard you try, there's nothing you can do about it. You just walk off the field thinking: "It's over, that's it. I can't wait till the next game."

And game after game, the whole experience repeats itself inside the same small green rectangle. It's a whole universe in there. When I leave society and I step into that 120-yard rectangle, I've just stepped into

a battleground. And I know every inch of it. I know where I can go, what the players can do, what I can do—everything about those 120 yards there is to know. It's the most well-defined, comfortable, natural place I can be in my life. It's home. Boy, if I could only feel that comforting security in my real life—that sense of "All is right in my universe as I wait for the next play to start"—I would be at perfect peace.

# 13. WHAT YOU DO AND HOW YOU DO IT

**I**t's guest night at the 1987 Central Officials' Association meeting when former members who made the NFL return to address the group. I'm about to be introduced and I'm looking out at the audience where I see all these eager faces, and I think: "My God, look how *young* these guys are. Thirty years ago, that was *me*. They don't know yet how good they're going to be."

Suddenly I'm standing at the podium and I say what I feel: "You're looking at me and you're thinking, '*That's* Jerry Markbreit? That's the famous official we hear so much about? He's just a little, shlumpy shlemiel! He doesn't look so tough. That's the guy who worked two Super Bowls?' Damn right it is. You don't have to be six-foot-five and two hundred eighty pounds to be a successful official. It isn't what you look like, guys. *It's what you do and how you do it.* And when you get the opportunity to step out and display your wares, that's when you show them what you've got. But if you're not prepared when the opportunity comes, nobody will ever know."

# CAL

Officiating demands endless physical and mental preparation. That's why, even though it's part-time, it isn't a
hobby. It's a vocation. I'm trade and barter manager
for the 3M Company and a National Football League
referee. That's all there is: a job, my officiating, my
family. I have no hobbies. I sacrifice many things: golf
and tennis with my friends; fall and winter weekends;
and vacations with my wife. Everything I do is geared
toward the current football season or the next football
season because I know how difficult it is to compete
every week with the best officials in the world. I know
I must study football 365 days a year. In fact, the older
I get, the more I have to do.

To be at the top of this profession, you not only have
to put in the minimum time for studying, meetings, and
games, you also have to put in that extra time. Extra
phone calls, extra reading sessions, extra emotional
preparation instead of playing golf in the spring. It's
that extra mile that provides the greatest rewards. The
men who put the most into it, whether through special
routines, or rituals, or even superstitious habits are usually the ones who get the most out of it.

My preparation includes all of the above, plus something extra. For instance: Cal LePore. Every season, Cal
and I talk on the phone several times a week. We discuss
the rules: which memo brought them to the fore; the
philosophy behind them; unusual plays; officiating
techniques. Whenever Cal takes the weekly rules exam,
he gets 99 percent of the answers right. And he's been
*out* of officiating since 1980 (he's now an NFL replay
man). He's been off the football field for eight years, yet
he knows as much about the rules as any official cur-
rently working in the NFL.

Cal is a stickler on terminology. We've spent hours
discussing the proper ways to announce fouls. He catches
everything. The NFL has a "five-and-fifteen" rule. If you

have a five-yard penalty on one team and a fifteen-yard penalty on the other, and there's no possession change, you disregard the five and penalize the fifteen. For years, teams were declining that penalty, even though there's no option. Technically it's called a disregard. Yet, as far as I know, I'm the only referee in the league who announces, "The penalty is *disregarded*." Nobody comments about it, nobody knows the difference—except Cal LePore. The next day, he'll call and say, "You had a disregard. *Excellent* call." Because, to him, it's important that it's done right. He always reminds me, "It doesn't matter if anyone else knows you did it right, as long as *you* know. Be as professional as you can."

He watches me like a hawk. One time, I switched the microphone on and, instead of saying, "There are two fouls. Holding, number sixty-four, and offside, number seventy-six," I said, "*We* have two fouls ..." Next morning, my phone rang off the hook. It was Cal. "What's this '*We*'?" he said. "*Nobody* says that." He was right. But I like to say "We" because it's more distinctive. Cal got all over me for that, so I told him I'd try to stop.

But I can't. After a recent game, Cal was very upset with me because twice I announced, "*We* have ..." on fouls. He said, "What's this '*We*' stuff I heard again? I thought *we* weren't gonna do that anymore." I needled him, "To be honest with you, Cal, the only reason I do it is because I know you're going to call me and aggravate yourself." He insisted, "There just isn't any rhyme or reason for using 'We.'" I said, "There probably *wouldn't* be if you wouldn't make such a big tsimmes out of it." He said, "What's this 'tsimmes' stuff? You're not gonna start saying *that*, are you?" I said, "Yes, Cal. Just for your benefit, I'm going to step out and say, '*We* have a personal foul on number sixty-two. *He* made a tsimmes out of nothing!'"

Raiders at Seattle, *Monday Night Football*, November 30, 1987. The same game as the Howie Long-picks-me-up-off-the-ground incident. Third quarter, the Raiders have just scored. Chris Barr kicks the ball sixty

yards to the Seattle five. The returner runs it thirty-three yards down the right side. But as he passes the last defender, Barr sticks his leg out and trips him. Bob Beeks, our line judge, throws a flag. It's a great tripping call, and I have a special way of reporting a trip. I step out, turn on my microphone, and give the illegal-use-of-the-hands signal. But I report, "Illegal use of the *body*. It's a tripping foul." With my right foot, I tap the back of my left ankle—the tripping signal. Then I say, "Number ten, offense," and I turn the microphone off.      .

Apparently, up in the broadcast booth, Al Michaels is caught by surprise. He says something like, "What is 'illegal use of the *body*'? I never heard that one before. Only Jerry Markbreit could come up with something like that." They laugh and make a big deal out of it. They think I just made it up. But the joke is on them; I've been using that for years. It's a Cal LePore-ism.

Technically, the signal is "illegal use of the hands, arms, or body." Cal feels that the tripping signal is so inconspicious that, unless someone is riveted on your foot, they'll never see you give the signal. But if you announce "illegal use of the body" first, it makes people aware that an important signal is coming and they're more likely to pick it up. So I've always done that.

Of course, when I got home from that Raiders-Seattle game, Cal called me and said, "*Excellent* signal. It's about time somebody recognized a unique signal." All signals are given with the hands—or are at least *preceded* with a hand signal—except the tripping signal. And tripping is not a personal foul, so all you do is tap the back of your leg with your other foot. I think that my way is more dramatic. To my knowledge, nobody else uses it. I owe it to Cal; without him, I never would've used that signal in the first place.

Cal's dedication to correctness and has helped me improve the thoroughness of my general preparation. I know his eye is always on me, so it's like having a second conscience to keep me sharp. Every time I leave for a game, the minute I get in my seat on the plane, I take out my booklet of personal reminders and spend

forty-five minutes going through it. I know it by heart;
it's like reciting "The Star-Spangled Banner." But I wouldn't
feel prepared unless I studied it. Then I review the rules.
Then all the signals. As well as I know them, I'm never
sure I'll know the one odd foul that might come up in
the next game, the one I haven't given the signal for in
umpteen years.

Two years ago I flagged a foul, stepped out, and
turned the microphone on: "Personal foul, number sixty-
four. Illegal crackback." I hadn't given an illegal crackback signal in five years. I thought: "What the heck is
it—front of the leg or side of the leg?" I looked around
for help—forget it, no help. I gave a signal, got in the
locker room at halftime, opened the book: son of a gun,
wrong signal. It aggravated me like crazy, but apparently nobody else had noticed. The next morning, I got
a call from Cal: "Don't you know the signal for illegal
crackback?" I said, "Cal, nobody caught that." He said,
"*I* caught it. You gave the illegal-block-below-the-waist
signal!"

Cal and I are both sticklers on knowing what to say
*before* the foul happens. So he taught me how to prepare while jogging. He said, "When you're out doing
your five miles every day, make up every kind of crazy
call in the book. Then turn your microphone on and
report it to TV and see how it sounds." The idea is to
practice the correct way to announce a foul that will
probably never happen so that, in case it *does* happen,
you don't fumble around trying to put it in the right
hopper. So every time I jog in the off-season, I invent a
strange play to announce.

In March 1986, while jogging through the park, I
dreamed up this one: "I have an eligible receiver who
goes out of bounds on a pass play. He's either bumped
out or he accidentally steps on the sideline. That makes
him ineligible to catch a pass unless it's touched first by
an eligible receiver. While the ball is still in the air, he
comes back in bounds, catches it, runs, and gets tackled."
Then I said to myself: "Okay, explain that one." I reached
down to my hip with my left hand and switched my

imaginary microphone on, and I kept making the call until it sounded right. Later I wrote the call down. And I kept reviewing it, along with my other notes, before every game of the '86 season. Then, amazingly, the play happened in the 1987 Giants-Broncos Super Bowl—which I refereed.

It was a wonderful moment. Without thinking, I stepped out, flicked on the mike, and announced, "We have an originally eligible pass receiver who went out of bounds and then returned to catch the pass. A flag was thrown for illegal touching of a forward pass. However, the ball was touched by an eligible receiver before the catch, making the play legal. There is no foul." Everybody in the stadium could understand what I said, and so could everybody watching on TV. I heard later that John Madden, who broadcasted the game on national TV, said something like, "That was an incredibly clear explanation of a complicated call. How did Markbreit figure that play out so fast?"

It was simple, John. I *invented* it.

## "WE ALWAYS KNOW IT'S YOU"

Everyplace I go—on planes, in restaurants, at airports, on the street—people recognize me. I can't go on a trip without strangers coming up to me and saying, "You're Jerry Markbreit." I was on a plane flying South for a speech without my NFL bag and dressed casually in jeans and a Zylon jacket. I thought: "Isn't this nice. Nobody can possibly recognize me." Just as I hung my suitbag up, the steward said, "Jerry Markbreit, NFL referee."

In the hotel after my speech, I was walking to the elevator and I passed the head of hotel security, a man in his sixties with a walkie-talkie. I nodded, pressed the elevator button, and glanced back at him. He smiled

and said, "You know, you're famous. I watch all your games on television." That afternoon, as I boarded my plane back to Chicago, the stewardess said, "Hi, ref." Later, as I sat reading quietly, a ten-year-old youngster turned around in his seat and said, "I know you. You're the football guy."

I'm surprised when *players* know me. Somebody says something to me in almost every game. A rookie kickoff-return specialist will position himself on the goal line, turn to me, and say, "You're Jerry Markbreit. I used to watch you on TV." I mean, these kids are twenty-two, twenty-three years old. I've been officiating in the NFL for twelve seasons; they probably saw me when they were ten!

What *really* surprises me is when somebody well known recognizes me. I was hurrying for a plane in Atlanta's Hartsfield International Airport when I spotted one of the most famous baseball players of all time: Ted Williams. As I ran by, his gaze caught mine and I acknowledged him by swinging an imaginary bat. He, in turn, gave me the holding signal, and I continued on my way. What a tremendous thrill to be recognized by Ted Williams—even if it was only by a signal on the run.

I'm often amazed when someone recognizes me because, at home, I'm a very quiet, ordinary, unassuming guy who shleps around the neighborhood minding his own business. Yet *something* makes me different. I think it's my refereeing style. Though *what* you do is the true test of your success, *how* you do it is important, too. While all officials do everything basically the same, I try to be distinctive on the field. I try to do things differently; I like to be creative. I have my own style of signaling and talking on the microphone and carrying myself on the field. I never draw attention to myself; I just try to present myself uniquely when the attention is already on me. When I was in the Big Ten, Howard Wirtz drummed a sense of style into me: "Don't be wishy-washy. Be decisive, be accurate, be orderly, be *memorable*." I think I'm now identified by those traits, be-

cause whatever it is that I do out there, people seem to remember it. All through my career, the one recurrent comment has been, "When you're out there, we always know it's you."

I've watched the other referees work and I don't perceive that I'm any different from them. On the rare occasion when I watch myself on tape, I don't like what I see. I think I look pudgy; I don't like the expressions on my face; my voice sounds wrong. To my eye, even my signals look cockeyed. For example, I don't give a straight touchdown signal. When I bring my arms up, no matter what I do, one arm is always off-center. When Tom Kelleher was on my crew, he used to say, "Mark-breit, can't you give a straight signal? Your left arm is crooked again. Next touchdown, lean to the *right*!" So the next time, I'd lean to the right and he'd say, "Next time, lean to the *left*!"

On the other hand, I *am* pleased with my microphone work. When I step out, turn my microphone on, and make a call, I know it'll be precise and understandable because I've spent years working on that kind of delivery. The secret to microphone work is to be brief, simple, and clear so that the stadium fans, the TV viewers, and the sportscasters can understand what you've said. I make an effort not to slur or swallow my words, or to use words that are difficult to pronounce. My tone is very stern and self-assured, denoting confidence that I know what I'm doing. My facial expression says just one thing: "This is serious business."

When I announce a call, I'm like a policeman letting you know that you're caught. I really let you have it: *"HOLDING! NUMBER EIGHTY-EIGHT! OFFENSE!"*—and I pause a second to let it sink in. It's like I'm saying, *"YOU WERE DRIVING TOO FAST! YOU'RE FINED! PAY HERE!"* I say it powerfully; I give it a little pizzazz, a little shmaltz. I don't want people who watch me on TV to say, "What did he say? Did you understand what he said?"

People respond to strength and authority. I am always decisive. And it's genuine; it's me. You can't contrive a personality just for the game. Under that kind of

stress and in that kind of action, your real self emerges automatically. Of course, every once in a while a "creative" announcement is liable to pop out.

Tommy Bell was firm, authoritative, and decisive on the field. That's why he was one of the most respected referees in the NFL. He was also a humorist, and his humor sometimes came out unexpectedly in his calls. When the microphone was first used in the early seventies, Bell added something special to the announcing of fouls. He had that shtikeleh with the microphone that no one else could get away with. He said things so naturally and inoffensively, the league just let him alone. One time, he announced in his heavy Southern accent, "Illegal use of the hands. Number sixty-seven, offense. He was tryin' to wring his neck!" He turned the microphone off, and the crowd was in stitches. Nobody ever said those things before. It was always very straightforward. Another time, he announced, "Personal foul. Roughing the passer. Number forty-four, defense. Boy, he cracked 'em on the head so *hard*!" Bellisms.

Ben Dreith is a veteran referee—twenty-eight years in the league, and a rough, tough individualist who teaches gym in Denver. His schoolkids are always giving him the business—that's his favorite expression: "Quit giving me the business. I don't care why you weren't in class, I'm marking you tardy." When you're with Ben at meetings, he's always talking about somebody giving him the business.

So here he is working a Jets game when Marty Lyons comes through on a quarterback sack for the Jets. But instead of just tackling the quarterback, Lyons also gives him a couple of extra shots. Ben flags him for roughing, steps out to make the announcement, and, on the spur of the moment, says, "Personal foul, roughing the passer. He had him down . . . *and he was giving him the business.*" A classic Dreithism. The league didn't criticize him because it was accurate. Lyons *was* giving him the business.

I remember when the press interviewed me after the Charles Martin/Jim McMahon incident. They asked

me what Martin did and I said, "He stuffed the quarterback into the ground." Afterward, I thought that wasn't as refined a term as I would've wanted me to use, but Martin *did* stuff McMahon, so that's how I described it. As far as I know, nobody had ever used that description before. In 1987, the league came out with a memo on quarterback roughing calls. In a section about continuing action after quarterback contact, one new prohibition was "stuffing the quarterback." Finally: a *Markbreitism!*

# WHISTLE WHILE YOU WORK

Whistles are a special part of everything you are and do on a football field. Having control of your whistle is a real art. There are three main ways to control it. Some officials have finger whistles mounted on an attachment that fits over two fingers. But to blow that whistle, they have to take the time to bring it up to their mouth. It's the safest way of doing it because you can almost never blow an inadvertent whistle. Then there's the official who carries the whistle in his hand. He, too, has to take the time to bring it up to his lips. Finally, you have the whistle-blower who carries the whistle in his mouth at all times.

I've always carried it in my mouth. I don't want to go looking for it when I need it. And I need my hands for signals. In fact, I buy rubber whistle covers by the gross because I chew through one cover in every ball game. I don't feel comfortable unless that whistle's in my mouth. Even when it's not in my mouth, it sits upside down on my lanyard so that when I have to yank it up, it's in the "blowing position" the instant it reaches my lips. I'm like a quarterback who wants the laces of the football facing *up* on the snap, so he can grip and throw in one quick motion, without fiddling with the ball.

Whistle-blowing habits are so engraved in your officiating persona that they're almost impossible to break. When the whistle is blown and you have to talk, you don't just let it drop out, you blow it out—"Poom!" Then the lanyard snaps it back to your chest. I remember working a college game when my lanyard broke. It was early in the second quarter and I didn't have an extra lanyard, and I couldn't just go to the sideline to try to find one. So I held the whistle in my hand until the next play started, put it in my mouth as the ball was snapped, and blew it to end the play. Forgetting I had no lanyard around my neck, I then blew the whistle out of my mouth and spent the next three minutes searching for it in the deep grass. For five consecutive plays, I whistled the play dead and then blew the whistle out of my mouth into the grass. Finally, I realized that there was absolutely no way I could learn another whistle technique.

Referees search far and wide for good whistles. I've always used the same ones I bought from Stu Popp— Acme Thunderers. They're English metal whistles with that shrill, powerful, booming sound I like. Of course, your pregame preparation includes adjusting your technique to the weather. On humid days, you have to be careful that your saliva doesn't stick to the little pea in the whistle because then you only hear the pea rattling around instead of the whistle. Occasionally an official will blow a whistle forty yards away and you'll hear the pea stick and everybody will start to chuckle. "Great whistle, Joe. What is that, a new signal? Blow that one again."

## PREPARING TO PREPARE

Preparation has no off-season. Even if you're not conditioning your body, your mind is always working out

for the coming season. After the Super Bowl in January, the season ends abruptly. It's a big letdown because the roller coaster ride is so exciting for five months and then, bang, it's over. It's just as sudden as someone turning the light out. As a younger official, I got very depressed when the season ended. But now I relish it because the season is so fast, so exhilarating, and so draining that, when it ends, it's like lying down for a long rest.

Immediately I pack my equipment away, put my official's briefcase next to my bed, and take a rest from football. I'm tired and sore; my legs hurt, my ankles hurt, my knees ache. During February and March, I take a sixty-day holiday from physical exercise and eat whatever I want. But I allow myself to gain only five pounds, tops. I don't want to show up at the first meeting the next summer and have my supervisor say, "Markbreit, do you know what a rolling referee is?"

In the off-season, I think about football every day. But for one week in February, I put my rule books and case books away and don't look at them. After a week, I get antsy and I start reading them again. After two weeks of this wonderful nowhere-to-go, nothing-to-do euphoria, I get that anxious feeling of: "Brother, I wish I was *going* somewhere. I wish I had a *ball game*." When the weather breaks in early April, I'm out running five miles a day. By midmonth I've run off those extra pounds and I'm almost at my working weight. I start reading the rules every night and reviewing for the annual officials' exam in May. At this point I'm receiving memos about rules changes from the league office, so I'm back into the season again. The only things missing are the games.

I get back to business around the fifth of May, when the league sends our practice exams for the coming season. All the rules are presented in 170 questions— multiple-foul plays with four or five parts to each question. Cal and I do it together. We have a ball working it out; we spend four weeks talking on the phone. Before I mail the exam in, I review it eight times. Mentally,

when I'm finished, I feel as if I'm in the middle of the regular season. Before I know it, mid-July arrives and I'm at the NFL officials' clinic—four days to review rule changes and attend meetings. After that, I return to Chicago for about two weeks, and then the exhibition season starts.

There are four weeks of exhibition games. For the first two games, nobody works with his regular crew. We're organized regionally, so we can be close to home. The purpose of these games is to get us ready for the regular season, just like the players. We take the games seriously; we officiate them as if they're regular-season games, although we're not graded. For the third and fourth weeks, we work with our regular crews so we can get a running start on the season.

In September, I'm ready to shed my regular personality for the next five months and transform into my football persona.

# THE TRANSFORMATION

My transformation takes place in stages. It begins every Saturday morning at a very unusual place ...

## STAGE 1: SARKIS'S

Sarkis's is a special restaurant in Evanston that I've been going to every day for the past fifteen years. It's a tiny, "Old World" neighborhood joint run by a wonderful Armenian named Sarkis Tashjian. He was born in Jerusalem and he speaks Arabic, Hebrew, Greek, Armenian, English, and about four other languages. He's a philosopher of sorts, and he likes to swear and holler, but it's endearing, not malicious. He does it to everyone who comes in there, from Bill Murray to Jimmy Carter. It's his own special language of friendship.

The same group of regulars is in Sarkis's every morning and, between six-thirty and seven-thirty, we have a little coffee klatch. We kibitz about the topics of the day—politics, business, everybody's personal life. The regulars are: Marcy and Connie, the preschool teachers; George, the gas cylinder man; Doc, the veterinarian; Don, the sporting goods manager; Dale, the factory worker; Joe, the retiree; and Norm, the undertaker. To us, it's not just a diner, it's also our private social club. It reminds me of *Cheers* because everybody cares about each other. For instance, when Norm comes in every morning, we ask, "How's business, Norm?" If he says, "We had *two* yesterday," we'll say, "That's *great!*" I mean, Sarkis's is the only place in the world where people are happy that somebody *died!* Because it's Norm's business, and we want his business to do well.

Sarkis has created this magnificent oasis of humanity where you can hear five foreign languages going at one time. It's the only place I know where I can walk in for a cup of coffee and a stranger will say in Armenian, "Hey, Jerry, have a good game this week." And Sarkis has an unwritten rule: If you don't talk, he won't let you stay. He personally likes to kibitz with everybody. He wants to know all about you: why you're there; who told you about the place; who you are; what you do. When you're ready to leave, he'll say "Oh, don't go. Stay awhile." Then he'll give you his famous saying: *"Stay until you go."*

For me, Sarkis's is a haven and a pick-me-up. Sometimes I'll go in there very down in the dumps and want to be alone. I'll sit at the end of the counter and sip my coffee and mope. Then somebody will ask me a question, and the guy next to him will realize who I am, and, boom, we'll be in a football discussion. It pulls me right out of my depression. Sarkis will see that I'm fine and he'll start bragging about me: "That's Jerry Markbreit, my good friend who did the Super Bowl!" He creates this warm atmosphere of support around me that boosts my morale.

The place is a good-luck stop-off because wonderful

things happen to me there. Recently I was having a cup of coffee when I noticed an elderly deaf couple signing to each other, and Sarkis talking to them and serving them breakfast. Finally the man got up and walked over to examine the pictures on the wall. He found my picture and studied it closely. Then he looked at me, threw his hands up in the touchdown signal, and pointed at me, as if to say, "Is that you?" I nodded yes and gave the touchdown signal. He smiled, walked over, and shook my hand. He told me his name and that he couldn't hear but that it was a pleasure to meet me. He walked back to his wife, and I watched as he told her in sign language that it was me in that picture. What a terrific moment. Nowhere else but in Sarkis's.

Another example: The morning after the Charles Martin/Jim McMahon incident, when I walked into Sarkis's at six forty-five, everybody stood up and applauded. Many of them are not football fans, but they all knew about the incident and they were proud that one of the "regulars" did well. Sarkis made a big deal out of it, even though he knows nothing about football. "I knew what a tough guy you were, Jerry," he said in his thick Armenian accent, "but I didn't know you were *such* a tough guy!" And he's been bragging about it ever since. When strangers come in, he points to me and says, "This is the guy that threw that Martin out when he hurt McMahon! He's *NFL*, this guy!"

Sarkis's is very important to me. It's as much a part of my football ritual as going to church. I go in there every Saturday morning before I leave for the airport. All the regulars greet me and we have coffee, and then they give me a rousing send-off: "We'll be watching you on TV!" "Have a great game, Jerry!" They sincerely want me to do well in my football game. And Sarkis and I have our own little send-off. He asks, "Jerry, are you leaving today?" I say, "Yes. I am leaving today." He says, "When will you be back?" I say, "I'll see you Monday." If I'm not in there on Monday, he'll call my home: "Where's Jerry? What's wrong?"

When I leave Sarkis's for my football weekend, I'm

in great spirits. In fact, if I miss a Saturday visit there during the season, I have this terrible, nagging feeling that I left part of my uniform home.

## STAGE 2: TRANSIT

Stage two in my transformation kicks in when I walk into the Red Carpet Room at O'Hare and a hostess says, "Hi Jerry. Where are you going this week?" I say, "I'm going to Green Bay." She says, "Have a good game." Bang, I'm in my football mode. Jerry Markbreit businessman, family man, father, and son, disappears. I am now Jerry Markbreit, NFL referee.

I sit down, take out an exam or my rule book, and start going over it. Somebody will invariably come up to me and say, "Who do you have this week, ref?" Other people will recognize me: "Hello, Mr. Markbreit. We love to watch you referee." One time, I was washing my hands in the men's room at O'Hare when I noticed a guy across the room, staring at my face in the mirror. He recognized me from TV, but he just couldn't put it together. Finally, he knew. He gave me the illegal-use-of-the-hands signal and pointed at me, hopefully. Without turning around, I nodded at him through the mirror, as if to say, "Yes, it's me." He gave me a big smile, patted me on the back, and walked out. That happens to me almost everywhere I go on football weekends. It's as if all week I wear a disguise but, on Saturday and Sunday, everybody recognizes me.

When I board the plane, usually there are only a few people in first class. A stewardess will see my Super Bowl ring and remark, "Where'd you get that beautiful ring?" She'll find out I'm an official and we'll talk a little while. I'm flattered, of course, but talking on the plane is like death to me. It detracts from my concentration on football. When I'm finally alone with my thoughts, I drift into my football world. The whole flight, all I'm thinking about is: "What time is my crew getting in?" "What are the topics for our meeting?" "When does our film study start?" At this point I don't talk to a soul, I don't kibitz

with anybody. For the rest of the flight, I study reminders of things you don't remember until they happen in the game: "Watch for this" and "Don't fall into that." From here on in, I don't speak English anymore. I just speak football.

## STAGE 3: CHIEF OF THE CREW

At the July 1987 officials' clinic, I looked at the crew lists for the coming season and discovered that I was losing four of my men. The league decided to regionalize its crews, instead of composing them of men from all parts of the country, as in the past. I was upset. I was losing four men I had grown to love. I'd spent five years with Ben Montgomery; five with Merrill Douglass; five, on and off, with Bill Reynolds; and eleven with Tom Kelleher. The only members of the crew I retained were Bill Stanley, whom I'd been with for six years, and Paul Weidner, who was a rookie in 1986. Everybody else would be new. It was very unsettling; I'd had one family and now I would have to build another.

Working with a group of adult men on an officiating crew is like going to war with them. You develop a unique bond of closeness because you need each other on the field of battle. That's why it was especially emotional for me to lose Tom Kelleher. He and I had worked every regular-season game together for the past eleven seasons. He was there when I was just a baby on Tommy Bell's crew. Tom made the difference; he gave me the confidence to excel. After Bell retired, Tom was the patriarch on our crew. For those eleven years, he was more than just a friend and fellow professional. He was a brother and a second father.

Even after eleven years, he never let up on me. One day in the locker room as we got ready to go out on the field, he said to me, "Your breath smells. Go rinse with mouthwash before you go out. You don't want to have bad breath when you talk to the coaches." Another time, he said, "Comb your hair. Never go out on the field without your hair neatly combed. It gives you

that neat, orderly image of someone in control." That's
how meticulous Tom was, and how closely he watched
out for me. Only a close friend would venture that kind
of advice.

I know that I will never have a closer friendship with
another football official. Shortly after Tommy Bell passed
away several years ago, it was Kelleher who offered
me the finest compliment I've ever had as a professional
football official. He said, "Jerry, if I didn't know better,
I'd think you were Tommy Bell reincarnated. I loved
Bell, but you are Bell personified—with something extra." How do you feel when you lose someone like that?

I was very close to Ben Montgomery, too. Ben is a
school administrator from Washington, D.C.; he's an outstanding official and a wonderful man. Rooming together, we became the best of friends, even though
we've known each other for only five years. There are
friends I've had for thirty years whom I don't feel as
close to as I do to both Montgomery and Kelleher. I
hated to lose them.

On the up side, the nice thing about getting a new
crew is the sense of renewal. It's the ultimate leadership
challenge: to re-create that special bond we need to
succeed. Already I've grown close to the new men. I
have Bob Beeks, a twenty-year veteran; Ben Tompkins,
a seventeen-year man; Bob Wagner, in his third year;
and Bill Quinby, a ten-year veteran who was on my Big
Ten crew for eight years. Bill and I are delighted to be
together again. In fact, we're all having a picnic with
each other: we're having a lot of laughs, the meetings
are fun, and we're starting to enjoy one another.

My transformation continues when we all gather at
the hotel on Saturday evening. All of a sudden, I'm chief
of this elite unit again, and I swing into my team mode.
In my regular job, I have freedom. I can be by myself,
I can think about anything I want. If I need to leave the
office early, I have the individual freedom to do it. But
in my team mode, I don't have that freedom because
I do everything as part of a *group*. It's like we're attached to each other for forty-eight hours. We do every-

thing together: eat meals; have meetings; share rooms;
drive to the stadium; dress in the locker room; work the
game. There's none of this "Well, I think I'll go be by
myself," or "I'm going to a movie tonight." We *never* do
that. It's important that we stay together because officiating a game requires such a concentrated team effort that if one of us isn't properly prepared, the team
doesn't do well.

For us, a football weekend is not glamorous. Nine
tenths is no-nonsense preparation, one tenth the actual
working of the game. We're so immersed in football,
we have no time for anything else. But I look forward
to that immersion; it's almost an addiction. We're not
concerned with anything in the outside world, just with
who we are and what we're doing *now*. We're in our
own little world.

These men are not looking up to me for guidance;
most of them have been around longer than I have. But
they do look to me for leadership. You identify the crew
by its referee. It's "Tunney's crew" or "Dreith's crew" or
"Markbreit's crew." Even though the referee has no more
officiating duties than anyone else—except for inter-
preting and announcing the foul calls—he's the chief
of the crew. He's the commanding officer and he's responsible for the whole unit, even though some men in
his command may have more experience. He tries to
get everybody comfortable enough with each other so
they can all do their best work. He gets everyone dining
together, telling jokes, communicating.

We start our weekend with a two-hour film review
of last week's game. Then we have dinner in the hotel.
At this point, we're so wound up, and our time is so strictly
budgeted, that even a meal can be an intrusion. Officials love to complain. What better opportunity than
while we wait for food at a restaurant? We complain
mercilessly: "The water is warm." "The food is cold."
"The rolls are stale." "The spoon is bent." I mean, we
gripe about everything. "The food on the plane was no
good." "The locker room is too hot." "The ball bag is
too small." It's like we're a group of prima donnas get-

ting ready to go out and sing the opera, and *nothing* is right: "The lighting is bad." "The makeup isn't right." "The *opera* is wrong."

It's so hilarious; it's a regular shtik. Last year, I said to the crew, "I never heard a bunch of guys—myself included—do more kvetching in my life!" But that's the nature of officials. It's just something we do for fun. It's a big part of our bonding, and it eases the tension of working a game. Either complaining relieves the tension or we're just a bunch of miserable grouches.

After the meal, it's back to the room to view a training film of unusual plays that occurred last week around the league. Art McNally narrates and tells us what the correct calls should be. Then we conduct a business meeting to review rules exams; set the meeting time for next week; discuss rental cars; and choose a church for next week's Mass. Then we turn in early. Some of us will even dream about football.

## STAGE 4: TOGETHERNESS DELUXE

Early Sunday morning, Bob Wagner, Pauly Weidner, and I go to church together. On my old crew, everyone went—first out of respect to Tommy Bell, then to Tom Kelleher. When I started going to church twelve years ago, I listened closely to the Mass and was delighted whenever they mentioned Israel or the Jews. Afterward, Kelleher would take me with him to shmooz with the priest. He'd say, "Thank you, Father. It was a nice Mass. We liked your homily. By the way, this is Jerry Markbreit. He's the Jewish member of our crew." The priest was always impressed. Tom would say proudly, "We wanted you to know that not everybody on the crew is Catholic, but they have so much respect for those who *are*, they come to church with us." Usually I'd remark, "That's true, Father." But sometimes, if I knew that the priest had a sense of humor, I'd add a little Jewish shtikl: "I also come here, Father, because in a job with so many Gentiles around me, I need all the help I can get."

After a while, I enjoyed going to church so much that I was afraid *not* to go. I didn't want to break the chain. I still feel that way. I've said many times in speeches, "I'm a modern Jew in a modern world who's reluctant to admit that he'd be afraid to work a football game without being in church the morning of the game." I even select the Mass we go to every Sunday morning. When the pope came to Chicago years ago and they had that tremendous rampart Mass, Bobbie and I watched it on TV. She watched in amazement as I mouthed the words of the Mass. Today, every time my rabbi sees me, he shakes his head.

It's funny; with our old crew, every time the priest mentioned Israel or the Jews, the guys would nod in my direction, as if I'd somehow influenced the priest. One Sunday, we were in church in San Francisco and there, attached to one of the banners behind the priest, was a Jewish star. When the Mass ended, we asked the priest why the star was there. It had something to do with the Jews' involvement with a saint whom the church was celebrating, and the star was a way of acknowledging the Jews' contribution. One of the crew said to me, "Wasn't it *coincidental* that you were in church today?" As if they suspected that I called ahead and arranged to have the star put up just for me.

When I walk away from church, I feel: "What a worthwhile hour I've just spent." I think about how peaceful I felt in there and how close it made me feel to the other guys on the crew. It gives me a relaxing, tranquil hour prior to going into the turmoil of a football game. When the Mass is over, I light a candle, make a donation, and say a prayer. I always mention my father and all our family members who have passed away, and every animal I've lost. Then I say, "Bless this crew and their families. Keep the crew safe today, and let our calls be correct. I know we can't be right on every call, but let's face it, that's what we expect. Let me do my very best in this game and for the rest of the season."

I'd be afraid to go out on the field if I didn't say that

prayer first. Maybe there's no correlation between praying and success, but it makes me feel good. There's
something about church that goes with officiating. You
often see athletes praying before going out on the
field—there's something very religious about being under fire. And the closeness you feel with your fellow
officials is almost religious. You spend a concentrated
Saturday together; on Sunday morning, you pray together; on Sunday afternoon, you officiate together. It's
togetherness deluxe.

There's also a lighter side to the churchgoing ritual,
and it contributes just as much to our camaraderie and
sense of togetherness. For instance, I always tell this story.
The league requires officials to dress formally on game
weekends—sport coat or suit and tie; or turtleneck, jacket,
and slacks. No open sport shirts, blue jeans, or lie-around
casual wear. And because we're a group of older men
always dressed so formally, there's a sort of off-field "aura"
around us. People always think they know us, but they
aren't sure from where. Especially in church.

Before a 1986 Giants game at the Meadowlands, our
whole crew went to St. Anthony's, a little Catholic church
in an old Italian neighborhood in Elizabeth, New Jersey.
There we were, seven shtarkers in suits and ties, piling
out of two big black Fords and marching toward the
church. Two Italian guys hurried across the street like
something important was happening. They probably
thought we were the Secret Service.

When we entered the church, people backed out of
our path. Inside, the pews were stuffed. Mass hadn't
started; people were talking up a storm. When we walked
down the aisle, it was like an old "B" movie—the talking
stopped and everybody turned to look at us. You could
hear a pin drop. The machers kept checking behind
us, like they expected the pope to walk in next. One
usher—a guy right out of *The Godfather*—kept pacing
back and forth, staring at us nervously.

Finally, the priest entered and noticed us from the
pulpit. "We have visitors today," he said. "Who *are* you?"
Tom Kelleher stood up—our Catholic spokesman. The

church didn't breathe. Tom said, "We're the officials for the Giants game today, Father." Everybody applauded. They were so *relieved*. A couple of times afterward, we went back to that church and the priest remembered us. He always pointed out, "We are so happy to have the *football officials* with us today." And they still applauded.

We'll go to almost any lengths to have a Mass before a game. Some years ago, I had a playoff game at Dallas on January 2. We flew into Dallas on New Year's Day. That afternoon we could not, for the life of us, find a church open for a six-o'clock Mass. Everybody on the crew was upset. One of the guys called a friend, who called a friend, and we eventually got a traveling priest who was in Dallas for the game. He came to our hotel and walked into Art McNally's room, carrying a suitcase. He opened the suitcase and out came all the wonderful paraphernalia of the Catholic Mass—candles, wine, communion wafers, even his robes. So there we were in McNally's room partaking of a traveling preacher's suitcase Mass. It was a strange sight. If a stranger walked in by mistake, he'd've thought he'd walked into a cult meeting! But it was just another classic case of official ingenuity at work.

## STAGE 5: DRESSING THE PART

After going to church, the whole crew meets for a relaxed breakfast. Then back to my room for a meeting, during which one of the crew gives a twenty-five-minute presentation, like the ones I gave for Tommy Bell. The next thing we know, we're driving to the stadium.

When football officials enter their dressing room and get into striped shirts and white pants, all of a sudden we meld into a unit. There's a strong feeling of bonding that always reminds me of the camaraderie I had with my childhood friends at O'Keefe Playground. I love that closeness. Everybody loosens up and, for the entire weekend, we joke and needle and complain and tell stories. Suddenly we're a family: confidential, ac-

cepting, supportive, trusting, loyal. That's a rare feeling among weekend friends.

Part of that special closeness is a sharing of personal stories that otherwise would never be shared. At any given moment in the locker room, we might be treated to a new revelation about one of the guys. Before a Cleveland game in 1987, we were getting dressed and we started talking about being in shape when we were younger. Bill Quinby said, "I was in great shape when I was in college. I was a boxer." Everybody was shocked. Here was quiet, modest, constrained Bill Quinby talking about boxing. We said, "You were a *boxer*?"

Then, out of nowhere, he told us this wonderful story about his two-fight boxing career. At Iowa, his friends talked him into going out for intramural boxing. He knew nothing about it, but in his first fight he knocked his opponent out. He won the next fight on a disqualification. All of a sudden he was fighting for the intramural heavyweight championship. He figured he was home free. But when he got in the ring and his opponent labeled him, Quinby saw stars. He was embarrassed just telling the story, so he started turning red. The redder he got, the more we laughed. And he acted out the whole thing. He tiptoed around the room in his official's outfit, hunched in this exaggerated boxing stance, throwing punches, ducking, getting hit, and looking hurt. Finally, he stopped and turned his back and said to us, "I was thinking: What am I doing here? This guy's gonna break my neck! But then I got an idea." Suddenly, Bill turned around again to face his imaginary opponent, threw this huge roundhouse right, and pretended to knock the guy out cold. He got this broad smile on his face and proclaimed, "And I was the intramural heavyweight champion of Iowa!"

We were hysterical; we applauded and cheered. We'd never seen this side of Quinby off the field before. Normally, Bill is quiet, straight-laced, and Cedar Rapids through and through. We couldn't picture him raising a finger to hit anybody; it was totally out of character. Yet here he had this Joe Palooka demeanor—tough,

aggressive, lethal—and he was bouncing around the locker room, conducting an imaginary fight. Afterward, as we headed out to the field, I walked up to him and said, "Quinby, I always knew you were punchy. That story just confirmed it."

It's funny how these things come out in the group. Once we get into our uniforms, we leave our outside lives behind and we change. We get younger. For a few minutes before a game, we're just a bunch of fraternity guys trading stories about ourselves that we'd never tell to anyone else. It's the same feeling of closeness I had as a boy in Camp Menominee when I shared a cabin for two months with the same fellas. It's ironic. If I had become the athlete I once hoped I'd be, that feeling would be over now. But as an official, I've been able to extend it through thirty-two years. And I dread the day it will stop.

Dressing for games is a major concern. The unwritten rule is: Bring your long-sleeve *and* your short-sleeve official's shirts. It's a cardinal sin to forget either one. Number one: You never know what the weather will do. When it's supposed to be hot, it gets cold; when it should be cold, it gets hot. Number two: Everybody has to wear the same shirt. If we have to wear the *wrong* one just because you forgot to bring the *right* one, we'll never let you forget it for as long as you live.

When we arrived in Dallas for the 1987 Dolphins-Cowboys night game, Bill Quinby announced that he *purposely* left his short-sleeve shirt home because the weather forecast predicted cold and because he wanted his bag to be lighter. Of course, we were overjoyed for him because we knew that his shirt must've weighed at least two ounces. Unfortunately for us, at game time it was 66 degrees in Dallas, so we boiled our *behinds* off. We rode Quinby's tochis all game. At every time-out, I walked over to him and I said, "Nice night for a short-sleeve shirt, eh, shmeck? It's okay, though, Bill. As long as your *bag* is light enough."

That brings to mind a classic Tommy Bell story. Late in the 1976 season, we had a November game in Shea

Stadium, and it was freezing cold. We were getting dressed when Bell informed us that he'd forgotten his long-sleeve shirt. In the cold, that's an official's nightmare. It's one of our worst fears. So everybody started complaining to Bell—except me, because I was the rookie. Kelleher insisted that under no circumstances would he go out and freeze his behind in thirty degrees. He turned to the crew and said, "All in favor of wearing long-sleeve shirts, say 'Aye.'" Everybody muttered "Aye" except Bell. So we got fully dressed in all our long-sleeve shirts, while Bell—our chief—dressed silently in his short-sleeve shirt.

Just before we were ready to go out and inspect the field, Nick Skorich, our supervisor (and former Cleveland Browns coach), came in and realized that we were five longs and one short. "What's going on, gentlemen?" he said in his very stern, low tone. Bell said, "I've decided to wear short-sleeve shirts today, Nick. But there's some insubordination on this crew." Kelleher chimed in, "But it's thirty degrees, Nick. And Bell forgot his shirt." Nick chuckled, standing there in a thick parka, gloves, and hat, with his pipe steaming hot. "Gentlemen," he said with a grin, "you'll all wear shorts today." Tommy loved it; he knew Nick would back him up. So we took our longs off, put on our shorts, and went out and worked one of the most miserable, bitter-cold days I have ever experienced. All because Tommy Bell forgot his shirt. The crew rode his tochis for a *year* about that.

Several years ago, we had the *Monday Night Football* Jets-at-Buffalo game. Twenty minutes before we were to leave for the stadium, our field judge, Bill Stanley, knocked on my door and said, "Jerry, I don't wanna upset you, but I forgot my pants." Everybody laughed hysterically. I pretended to panic. "Geez, Bill," I said. "We're leaving in twenty minutes. What should we do?"

That afternoon, we had gone to the local high school and donated our fourteen complimentary tickets to the athletic department's coaching staff. One of them was a high school official, and he'd given me his card. So I called him up and told him we had an emergency, we

needed a pair of pants. He immediately called the chain crew that was scheduled to work the game, some of whom were also officials. Then he called me back and said, "Don't worry, somebody will bring a pair of pants down for your man."

We needled Stanley all the way out to the stadium. I mean, Bill Stanley never forgets anything. He's the athletic director of a junior college in California; he's always got *everything* in perfect order. We said, "Stanley, how could someone as fastidious as you *possibly* forget his pants?" We drove him crazy.

We got to the stadium, and within a matter of minutes an entourage of *fifteen* men showed up in the officials' room with white officials' pants. The guys at the high school had called everybody they gave tickets to—all of whom were also officials—and asked each to bring a pair of pants, figuring at least one of them would. They *all* did. It demonstrated the solidarity among officials, and our universal obsession with dressing properly for a game.

In the locker room, dressing is a ritual. When Markbreit walks into the Philadelphia stadium, his stall is always the second one on the left; Stanley's is the last stall on the right; Beeks' is the first on the left. Every stadium is our home stadium, every locker room our home locker room. If there's a rookie on the crew, he always stands and waits for the veterans to take their usual spots, then he takes whichever one is left.

And he'll study what the veterans do. For example, he'll look at everybody's flags the first couple of games to see how they're weighted. The position dictates how much weight you use in your flag. The farther you have to throw, the heavier the weight must be. The deep officials—field judge, back judge, side judge—may have to throw their flags twenty-five to thirty-five yards. They need a very heavy weight. The referee, who rarely throws any great distance, has a lighter weight. The head linesman, line judge, and umpire use medium weights. Some guys use golf balls, others use heavy fishing sinkers. I tape a cloth bag of BB's inside my flag.

I know that to be a great official, I also have to dress the part. When I first became an official, Ellie Hasan told me, "Always look good. Everything about you should look neat and clean because people will think of you as efficient and sharp." He was right. If you look good —shoes shined, pants tapered, stripes matching on each leg—you at last *appear* to be a good official. Your work is the real yardstick, of course, but appearance is a big factor. That's why, to me, dressing for a football game is like dressing for a formal affair.

Shoes are an important concern. Ellie advised me, "Always have your shoes shined, even if two minutes later you'll be working in a mud pie. In those few seconds when you walk from the dressing room to the field, people will notice that your shoes are shined." Every Monday morning after a game, I take my shoes to Mike the shoemaker for cleaning and polishing. He loves to see those shiny shoes on TV. I do, too; I would never go out on a football field without shined shoes.

Suiting up for a game takes us a good half hour. It's a very personal ritual. The uniform is part of your character and style, from shoes to cap. Some guys roll their sleeves up a little bit; I never roll them up unless it gets really warm. Your flag has to be placed neatly in your pocket. Some guys put the flag in the back pocket; I wear mine in the side. When I throw the flag underhand from the side, it looks quick, efficient, smooth. Everybody wears their socks in a different way; they can't be wrinkled, because a wrinkle can cause a blister. Everyone wears their pants differently; I wear mine tapered so they don't look baggy at the bottom. Some guys use garters to taper their pants; I use tape. Everybody wears their cap differently; I fold mine baseball style, so the peak pops up crisp and sharp. It makes me appear alert and strong.

The referee is wired with a very complicated sound system. Once I get dressed, it's very difficult for me to use the bathroom. I have to detach the microphone and then pull the wires around—there's just no room for it. So I try to prepare for that, too, by taking care of my business before I wire up with the mike. People some-

times ask me, "Don't you ever have to go to the toilet when you're out on the field?" I always say, "When officials are out on the field, they never go to the bathroom because we're immune to those needs. It's one of life's strange phenomena. I call it 'official holding.'" In fact, in my thirty-two years of officiating, I can't remember a single instance where an official left the field to use the bathroom. That's because the pregame anxiety takes care of this problem.

But the butterflies and excitement are also exhilarating. I feel like a kid getting ready for my first ball game. And it feels that way for every game. It never wears off. How many people feel that way on their jobs? That wonderful nervousness tells me that I'm about to enter another avenue of my life, something more real to me than any other aspect of my existence. And once I'm fully dressed in my outfit—hat peaked; shirt taut; pants tapered; shoes shined—I slip into another identity.

## STAGE 6: "THE INCREDIBLE GROWING MAN"

As we finish dressing, the footballs are brought in: two big bags of twelve each. The head linesman (Paul Weidner) and the side judge (Bill Quinby) wipe the balls down with damp towels to remove the natural oily coating. Then I use a gauge to make sure that each ball is infalted with between 12½ and 13½ pounds of pressure.

At about this time, the PR directors of both teams come in to accompany the officials to the team dressing rooms. The side judge and the field judge (Bill Stanley) go to the visitors' locker room; the line judge (Bob Beeks) and the back judge (Ben Tompkins) go to the home team locker room. They deliver the correct time to the coaches; tell them when the teams have to be out on the field; and get the captains' numbers. They then return to our dressing room and we go over the captains' numbers and anything else the coaches may have mentioned: "Please ask the referee to watch for our special punt formation" or "We have a trick play" or

"We'd like a clarification on a rule." I make notations of these requests because, when I go out on the field a half hour before kickoff, I'll discuss them with the coaches.

After the PR guys leave with the officials, an entourage of about twenty people flows in: league communicators, replay men, TV people. Usually I talk directly with the TV producer, the sideline coordinator, and a club rep who's in charge of liaison in case the microphone fails. We discuss the procedure for inserting commercials into the game and how many commercials they want. Generally, we go through the same spiel every week just to remind everybody where the coordinator stands on the field and what his proper signal is.

By this time, Bill Stanley has returned. He's our TV coordinator on the field. Once I go into commercial, Bill times it on his watch. When the two minutes are up, he'll signal me and I'll start the game again. Now it's twelve-ten and we've got fifteen minutes to go. At this point, the officials are engaged in officials' conversation: "What about penalty enforcements on scrimmage kicks?" "How about double foul after possession changes?" At precisely twelve twenty-five, Bob Beeks announces, "Gentlemen, it's twenty-five minutes after the hour. Let's go."

We start out to inspect the field. When I walk from the dressing room to the field with my crew, I always experience the same amazing sensation. I'm aware that I'm the shortest man on the crew because everybody else is at least six feet tall. Bob Wagner is six-seven, and whenever he and I walk into a hotel or to the car, I feel very short next to him. But once I get out on the football field, I suddenly feel the same size he is. When I get out there in my Superman uniform, I know that I'm also wearing my six-foot-seven personality.

## STAGE 7: TESTING

Once we're on the field, the head linesman, Paul Weidner, talks to the chain crew; Quinby talks to the ball boys about the procedure for changing balls during

the game; Ben Tompkins makes certain that the goal-posts are straight and properly padded, and that the wind ribbons are on top of each upright. Then we make sure the field is lined and numbered correctly and that the end-zone pylons are in the right place.

I immediately go to the press box side of the field to do a microphone check. I test it so they can hear it in the stadium and in the sound truck outside: "TESTING, TESTING." There are other things you can say, but some-times they backfire. One time in Tampa Bay, Tommy Bell turned the mike on for a test and said, "Testing, testing. Holding, number sixty-nine, Tampa Bay." And sixty-nine, who happened to be limbering up at the other end, turned around and smiled, and Tommy smiled back. When the game started, on the first offensive play we had holding on Tampa Bay's right guard. Tommy stepped out and announced, "Holding, number sixty-nine, Tampa Bay," and the guy went crazy. He hollered, "You had my number picked out before the game started!" Bell turned to me and said, "See that, kid? I did that to teach you that you *never* give a number on a test."

I pay close attention to the microphone check. Every microphone in every stadium has different feedback. Some have an instantaneous report, some a delay. I key the way I speak during the game to the specific kind of feedback. Sometimes I'll say, "Holding," and I'll hear the report two seconds later, so I have to wait. I can't say, "Holding, number forty-seven, offense," be-cause it will all run together and nobody will under-stand it. In a stadium that has that delay, like in Chicago, I pace it accordingly: "Holding . . . number forty-seven . . . offense." Whereas at the Meadowlands, it's an instant report: "Holding-number-forty-seven-offense." Totally different timing.

So the first thing I do is test the report on the mike to see what I'll sound like in the game. It matters, because if you look good and you sound good, people perceive you as better than you are. I think that's fine. The better the players think you are, the more respect they show

you, and the easier it is to control a football game. In the NFL, you might have the strongest personality in the world, but if you don't come across strong, you lose the power of control.

After the mike check, I go out on the field to talk to the coaches. Whenever I do that—even after all these years—I still feel like a kid. For example, in the 1987 Dallas-Miami game, I remember going over to talk to the coaches, thinking, "I can't believe I'm about to talk with two of the greatest coaches in the history of the NFL." I went to Tom Landry first and said, "Hello, Coach." He said, "Hello, Jerry. How are you?" I said, "Do you have anything unusual today?" He said, "No. We have a lot of motion and an occasional backward pass, but that's all. Nice to see you again, Jerry." I said, "Nice to see you, Coach. Have a good game."

I walked down to Don Shula, who greeted me with a big smile. He always smiles at me. I said, "Hello, Coach. He said, "Hi, Jerry." I said, "Anything unusual?" He said, "We may have some unusual plays, but you'll see them when they happen. And I know you'll do the best you can possibly do today." I said, "You *know* that." He said, "I know it" and he gave me a warm smile. I walked away, thinking: "Isn't this something? Here's Jerry Markbreit from Skokie, Illinois, out in the middle of a football field in front of sixty-three thousand people, having casual conversations with two of the biggest coaching legends in the National Football League." It's a thrill I can't describe. There's just something about hearing these great men call me by my first name—as if we'd been friends all our lives.

## STAGE 8: THE GAME IS MINE

After all the field checks are done, we go back inside. We have about ten minutes before the toss of the coin, so we just relax. We make sure that the guys who have to notify the teams when to come out know the exact time to deliver the warning. For a one-o'clock kickoff, one team is warned at twelve fifty-two, the other at twelve

fifty-three and thirty seconds so the field introductions are correctly staggered. Just before we leave at twelve minutes before the hour, we get a football and we all put our hands on it and I say a prayer. Most of the time, I say something short and fast: "Dear God, bless this crew and let them all be right."

We all shake hands and out we go. Quinby, Tompkins, Beeks, and Stanley go to their respective team locker rooms to get them out for introductions. Weidner, Wagner, and I wait one extra minute. Then Wagner grabs a bag of footballs and the three of us go out. On the field, a ball boy takes the footballs from Wagner, and we all get in position on the sidelines for the national anthem. After the anthem, I wait for the TV coordinator to cue me for the toss of the coin. At two minutes before the hour, he says, "Okay, Jerry. It's time." I step onto the field and I leave everything and everyone else behind. I run to the middle of the field all by myself to conduct the toss. When I get there, out come Ben Tompkins from one side and Bill Stanley from the other, escorting the respective team captains.

I feel a surge of power because now I'm in charge, I'm running the entire show. I say, "Captains, introduce yourselves. Who's going to call the toss?" I turn my microphone on, announce the toss, and away we all go to our spots on the field. I wait for TV to clear us, and then I start the game. I can really feel it now. I'm inside the rectangle. The game is mine.

## STAGE 9: "THE INCREDIBLE SHRINKING MAN"

When the game is over and we leave the stadium, I still have that six-foot-seven feeling—that supercharge of bigness and importance and strength. I have it until I reach my car at the airport after midnight Sunday. But once I start driving home, I'm "The Incredible Shrinking Man." I start shrinking back to my normal self. By the time I walk into my house, I've shrunk all the way back down to the shlemiel who walked out the door on Sat-

urday morning. When Bobbie greets me with, "How was the game?"—even if it was the most exciting, gang-busters game ever played, with the biggest crowd and the toughest calls—all I can say is, "Oh, just another game." I drag myself downstairs to unpack wet under-wear and a jockstrap.

I've been in a two-day football trance, and now I've awakened to regular life. I was a weekend celebrity, but the weekend is over and now I'm just Joe Ordinary again. It feels like I just walked into a store and, instead of, "Hi, ref, we loved watching your game," it's, "Get in line." And I want to say, "What do you mean, 'Get in line'? I'm *Jerry Markbreit, NFL referee!*" But they'd just say, "Who *cares*? This is the line for leftover gefilte fish. Get to the end of the line."

# 14. BOBBIE AND JERRY

## SKOKIE, ILLINOIS, 1987

Jerry is very much like the sabra plant. I think of him that way. The sabra is a plant of the desert that is tough and prickly on the outside and soft and tender on the inside. Native Israelis are called "Sabras" because they've had to be tough to defend Israel but, inside, they're sensitive, warm, and caring. And that's what Jerry is. I remember a neighbor telling me that, for two years, she was terrified of Jerry because he's so tough. She was even afraid to cross the street to say hello. Then he did something sweet for her and she realized he was very sensitive and kind. He's an intensely private, complex man—though you can't see that on the surface. I have learned this by living with him. I have forced Jerry to express himself, drop by drop. And I notice that when he comes out of his shell and lets his feelings out, he feels better for it. He's relieved to get them out. But I have to do it in small doses. All his life, he has kept everything in—like so many men of his generation.

—Bobbie Markbreit

# SKOKIE, ILLINOIS, 1987

Bobbie is an integral part of my officiating career. Even though she probably doesn't think she's given me the support over the years, she really has given me the opportunity to get out of here and go do my officiating. In this profession, you can't do it all by yourself. You've got to have someone behind you. Although Bobbie hasn't been happy with my being away on weekends for the past thirty-two years, she's enhanced my career—maybe more than she realizes.

Yet, I still bully her emotionally. I'm aware of it, but I can't stop doing it. She, in turn, complains about me a lot. If I'm away, I'm away too much. When I'm home, she doesn't like the way I behave. Her complaining gets progressively worse every year, and she gets stronger every year—which scares me. Because as tough as I am on the field, she's tougher at home. She absolutely will not take my bullying. But it's hard for me to switch personalities. I have not learned how to switch successfully from Jerry Markbreit, referee, to Bobbie Markbreit's husband.

—Jerry Markbreit


Bobbie always tells me, "Your problem is that you can't separate your home life from your officiating life." She's right. I think the great officials have to be just as tough off the field as on. If you're soft at home, you'll be soft on the field. I can't afford that. As referee, everyone's looking to me for leadership. If I don't have it, and those players sense that their game isn't in strong hands, I'll constantly lose control of the game.

The thing is, I want the same control and authority at home as I have on the field. But I can't have it because I'm living in a relationship with someone else who's on an equal footing with me. On the football field, I am the policeman, I enforce the rules. When I blow the whistle, the play ends, and that's it—it's over.

But I am not a policeman in my own home, I'm just an equal partner. I have no control, and that's that.

For example, Bobbie will get me aggravated and we'll start one of our classic arguments:

ME: It's impossible to live a split life.

BOBBIE: Why?

ME : You can't be in charge of everything that you do on the football field and then come home and not be in charge.

BOBBIE: Why?

ME: You'll have to knuckle under and I'll be in charge here, too.

BOBBIE: In charge of who? The *cats*?

ME: No, *you*!

BOBBIE: It'll be a cold day in hell.

ME: I wish I could throw a flag when you aggravate me like you always do.

BOBBIE: You do all the time.

ME: No, I don't have any authority here. I don't have any power here.

BOBBIE: Why should you? Why do you feel you have to control everything in this house? That's bizarre.

ME: You know what really upsets you? That I am a success at something. It eats your kishkas out. You hate it.

BOBBIE: I don't hate it, but I was the one who had to stay home and take care of the children all those years. And I used to look at you going out the front door and I'd think: "How does he have the luxury of being born into that species that can walk out the door without feeling guilty?"

ME: And how does he have the nerve, the guts to walk out in front of a hundred million people and be exposed to the most ridicule that an individual can have, week after week?

BOBBIE: I don't know. That's wonderful. I'm overwhelmed.

ME: *You* don't have to embarrass yourself
in front of anybody. *You* don't have to
get up in front of thousands of people. I
do it every week!

BOBBIE: I never had that opportunity. I
stayed home with the children.

ME: That's your fault.

BOBBIE: Yeah, I was born a woman and I
married a referee.

It would be great if I could blow the whistle on Bobbie whenever she irritates me. But she won't tolerate it.
If I say, "That's enough, I'm sick and tired of that conversation," she says, "You can't tell me what to say. You
can't tell me what to do. You don't have any authority
over me." So I can't act the same at home as I do on
the field. And because I'm a take-charge kind of person, even though she's very much my equal, I find it
hard to live in an equal environment with anybody.

My referee's persona has taken over my entire life.
For instance, just before the kickoff, everybody gives
an "all clear" with a flick of the hand and, as they clear
one at a time, I flick my finger back to acknowledge
them. Well, I do that to Bobbie all the time. I'll come
over and flick a finger at her face and say, "Let's go!"
She hates that. But I don't realize I'm doing it. Another
example: During a game, I'm always flicking at someone, calling for the ball. I keep doing that at home,
and it drives Bobbie nuts. She says, "What are you flicking at? You're not on the football field." Recently I tried
to direct her to a parking spot near the bank and I
gave her the first-down signal, like: "Over *there!*" She
rolled up the window and said, "Call me when the
game ends"—and drove away without me.

We have totally different personalities. I think I'm
very uncomplicated. But Bobbie is so complicated that
she analyzes everything. After the Charles Martin/Jim
McMahon incident, she was at the dentist's office and
the technicians teased her about how funny it would've
been if *she* had been the referee on that play. They
were right. Because she would have said, "Now, Charles,

you should be ashamed of yourself. Why did you do that to nice Mr. McMahon? Are you mad at your mother? You really didn't mean to hurt him, did you? Would you like another chance? Try to be nice this time, all right?"

I know I'm hard to live with. I always have to know what the rules are. Bobbie is operating on a totally different set of rules. For example, I get impatient with her because she does things slower than me. She's gentle and spontaneous and patient. But the officiating world I come from is a tough, masculine world of calculated order. Everything better be in the right place at the right time or you can't function. Decisions are made and things get done immediately. Time schedules are followed meticulously. At our home, I don't have the authority to make all the decisions, and time schedules are almost nonexistent.

Seven officials go to dinner, we sit at the table, the waitress comes, we give the order in one minute. Two minutes later, we're hounding, "Where's our food?" We're hocking her to death until it comes. When the food gets there, it's gone in five minutes. Everybody gets up and the designated banker pays the bill and we're gone. We don't waste a minute on *anything*. But here I come home, and my life is controlled by a woman who operates at a third of my speed. We sit down to have dinner and it takes me five minutes to finish. If I make an extra effort not to eat fast, it takes me seven minutes. It takes Bobbie *forty* minutes. She's picking at the food and, when she gets done forty minutes later, I've already cleaned my dishes, changed the cat litter, taken out the garbage, and shoveled the snow. I come back inside and she's still got the same six pieces of food on her plate.

To illustrate the conflict, here's a typical dialogue between us when I'm getting ready to leave for a game:

BOBBIE: What time are you leaving?
ME: I've got a one-o'clock plane. I'll leave
    at eleven-thirty.

BOBBIE: It's ten o'clock. Will we have time
   to go out for breakfast?
ME: No.
BOBBIE: Why not?
ME: You're not dressed yet. I can't go out
   and have breakfast with you for twenty
   minutes and then have to rush home and
   worry about getting to the airport on
   time. What if there's a problem with
   parking, or something?
BOBBIE: I can be ready in fifteen minutes.
ME: You cannot be ready in fifteen minutes. You won't be ready in an *hour* and
   fifteen minutes. If you wanted to have
   breakfast with me, you should've been up
   and dressed at eight, and we could've
   spent a couple of hours together.

Now, I know how bad she feels because I feel bad,
too. I *want* to have breakfast with her. But she takes
her time, so she's often late. It's like she purposely doesn't
leave enough time just so we can argue about it. I once
came back at 8:30 A.M. from a speech in Moline. She
had a ten-twenty appointment for a newspaper story
she was writing. I took my cleaning in and picked up
my football shoes and got back again at nine thirty-
five. She was all dressed. I said, "Gee, I'm sorry I'm
back so late. We won't have time for breakfast." She
said, "Yes, we'll have time."

We got in the car, drove three blocks, and she said,
"I don't have time." I turned the car around and drove
back to the house. She said, "We never have time for
breakfast." I said, "You were up at eight this
morning—why weren't you dressed? We could've gone
then." She said, "I don't know. I was thinking about the
appointment. It never works out." Then she stormed out
of my car. As she marched to the house, she saw me
pulling out again and she said, "Where are you going?"
I said, *"Out for breakfast."* She was furious. She jumped
back in her car and roared away.

The focus of most of our conflicts, though, is the fact

that I'm away a lot. What Bobbie does is create a neglect syndrome. She thinks I am the ogre who leaves on the weekends, and she's the neglected wife who can't stand to have me away. Ninety-nine times out of a hundred, before I leave home for a game, we have an argument and I storm down the driveway in a state of irritation. Half the time, I don't even know what started it. It's really Bobbie being angry with me for leaving, and I can understand that. It happens so regularly, it's part of our shtik now. It's like, "Well, we had another argument. I can work my game now."

They're really not arguments; they're little crises that aggravate me because, in her mind, she believes I'm abandoning her again. She'll suddenly get insistent: "Oh, the bathroom faucet's clogged again!" We'll look at each other and grin; we both know exactly what she's doing. She knows I can't stand it if something's out of order in the house, and that I'll put down my bags and fix it. It keeps me there another ten minutes. Then she'll find something else. She'll say, "Why don't you change the cat litter?" I'll say "Why?" She'll say, "Because I always do it. I've been doing it for twenty years while you were away officiating!" It's like a little game now. Sometimes it's so obvious, we get hysterical with laughter. Yet, every football weekend, we run through the whole routine again.

When I'm away, I miss my home and I miss Bobbie so much, I can't wait to get back. I shlep through the airport and I'm exhausted and I can't wait until I pull up in my driveway. But the minute I walk in the house, all those terrific feelings disappear. Because, immediately, she's on my tochis about thirty-five things that happened while I was away. I'll come in and she'll hit me with a bunch of basic things like "I went to the play" or "I wrote this fascinating article today" or "I met this woman who's into animals like we are." When I'm not home, she has nobody to tell these things to. So she keeps them to herself for a few days, gets angry with me for not being there, and explodes on me the second I walk through the door. I come home excited to see her, but she doesn't know that. I never get a chance to

tell her because we're always debating about who's going to clean up after the cats.

One game in 1987, I left home and it was the first time all year we didn't have an argument. We were both preoccupied with plans for our daughter's wedding in June so, before we knew it, I was gone. But she did something bizarre when I was at the hotel in Cleveland. The crew was right in the middle of our three-hour film session when the phone rang. It was Bobbie. She *never* calls me on the road. She said, "Can you talk?" I said, "No. I'm in a meeting. The film is running, there are six other guys in here."

She said, "I have something important to tell you." I said, "What is it?" I thought something was wrong. She said, "I just came from the wedding consultant and I'm really excited about it." And she gave me this whole spiel about the wedding plans. I said, "I'm interested, but I'm in the middle of a meeting. I'll be glad to call you back about this later." She got offended: "Well, if you're not interested in your daughter's wedding, then I'm sorry I bothered you." I said, "Thank you very much," and I hung up. She used that phone call to create a little crisis. That was her tactic—probably to make up for the argument we missed.

Even when we're both nice to each other, we end up in the same old argument. I called her *before* I got home one time and I was very pleasant on the phone. When I got home, she said, "You were very nice on the phone," and here's what developed from that:

> Me: I was trying very hard to be nice.
>
> Bobbie: You never used to try. You used to be all over me. And I took it personally.
>
> Me: That's my personality, Roberta. I can't change it.
>
> Bobbie: I don't want you to change your personality, just your tough-guy behavior at home.
>
> Me: That *is* my personality! You think I could do what I do by being a laid-back shlemiel? You think I could be in the National

Football League if I were just some shlump
who sat back and contemplated his na-
vel for thirty years?

BOBBIE: I'm impressed. When are you going
to Hollywood?

This is all because she says she doesn't like me being
away so much. In reality, Bobbie *enjoys* having me
away. She likes the privacy. She likes to write and do
what she wants to do—and I'm not home to nudge her
to do things or to complain about anything. So things
aren't as bleak during the football season as she makes
them out to be. I don't know how it affected her years
ago because it's hard to weed out what is serious and
what is just discussion. Here, at the pinnacle of my career, instead of accepting what I do, she's just as distressed about the football season as she ever was. So,
to compensate for the lost time together, she tries to get
me more socially involved.

One morning, I asked Bobbie what we were doing
the next night, and she said we were going to another
play. Some little feckucteh play in Lincolnwood. And I
said, "My God, haven't we seen enough of these little
grubby plays that are all so lousy? They're so terrible,
I can't stay awake!" And she says, "I'm raring to go at
nine o'clock at night and you're *sleeping*. Why is that?
Why am I getting younger while you're getting older?"

Bobbie is very social and she likes to dress up and
be with people. She's the best-looking fifty-year-old I've
ever seen. She's very stylish and refined. She's a real
lady who always dresses beautifully and takes wonderful care of herself. She's terrific with people, she knows
how to communicate, and everybody who meets her
loves her. I'm exactly the opposite. I'm more of a grouch
and a ferkrimpta punim, and I'm always complaining.
She's with the wrong guy; she should be with some night
owl who loves to socialize. I'm a guy who gets up automatically at five-fifteen every morning. But at nine-
thirty, ten o'clock at night I'm tired and I'm ready to go
to sleep. So if I'm sitting in one of these lousy plays she

drags me to all the time, I fall asleep. And she gives me a shot in the ribs, "Jerry, wake up. You're breathing too loud. You're snoring." Why do I even have to go and sit through that? I go because she buys the tickets and I feel guilty. But I complain about it.

She loves getting dressed up and going out dancing. One time, I came dragging home from my football game and I was in such agony. I got knocked down in the end zone and every bone in my body hurt. I dragged in at about ten o'clock, I couldn't even get my shoes off, and she said to me, "Why don't you take me dancing?" I said, "Dancing? I can't even *walk*!" I come dragging home, I'm fifty-two years old, I'm worn out. I want to lie down and relax. I don't want to get up and hurry out to the Ritz to break both my legs.

I am just not a social butterfly. For one thing, I can't stand to make small talk. It absolutely kills me. But Bobbie loves to shmooz and she knows how to use her small talk as a vehicle. If she has to, she can small talk about a can of mixed nuts for thirty minutes: "Oh, they're wonderful nuts! . . . buh-buh-buh . . . and *salt* on 'em! . . . buh-buh-buh . . . and he ate *one nut*!" Four hours later, she's still talking to the same people about the nuts. And they won't let her go.

Except for the fact that we're both kindhearted and we love animals, we're complete opposites in everything. What is love, and what keeps people together? She has never patronized me or tried to drive me to success. She has always gone along with whatever I did. Yet she always hated the travel I had to do—in officiating and in my job with 3M. But despite our different personalities, we've stuck together for thirty-two years. She's the stabilizer in our relationship. She brings me back to normal when I come home. And that's not easy. She leads me back to the activities of a normal guy who has to share everything with his wife. I fight it, but I respect her for not letting me intimidate her about everything.

In fact, she's really not the pain in the behind I make her out to be. I like the arguing and the disagreements.

I think it's healthy. She doesn't. I like needling her, but she can't take the needle very well. I love just to mutter at her under my breath, and she gets so aggravated because she knows I'm calling her some Yiddish name—a shmeck or something else. To me, that's fun, that's affectionate. And knowing it aggravates her makes me do it more. I love her dearly, but I have a hard time telling her because I enjoy irritating her so much. For example, she'll ask me, "Why do you think we never got divorced?" And instead of admitting, "Because I love you," I say, "Because I never quit *anything*."

That's the referee in me. I have to have the last word.

# 15. THE LAST WORD

Why do I go out every Sunday and take the physical punishment of being on a football field? Why do I expose myself to the physical risks and the national media and instant replay? I have a nice home; a terrific wife; travel is a pain in the neck. Why am I constantly going away?

Because I love risks and I love the challenge of not knowing how good I can be. Do you ever really know how much success you can accomplish at your job? The answer is no. That's why I officiate. I never know, from play to play, whether I'll make the wrong move or the right move. Every Sunday, I'm in a position to show what I can accomplish. Nothing feels as exciting as that.

I don't think I'll ever find anything more exhilarating in my life than officiating. It is ten times more fulfilling than playing. I never played on a championship team in high school or college, but I played on intramural championship teams, and it was a terrific feeling. But that was a team effort. When you are rewarded for your officiating efforts with a Super Bowl, for one whole year, you have the satisfaction of knowing that you did the best job among the fifteen men who wear the black cap. It's all yours.

After I worked Super Bowl XXI, I felt like I had won the lottery. Nothing else could have happened to make me feel better about myself. It was fifty times more powerful than my first Super Bowl because, the first time, I was too nervous to enjoy it. The fear of making a mistake, of embarrassing the league and myself, was much more apparent. The second time around, I was older, more mature, more confident, more proud.

That feeling hasn't left me yet. It confirmed for me, finally, that I had arrived, that I really *was* good enough to referee a Super Bowl. I just wish that the people who helped along the way could've been around to see it—especially my dad and Ellie Hasan. They were responsible for my becoming an official, and they would've been just as proud.

The day after that game, when Bobbie, my daughter Betsy, and I drove our rental car back to the airport to fly home to reality, I remarked, "Well, it's over. We'll park the car, get on the bus, and fly home, and I'll just be plain old Joe Shlumpmeyer again." I wanted the thrill to last. After we returned the car, we were the last people to board the shuttle bus. As we stepped on, the entire bus erupted into applause. It was loaded with New York Giants press and fans who recognized me. That made me feel so terrific. I wasn't a player, I wasn't a celebrity, I was just the referee. That round of applause made me realize that working a Super Bowl game really *was* prestigious and that it would be an indelible mark I would carry for the rest of my life. No matter what happens, I will always have those two Super Bowl games.

When I'm through officiating, I will know that I don't need anything more from it. I will have given it everything I could and gotten as much out of it as I put in. I'll walk away with a warm feeling in my heart that should last the rest of my life. Right now, I still need it. It takes a lifetime to become a competent official, and I haven't officiated a lifetime yet. There is no perfection in this work. I'll never be perfect—but I still love the challenge of finding out how close I can come.

I know that when I retire from officiating, I will be

replaced instantly and the game will go on as if I never existed. But I'd like to be remembered like Norm Schachter and Tommy Bell. I bump into fans today— *years* after these great officials retired—who believe they're still officiating. Ask them to name NFL referees and inevitably they say, "Norm Schachter, Tommy Bell." Schachter has been retired for twelve years and Tommy Bell passed away a few years ago. But they left such a deep mark, people still think they're around.

Norm Schachter relayed a story to me about the time recently when he and Gordon Wells, a Super Bowl official himself, were flying back from San Francisco. Someone recognized Schachter and congratulated him on a well-worked game. Schachter got a big chuckle out of it. Then the guy turned to Wells and said, "Oh, are *you* an NFL official also?" And, of course, Schachter always tells the story about the time, years after he'd retired, when a guy tapped him on the shoulder and said, "Excuse me. Didn't you used to be Norm Schachter?" Apparently the guy felt that when you retired from officiating, you also ceased to exist.

Well, twenty years from now, as I come strolling down the street, minding my own business like any other local shlemiel, I'd love for someone to come up to me and say, "Excuse me. Didn't you used to be Jerry Markbreit?"

# GLOSSARY OF YIDDISH MARKBREITISMS

bulvon: a gross, thick-headed oaf

bupkes: baloney; nonsense

chutzpah: gall; nerve

cocker: dummy

feckucteh: crappy

ferkrimpta punim: a sourpuss

gefilte fish: fish balls (a Jewish tradition)

hock: to hound

kibitz: joke; comment; socialize; tease

kishkas: intestines; guts

klutz: inept blockhead

kvetch: complain; whine

macher: a big wheel; someone active in an organization

mechaieh: pleasure; great joy

megillah: the whole works

meshuggeh: crazy; nuts; absurd

meshuggener: crazy man
mishegoss: absurd belief; nonsense
narrishkeit: foolishness; triviality
nebbish: weakling; ineffectual person
nebechel: a pitiful nebbish
nudjel: badger
pisherkeh: a young squirt; inexperienced
shlemiel: a loser; an unlucky person
shlep: to drag or carry; to do an errand
shlepper: the rookie; the errand boy; low man on the totem pole
shlepperdik: a nobody
shlocker: a cheap person or place
shlub: clumsy oaf
shlump: a small, innocuous person
shmaltz: corn; show business
shmeck: a dope
shmeer: the entire package; everything
shmendrick: a Caspar Milquetoast; an apprentice nebbish
shmo: boob; fall guy
shmooz: chat; gossip; talk
Shmuckmeyer: alias for Jerry Markbreit
shmutzik: dirty; soiled
shnook: a patsy; a dope
shpilkes: anxiety
shtarker: big, strong person
shtik: characteristic way of doing things; a routine
shtikl: funny business; needling
shtikeleh: a small piece of funny business

spiel: a talk; a speech

tochis: rear end

tsimmes: fuss over nothing

tsuris: trouble; misery

ungeladen: covered